Promises
of the
Constitution

Yesterday, Today, Tomorrow

PROMISES
OF THE
CONSTITUTION
YESTERDAY, TODAY, TOMORROW

Pamela Romney Openshaw

— ∞ —

Provo, Utah 2015

Promises of the Constitution: Yesterday, Today, Tomorrow
Pamela Romney Openshaw
Second Edition
Copyright © 2015, Openshaw Enterprises, LLC

Two additional books turn this volume into a study course for families and homeschools. *Lessons of the Constitution Student Workbook* poses three questions for each vignette in *Promises of the Constitution* to bring out the moral principles and application of the Constitution. A Bible scripture is applied to each vignette. The *Parent/Teacher Resource* gives the answers plus discussion questions, books, DVDs and projects for extended involvement and learning.

Contact Openshaw Enterprises for additional copies of the book, volume orders, other constitutional materials, and to book a live speaker presentation.

www.promisesoftheconstitution.com
openshawenterprises@gmail.com
(801) 373-0240

ISBN 978-0-9882550-6-7
LCCN 2015909915
Cover design and interior art by:
Douglass Cole of Ninth Floor Design

2nd Edition
Printed in the United States of America by:
Peczuh Printing, Lindon, Utah 84042

Dedicated to
all the people who, like me,
want to understand what we once had,
what has gone wrong,
and how to regain our liberties.

CONTENTS
ભ

PREFACE

⸿

S OMEDAY, perhaps I'll write a book about how to write a book. The creation of this volume has been one of the great experiences of my life, and I would like to record its birth.

To write a book, one must become immersed in the subject at hand. In my case, that subject has been the United States Constitution. This book is its biography. Within these pages, I've portrayed the life of the Constitution—its ancestry and birth, its vigorous youth, and the infirmity of its sullied middle years. I've outlined its necessary healing and trumpeted the vigor of its renewed future years.

The Constitution has consumed my interest. It has been my last deliberation at night, my dreams in sleep, and my first reflection in the morning. The promises of the Constitution have worked their way into my soul and formed the warp and woof of my heart. It has been a joy to embrace and invest myself in this great founding document.

In the process of writing this book, I have fallen in love with the English language. I've come to love the combinations of its words and relish their meanings. I've played with words, experimented with them, and even teased them to bring life to thoughts that must be laid to paper. Words are tools to excite, instruct, even inflame, should they be chosen for such. With words I can paint reality; with words I can reveal or censure.

Through writing a book, I've come to know myself—my limits, my talents, my weaknesses. I've found boundaries to my patience and have learned to trust my opinions, but not my spelling. I've uncovered my priorities and located the inner windows to my mind.

I've learned to relish others' opinions, for they hold the life and future of my creation in their hands. Some share my fascination with the Constitution, and that is sweet. Others find it unimportant, obsolete, or worse, mundane. I am saddened but unshaken by their indifference. It is a part of life that diamonds sometimes lie undiscovered in the dust.

Writing this book has been like giving birth to a child. From its conception, the nurture and protection of my creation has taken center stage. My life has focused on the future of this "child" I carry—this child of my heart and mind. It has slowly taken form in the verbal landscape emerging one page at a time before my view. It has been a wondrous thing to participate in this creation.

Promises of the Constitution now enters the world of ideas to find its place among those who will embrace its message. It carries my reverence, my love, my longing for liberty. This book is woven into my heart. I pray that those who open its covers will be kind, that they will be changed by its message and love the document whose biography it is.

As with my child, I have prayed for this book. The decision and intent to write it were God-given. Its form and figure were set by the divine impression that gave it birth. While the book bears my imprint, it also bears His.

To the reader: learn and enjoy. Give your heart to the Constitution that God created for us. Relish it; restore it!

ACKNOWLEDGMENTS

N o BOOK arises in isolation, and this one is no exception. Many people have given unselfishly to bring this work about.

My grateful thanks go to my husband, Bob, for his support. He has kept the home fires burning, run interference for me, made sure I got at least some sleep, and stepped in at critical points to offer key assistance. He has been my sounding board and the source of critical insights at key junctures. His attention to the details has lifted a load from my shoulders.

Val Arbon and Marilyn Harris, my cohorts and fellow patriots, have given generously and unfailingly. I could not have written this book without them. Each gave me valuable insights and taught me key skills when needed. They have spent long hours giving freely of the help I needed. Both are dedicated authors and actors on the modern freedom scene and each is a valued and valuable associate. In addition, Marilyn taught me a new style of writing and Val, along with my daughter, Betsy and her husband, Matt Moore, kept my computer alive and smoothed away the glitches.

Pat Sheranian lit a fire of belief and self-confidence in my soul and fanned the flames when they sputtered Beverly Arbon brought her eye for detail to my aid. Valuable assistance was also given by Debby Swan, Jeff and Cyndi Looman and Shirley Van Leuven, who read the original version of the manuscript, and Kristen Bishop and Annie Penrod who gave valuable research skills when needed. Kathy and Bert Smith, Robert Arbon, and Oak Norton gave me understanding of what life would be like without government intervention. Others have helped along the way, and I thank them for their efforts.

I have had solid professional assistance. Editors Elizabeth and Jaime Watkins polished the rough edges of the manuscript and brought simplicity and accuracy to the project. They, particularly Elizabeth, have been wonderful. Ben Welch and Sean Graham through Angela Eschler, designed the look of the book and went the extra mile, and Douglass Cole of Ninth Floor Design lent his creative artistic genius to the artwork.

I would like to express my thanks to our Founding Fathers, whose lives and sacrifices set the tone for our original Constitution. I am grateful for their studies, time, effort, and attention to the details of wise political government. As I have studied their lives and works, they have become my friends. Their integrity and honor have instructed me and given me a desire to embrace those virtues.

Lastly, I would like to offer my gratitude and love to the eternal, omnipotent God I worship. I have asked for and received His instruction, direction and steadying hand throughout the creation of this volume. My appreciation for His influence knows no bounds. It has been my great desire to earn His approval for this book. I sincerely pray that I have.

Prologue

———————— ☙ ————————

PERSONAL PERSPECTIVE

I GREW UP in the southwestern United States as the daughter of a former World War II pilot. My dad had flown C-47s across the English Channel as he delivered fifty-five-gallon drums of fuel to General Patton's tanks near the end of the war. Those stories are my heritage, along with the story of my birth.

Daddy wanted to "join up" when Pearl Harbor was bombed by the Japanese on the day my older brother was christened in church. Mom finally gave her very reluctant approval, and Daddy went immediately into the Army Air Corps on the West Coast.

To support their son, since military trainees were unpaid, Mom worked as a bank teller until her advanced pregnancy with me and the accompanying facial paralysis of Bell's palsy forced her to quit. She rented out her two bedrooms for income, while she and my brother Barry slept on the couch. Daddy went AWOL to visit us in the hospital in Arizona after my birth. He told mom that he knew he wouldn't return. He did, and fathered five more sons.

I married my high-school sweetheart when we were college students. His Air Force career put us in the middle of the Vietnam War, where we lived our parents' experiences firsthand. I gave birth to our third child while my husband flew reconnaissance missions out of Korat Royal Thai Air Base in Thailand.

Decades later, that grown child also experienced war. He was in the World Trade Center on September 11, 2001. Had American Airlines Flight 11 come one hour earlier, he would likely have been a casualty in that attack. We are deeply grateful that he was not, and we mourn for those less fortunate.

So, these many years and their accompanying experiences have infused my heart with patriotism. I gave it little thought when I was young. I heard my father's animosity over the Wilson and Roosevelt years—1913, the Year of Infamy for personal rights and limited government. Both were dismembered by the implementation of the Federal Reserve System and the passage of the Sixteenth and Seventeenth Amendments, all in the same year. It took me decades to understand my father's angst. He feared that the United States would never recover from those disasters. It never has.

My husband and I lived in Italy from 2007 to 2009. We returned to worrisome changes in our own government. Our country was sidetracked and in dangerous waters. I began my search for answers to what and why.

Now it is very clear. We are in crisis.

In reality, I wrote this book to me—the way I felt as I was eight years ago, and to all those who are now where I was: filled with worry, concern, and confusion.

What is the answer to the dilemma that surrounds us? The answer is to love our Founders, our country, our founding document, and the God that gave them to us. We must teach that love to our children, pray for our leaders, and plead for help. The answer is to get involved.

I invite you to journey through these pages and find the hand of God in making America great. Mourn for the changes that have since taken place. Join your heart and hands to the great work to bring back our freedoms and prosperity. Resolve to make a difference.

God will help us. It can be done. It must be done!

Pamela Romney Openshaw

Section One

───────────── ◌◌ ─────────────

WAITING

THE YEAR WAS 1787. The air hummed and crackled with anticipation as America awaited notice of a new birth.

Thirteen colonies held their collective breath. The long ordeal of waiting was about to end. This birth of a new government had been years, even centuries in coming. The colonists could scarcely contain their excitement, nor hide their fears. This test of endurance, this hanging in suspended animation before they could view the finished product, would soon be over.

Beyond their shores, the Western world watched and waited as well. This birth held great possibilities, yet was fraught with dangers for them. Would this new government be weak, providing opportunity for conquest? Would it be aggressive and try to reach beyond its shores for those who had previously been its masters? Hopefully, it would not be brassy, arrogant, or simpering. Hopefully, it would be a government that wanted trade and friendly relations with its neighbors across the seas. Time would tell. Europe waited with calculated, attentive ears.

This was not the anticipated birth of a country. That had happened years before, when the fledgling colonies had refused to flinch at England's tyrannical whip. Though the colonists suffered and bled, they had stubbornly held the course. They had claimed the improbable victory.

Now, eleven years later, America waited for a new, deliberate creation to guide its government. The country had struggled in the interim with a timid political system that left its people fighting each other, nearly destroying them and all they had worked and sacrificed for. The Articles of Confederation had given them bitter experience in what would not work. Now, surely, the fifty-five men closeted in the Pennsylvania State House would find what did work.

Life moved on that summer of 1787. The people, expectant and anxious, willed themselves to their daily tasks as they waited on the process secluded behind the protective convention doors. There was nothing to do but wait. The common question that united them was this: would they like the creation taking form behind those doors?

1.1 | America in June of 1787

WHAT WERE AMERICA and her people like during that summer of 1787, when her democratic republican government was being born?

America was vast—a bold, fresh, wild land. Her people were rugged individualists, liberated from the rigid dictates of European society. They created a new philosophy and language to match the land, with strong words such as *federal* and *national* common among the people.

America was a world largely devoid of sophisticated elegance. It was home to a new breed of women that shunned the wanton ways of European aristocracy and chose, instead, solemnity and austerity unadorned by wigs, rouge, and powder. Bathing was minimal. A lady's brocade dress lasted years and then was willed to her children. The European author Médéric Louis Moreau de Saint-Méry, schooled in the feminine standards of Europe, bitingly described American women as "charming . . . at fifteen . . . faded at twenty-three . . . decrepit at . . . forty-five."[1]

Frenchman Marquis de François Barbé-Marbois contrasted the robust American men who could fend for themselves, then take musket in hand and march to meet the enemy, with their European counterparts: "I am not sure that [men] who have porters, stewards, butlers, and covered carriages with springs would have offered the same resistance to despotism."[2] Men of principle, common and valued in America, seemed in short supply in Europe.

Learning tended toward the practical and useful. During illness, neighbors treated each other with home remedies and summoned doctors as a last resort. Bleeding by the quart was common, and patients sometimes were bled to death. Unaware of basic sanitation, many new mothers died after childbirth from infections spread by unsuspecting doctors.

America had no love for its forests and trees when clearing them spoke of progress. They chopped them down whenever possible, leaving two-foot stumps to mark the spot. Crops grew right up to a farmer's front door. The land was hostile to any who would not conquer it with hard work, yet potatoes grew wild in open fields.

The steam engine was touted that summer, although its practicality was a matter of speculation. Toothbrushes were coming into fashion to replace cloths dipped in snuff and rubbed on the teeth to freshen breath. Chinese imports of silk, ivory, tea, and cocoa appeared in the local shops, and the booths at street markets were flush with goods. Drinking water was foul-tasting; it was deemed unsafe, even fatal, to drink too much too fast. The drinking of "spirits" was considered safer, and most Americans drank them in quantity.

In Philadelphia, site of the Constitutional Convention, flies and mosquitoes were a constant torment, exacerbated by slops and garbage routinely thrown into the city gutters. Sleeping rooms had to be shut tightly at night for protection from the pests, making the summer heat unbearable. Bedbugs added to the discomfort. Northerners in their woolen clothing suffered most; Southerners, clad in linen, fared better.

Philadelphia was a city of parties and drinking. All livelihoods jostled one another on the streets—farmers, sailors, gentlemen and their ladies, Quakers, frontiersmen, and Indians from the backwoods. Bells rang everywhere. Watchmen called the time hourly all night long and awakened travelers who needed to catch the early coach out of town.

These were the people who gathered to watch and wait for news from the Pennsylvania State House.

1.2 | A Pattern of Freedom

POWERFUL MOMENTS of history are often lost on those who live them. It is unlikely that the American people realized the greatness that emerged among them as they embraced a new governing document.

The people of the newly formed United States sought their own liberty, unaware of the modern pattern it would set for generations and nations that followed. Throughout history, humanity had sought freedom but had rarely found it. Many political systems had taken it away; few had deliberately created it.

The great men who created our Constitution discovered the pattern for wise government in the Bible, which they knew well. Like other early settlers of America, many of the Founders governed their lives according to the "Good Book." Its pages gave them their basic education, their spirituality, and their common reason. Bible study guided their everyday actions and provided instruction and practical application in such matters as their use of time and the conduct of their relationships. Many could quote long Bible passages from memory.

The Founding Fathers drew heavily from the Old Testament for inspiration and instruction in forming our constitutional government. They scoured its pages to learn the concepts of divine governance. This was particularly true of Thomas Jefferson, who began his study as a young man and continued it throughout his life.

In the Bible, they found God's political pattern for representative government, without which their task to create a political system of liberty for America would likely have been impossible. No group of people could hope to create a stable, balanced government without wise direction and guidance. This pattern for liberty included a system of wise self-rule, principled leaders, and virtuous people. That pattern could be found in two previous civilizations whose records were available to the Founders: the people of ancient Israel, and the ancient Anglo-Saxons.

The first element of the pattern, a system for representative government, came to the ancient Israelites by direct revelation from God. This law is recorded in the five books of Moses in the Old Testament. This is the only place in holy writ where God outlines in detail His plan for civil government.

Another civilization offered its example to the Founding Fathers. Though its origin is unknown, the Anglo-Saxons in 450 AD had embraced a system of representative government in England. Their records and a remnant of their system survived the Norman Conquest in 1066. Their governmental systems became part of our Constitution through the diligent study of the Founders. Again, Thomas Jefferson led the way in this discovery.

Leaders of courage, wisdom, and virtue form another essential part of the liberty pattern. America has had many of them: George Washington, Thomas Jefferson, John Adams, and James Madison. Less familiar were William Bradford, John Winthrop, and George Whitefield. They and others who inhabited the land were giants—great men carrying a great movement upon their shoulders.

The third part of the pattern for liberty is the people. Freedom cannot remain long among people who do not bring virtue into the governing process. God requires a covenant-making, covenant-keeping people. The stories of America's people are written in histories, in journals and letters, and on their hearts. We are among those people, and we are writing our stories to join with theirs. We must write them well.

1.3 | Announced, at Last

S HORTLY AFTER 3 p.m. on September 17, 1787, the Constitution was signed. The people would meet the new Constitution at last. Rarely had a political system roused such interest among the common people. Set before these Americans was a set of rules for the United States of America—thirteen entities joined together, yet separate and independent. Fifty-five men with unparalleled understanding of what does and does not work in government had created it.

They were not ordinary men. On the one hand, they were farmers, soldiers, merchants, lawyers, and landed gentry. They were also political dissidents, philosophers, and emboldened patriots. God had raised them up to create a government that would give freedom, protection, and prosperity unequaled in any government since antiquity.

Other systems of government had evolved by catch-as-catch-can. The rule of law had been formed by wars, political expediency, intrigue, and the demands of aristocracy. Most were patches sewn upon patches—convoluted conglomerates of temporary fixes that became "the law." Charles Pinckney of South Carolina, one of the youngest of the Founding Fathers at the Constitutional Convention at age twenty-nine, expressed it well: "To fraud, to force, or accident, all the governments we know have owed their births."[3] Under these systems, the condition and needs of the people mattered little.

But this was not the case with the Constitution of the United States. This dynamic system of rules was based upon worthy principles. It was designed to promote the immutable goals of all men everywhere: freedom, protection, and prosperity. With freedom came self-determination. With protection came the defense of life and property. With prosperity came liberty from want, providing that one applied individual effort. The sum of these goals was peace.

The convention that drafted the Constitution released an announcement directed to the Congress of the Confederation, which governed the former colonies under the Articles of Confederation. Upon its approval, the Congress would send the new political system to the states for ratification. The statement bore the signature of "George Washington, President. By unanimous order of the Convention."[4]

The Constitution would not be submitted to the people for their popular vote; instead, it would be ratified by their representative bodies. This was fitting for a newly formed constitutional republic in which the general body of the people elected representatives to conduct their governmental business.

The announcement read: "We have now the honor to submit . . . that Constitution which has appeared to us the most advisable." The statement explains the tradeoffs of government:

> *Individuals entering into society must give up a share of liberty to preserve the rest . . . It is at all times difficult to draw . . . the line between those rights which must be surrendered, and those which may be reserved . . .*
>
> *In all our deliberations . . . we kept steadily in our view . . . the greatest interest of every true American, the consolidation of our Union . . . and thus the Constitution, which we now present, is the result of a spirit of amity [friendly relations].*

The drafting members had done their best, but they admitted that the needs of all states could not be fully met. They concluded, therefore, by saying: "We hope and believe . . . that [the Constitution] may promote the lasting welfare of that country so dear to us all, and secure her freedom and happiness, [which] is our most ardent wish."

Every newspaper in the thirteen states ran news of the Constitution on the front page. Public scrutiny began in earnest to determine what this new system meant for its people.

1.4 | Freedom under the Constitution

T The Constitution was analyzed, reanalyzed, and then analyzed again. Slowly, the details of its character emerged, offering exciting new advantages. Perhaps the greatest blessing was freedom.

All people want to be free. They want to make their own choices about how to create, live, and think. This has been true the world over, present and past, and it will always be so. All of us want to be free.

The God who gave us life intended that we be free to act for ourselves. Freedom is His gift, designed for all people everywhere. When people are free, they enjoy their lives—they "rejoice", as the Bible explains. The Founding Fathers wrote their yearning love of freedom into the Constitution as the inalienable right that it is. First, however, they had to determine what freedom is and how to keep it.

The Founders studied the works written over centuries by the greatest minds of Western wisdom. They looked for the basic truths of political thought. Many of the fifty-five men who later sat in the Pennsylvania State House to draft the Constitution had lived under oppressive government and knew its misery. They sought out the fountains of freedom to bring liberty to thirteen thirsty former colonies.

The principles of liberty existed long before our Constitution in what Thomas Jefferson called "the ancient principles."[1] While some say the Founders "invented" self-government, they did not. The Constitution was a restoration to bring back the divinely given principles presented to ancient societies. Thomas Jefferson made it his life's work to trace freedom to its source: the people themselves.

Freedom exists when people preside over themselves and do what they decide is in their best interest. Then, using their God-given freedom—the right to make their own choices—the people create liberty, which is the wise use of freedom. When we use our freedoms coupled with morality and virtue, we create liberty.

Government's measure of success is its ability to first protect freedom and then guarantee that none take it away. This is why government exists. Its purpose is to cover its citizens with an umbrella of protection under which they can safely operate to achieve their desired goals. It was not intended that our government fix the people's ills, feed them, and regulate their everyday affairs. These things are for us to do ourselves. The Founders intended that we be given opportunities, not custodial care.

The Constitution made freedom available to the former British colonists, and to their future descendants, in essentially every aspect of their lives. So great and powerful was this system of government that in 1905, just 116 years after its inception, the United States produced almost 50 percent of the world's goods with only 5 percent of the world's land mass and 6 percent of its population.[6]

The new American Constitution embodied the idea that freedom, and the liberty that can be produced from freedom, belongs to everyone. A sense of "manifest destiny" arose in America as people accepted their duty to assist other national governments to promote freedom. Over time, these political principles of the Constitution would spread to many other nations.

As the earliest settlers of America intended, our United States Constitution has stood as a light on a hill in an otherwise dark world.

1.5 | ## Protection under the Constitution

As the people pored over their new governmental birth certificate, they found protections available that had been denied them under British rule. These safeguards had also been missing from their crippled Articles of Confederation. They had been unknown in governments for most of the world's history.

An unethical government can do many destructive things, as the former colonists well knew. The divinely inspired Constitution would protect the people from these oppressions.

The British Parliament had set colonial America's laws and then, through "salutary neglect," had left the colonies to largely govern themselves. Had that continued, the colonies might never have broken with the mother country.

Parliament changed course, however, and imposed taxes without colonial consent. It wanted the colonists to pay for the costly war England had recently concluded with the French over ownership of America. When the colonists revolted, Britain sent troops to quell the insurrection. British leaders demeaned, abused, and ignored the colonists' diplomats. The Revolutionary War erupted, and ultimately America became independent.

Now, under their new Constitution, Americans had a governmental system that put limits on power so that their inalienable rights would not be violated. These inalienable rights, given to all people by God, cannot be taken from the people without accounting to God for having done so. Written into and throughout the Constitution, these rights were later clarified and reinforced in the Bill of Rights, the first ten amendments to the Constitution.

Under the Constitution, the people could choose their form of religious worship. Government could not forbid or intervene in religious affairs in any way. There would be no taxes to support a government-sponsored church. Religious leaders could not influence the course of government. Americans' knowledge of right and wrong, of good and evil, could remain untainted by politics.

Americans could own and bear arms to defend themselves. That protection was essential to farmers and shop owners who would be called up to defend their homes and families and preserve national freedom. A century later, this principle of home defense by the common man would be formalized when all males between the ages of eighteen and forty-four would be officially organized into a resting militia.[7]

Treason was a serious issue of the day. Unethical governments used it to threaten political enemies, resulting in lengthy imprisonment without trial. Personal property was often seized by government. Today we rarely deal with this issue but we should understand treason and be alert to its tyrannical possibilities.

The Constitution guaranteed legal protections. Citizens could not be jailed without a trial or tried twice for the same crime. They were protected from secret trials, "rigged" juries, and trials without legal assistance. Punishment was required to match the crime. Those accused must be told the charges brought against them. Consequently, Americans were protected in the courts of law, where the common citizen could easily flounder.

Americans could speak their minds and gather in groups. Their property could not be searched or seized without legal consent given for good reason. Citizens could not be compelled to billet military troops in their homes.

These satisfying, previously unavailable protections were essential then, as they are today. We are fortunate that these rights are available to us in our founding document.

1.6 | Prosperity under the Constitution

ALL PEOPLE desire prosperity. Colonial-era Americans were no exception. When they understood the prosperity available through the Constitution, they embraced the new government.

The inspired Founders planned for prosperity for all Americans. Prosperity was not defined as wealth, however. Wealth consisting of things—mansions, land holdings, and sophisticated society—did not then, and does not now, constitute prosperity.

Real prosperity is a sense of well-being, a pattern of life where people are content and all proceeds well. Individuals may move about freely, pursue what interests them, and provide for their own basic needs without undue restraint. When prosperity prevails, citizens anticipate that they will continue to live in a comfortable, pleasant world. They are free from enemies that could overwhelm them or take what is dear to them. This state of well-being leaves people free to respect themselves, others, and God. Prosperity requires that citizens are secure with those who lead them.

Prosperity always results from the integrity of a nation's citizens and government. This is an unchangeable law of the universe, just as the law of gravity is unchangeable. Only a virtuous people will treat others with the fairness that well-being requires. Only a principled government will respect their rights. Prosperity comes only to those who live with integrity, and no nation maintains its prosperity without upholding integrity.

Laws are necessary for us to prosper. The purpose of government is to enact laws that structure society in rewarding ways. Laws set boundaries on our actions and those of others. A virtuous government will enact virtuous laws, and the people will thrive. Once a government abandons virtue, its laws become unfair and constricting, and prosperity wanes.

This true definition of prosperity was well understood in colonial America. The new Constitution provided fertile ground where prosperity could flourish. It required leaders to exercise their power wisely. The Constitution restrained those who would enslave the people—either knowingly, to gain power, or innocently, in a misguided attempt to keep them "safe." It divided power to prevent self-interested individuals from seizing and abusing it.

Laws that governed people's day-to-day lives were kept as close to them as possible to secure the conditions needed for them to prosper. Prosperity diminishes when people are governed from a distance by those whose priorities are different. Those local to us know our values and needs. They are best able to create and enforce our laws.

Prosperity does not mean freedom from adversity. Adversity is the common lot of all people. Hard times come, businesses fail, calamities strike. The role of the national government is not to atone for these disasters. The Constitution creates a stable environment in which a person can safely operate. This allows each individual to conquer personal adversity and prosper.

The poignant evidence of history shows that few nations have maintained prosperity indefinitely. Comfort leads to complacency, and internal decay always follows. America is proving this sad principle. Detrimental changes made in our success formula during the last hundred years have seriously impaired our prosperity.

To colonial-era America, however, with its vibrant work ethic and strong moral fiber, the new Constitution and its Bill of Rights offered all the freedoms needed to thrive.

1.7 | ## Peace under the Constitution

W
HEN GOVERNMENT provides freedom, protection, and prosperity, peace will inevitably follow. Americans under the new Constitution had every possible opportunity to live peaceful lives because their new government gave them these blessings.

With political peace comes the opportunity to find personal peace from within. It is not the function of a political system to offer personal peace, but government should provide the umbrella under which a person can find peace. Sound government gives us national peace, and we make our own personal peace within it.

John Widtsoe, a college president and noted theologian who lived a century after the drafting of the Constitution, addressed this topic: "Peace . . . is not to be established by Congress . . . Peace cannot be legislated into existence . . . Peace comes from within . . . The only way to build a peaceful community is to build men and women who are lovers and makers of peace. Each individual . . . holds in his own hands the peace of the world."[8]

Government has two responsibilities to its peaceful citizens. The first is to create an environment that fosters peace. The second is to protect its citizens from anything that destroys peace. Unwise laws destroy peace; good laws promote and encourage it.

Government encourages peace when it controls actions rather than beliefs. Laws should protect our property and our lives. They should restrain crime and punish guilt. It is not the duty or jurisdiction of government to control the minds and hearts of its people. Any government that does so oversteps its bounds. Laws based on sound principles will never dictate thoughts, beliefs, and opinions. Each of us is entitled to believe as we choose.

Wise political rule requires a second component to encourage peace. Good government must be paired with virtuous people—those who abide by godly principles. The relationship flows both ways. Virtue in government protects the people. In return, people of virtue keep the laws of the land. Each has integrity in the process, and both work in harmony. Virtuous people and limited moral government unite to promote peaceful living.

We are largely responsible for whether we have peace, both national and personal. Few things are more desirable than a peaceful existence. Our part of the arrangement is that we must earn our peace. Once we have earned it, we must maintain it. If we abandon virtue, we also abandon peace. The Constitution was created for a moral people and will not be effective for any other. Violating moral principles does not bring peace to any people under any system of government.

Isaiah details the relationship between personal virtue and peaceful government: "O that thou hadst hearkened to [the Lord's] commandments! then had thy peace been as a river, and thy righteousness as the waves of the sea" (Isaiah 48:18).

Virtue and peace are synonymous. It is that simple. It has been so from long before the writing of our founding document. It will continue to be so as the freedom principles of the Constitution endure throughout time.

Section Two

━━━━━━━━━━ ❧ ━━━━━━━━━━

PREPARING FOR FREEDOM

Looking at the foundations of the grand document that would guide America is much like reviewing the ancestry of a great historical figure.

Greatness does not arise in isolation. It is rooted deep in soils rich with tradition and watered with virtue. The lineage and destiny of greatness must be understood in order to understand the United States of America.

God established America's ancestral line in preparation for her divine stewardship. Her grand privilege was to restore the elements of Christ's government of freedom as He taught them to Old Testament Israel.

The American continent and its people required cultivation before liberty could blossom from America's soil. The land itself must be nurtured and governed by people with character who would bear the standard of virtue. Their devotion would be manifested in making covenants with their God. Individuals of integrity and unflinching courage must emerge to lead. Tyranny had to be repressed, sound economic policies put in place, and colonization advanced. Sacrifices made by individuals and communities would dedicate and sanctify the land for both political and religious freedom.

God's hand is evident in the preparation of this ancestral line, beginning centuries before the creation of the Constitution. Ezra Taft Benson, secretary of agriculture under Dwight D. Eisenhower and a committed religious leader and patriot, emphasized the link between these spiritual and political truths when he said: "When a man stands for freedom, he stands for God."[1]

The following pages reveal America's ancestry of liberty. The evidence of God's hand is abundant in populating America and guiding the people and events that constitute our American heritage.

2.1 | Settlers in America: Jamestown, 1607

For centuries, the Americas remained unknown to the rest of the world, held in reserve for God's purposes. After their discovery by Columbus, who declared that he was on God's errand and was directed by Him to find the New World, God slowly began to bring specially prepared individuals into their vast domain.

For over a hundred years, between the four voyages of Columbus that began in 1492 and the founding of Jamestown in 1607, Franciscan and Dominican friars from Spain and French Jesuit priests explored and charted North America. They came with the purpose of serving God. Tens of thousands of Native Americans embraced Christianity through their influence and benefited from the schools and orphanages they established. Loved by the indigenous people, these Christian missionaries began to steer native traditions toward a belief in Jesus Christ.

By the early 1600s, God was ready to begin the colonization of North America. Three main groups of colonists sailed to the New World as strangers in an untamed new land. The first of those groups was the colony of Jamestown.

Jamestown was established in Virginia in 1607 as a business venture by The Virginia Company of London, an English investment group. They professed piety and stated that they came to seek God, but their true objective was gold. Some were down-and-out "gentlemen" who hoped for a rich new start in life. Others were convicts and professional soldiers without a war to fight. Unfortunately, none were farmers who could grow food for survival in a savage new land. All property was community-owned, and each settler was allotted his necessities from the results of common effort (in modern terminology, communism).

Many of the gentlemen refused to labor, though starvation loomed. The rest of the colonists worked half-heartedly, unwilling to exert themselves when their idle neighbors would benefit as much as they from the labor expended. With meager crop yields, every winter brought starvation. Each summer, ships brought new settlers, most with no food production skills and scant supplies. Though their system of communism was eventually abandoned, the preoccupation with wealth continued for twenty years. At least half—sometimes many more than half—of the colonists died each winter. One minister accompanied the original group. Though he tried, he failed to turn their hearts from riches to God and died the second winter.

In the beginning, the natives gave limited help, which eventually vanished altogether. The colonists began to steal food from the Indians and then killed them to compensate for their own negligence in food production. The Jamestown colony became a desolate, death-ridden place that frequently found itself under attack by the natives. It and the Pilgrim and Puritan colonies that followed struggled with high death rates and insufficient food for years after their founding. By far, Jamestown took the brunt of the difficulty.

Help arrived in 1609 in the form of a new governor, Lord De La Warr. When he arrived, the people of Jamestown had food sufficient to last—at near-starvation levels—for only sixteen days. Taking control, he imposed martial law. He implemented a rigid work schedule, requiring all hands to labor. Without his intervention, the colony would very shortly have perished to the last man. Officials continued to mistreat the Indians. It was two decades before the extreme crisis stage passed for Jamestown.

The colonists' situation might have been less difficult if the settlers of Jamestown had attended more to spiritual matters, as well as to hard work, to qualify for God's help. Divine assistance could have softened their burdens.

2.2 | The Pilgrims of 1620: Christian Unity

IN 1620, one hundred two Pilgrims arrived in Plimoth (Plymouth) Colony, in present-day Massachusetts, as indentured servants under temporary contract to their English business sponsors. They were led by William Bradford, one of the greatest of America's Christian ministers. They sought God's will to raise their children free from worldly influences. They desired to carry the light of Christ with hope and zeal to a remote continent. Their founding document, the Mayflower Compact, voluntarily committed all aboard the ship to a government based on biblical principles. It established a pattern for our American representative government.

The Pilgrims also practiced religious "communism," with all property in common, as Jamestown had done. But Governor Bradford said of their experiment: "[This] experience ... was found to breed much ... discontent and retard ... employment."[2] A fundamental facet of human nature is the need to own things. We need the opportunity to call them ours and the responsibility to protect them. When we own property and must account for it, we work harder. After three years, the Pilgrims' communal system was abandoned, and each head of household received private land to farm. Only then did they begin to flourish.

The first months on land brought the "general sickness," when many died from scurvy and exposure to the elements. Unlike Jamestown, the Plymouth colonists turned repeatedly to prayer and service to their fellow settlers. Blessings came, and their fortunes began to turn.

One day in early March, the Indian Samoset, an Algonquin chief who was visiting a nearby tribe, strode into their common house, wearing only a leather loincloth. To the startled Pilgrims, he boomed: "Welcome!" He further stunned them with his next words: "Have you got any beer?" Samoset, in traveling with exploring Europeans, had learned the English language and some of their habits. He brought them another

English-speaking Indian named Squanto, who had been kidnapped and taken to Britain for several years, had learned Christianity there, and had returned to find that his entire tribe had perished.[3]

Squanto became their passport to survival. He introduced the colonists to local vegetable crops and taught them to extract maple syrup, stalk deer, and use native healing herbs to treat illness. He showed them how to collect beaver pelts, which brought them valuable funds in the British markets. Through his influence, the local Indians lent protection from more hostile tribes. Squanto's arrival on the Pilgrim scene is evidence of God's mercy to the faithful. He greatly improved their lives and reduced their trials in the new land. He died twenty months after the arrival of the Pilgrims. Before his death, he asked their governor to pray that he could go to the Englishmen's God in heaven.[4]

Unlike the Jamestown colonizers, the Pilgrims worked together to promote a Christlike society. Their virtue extended even toward their sponsoring investment company in England, which dealt with them unfairly. Rather than bring animosity into their midst, they forgave and submitted to the unfairness. They consequently paid twenty thousand pounds to retire a debt of eighteen hundred pounds.[5]

Miracles attended the colony because of their commitment to God. One example occurred during their second summer. A devastating twelve-week drought threatened their food crop. The entire congregation of Pilgrims humbled themselves in personal repentance. They held a nine-hour prayer gathering. At its conclusion, clouds were forming. The rain came without wind or violence and soaked the earth for fourteen days. The dying plants revived and produced an abundant crop for winter.

2.3 | Arrival of the Puritans, 1630

THE PURITANS came to America to be a light on a hill—a covenant people. They sought to leave behind the worldliness of the common man. They intended to build a new life in an untainted new world.

The Puritans were the third major group to come from Britain to America in the early 1600s. They arrived in the area of Boston, Massachusetts, in 1630 and settled just forty miles north of the Pilgrims. Their leader was John Winthrop. Their arrival began the Great Migration, which eventually brought twenty thousand Puritans and forty-five thousand other Englishmen to American shores during the next sixteen years.

While the Pilgrims had fled because of religious persecution, the Puritans left by choice. They came to separate from and purify the corrupt English church. They believed that England's lack of virtue in government, religion, and public and private life had left it without a soul. The Puritans trusted that their reformation would travel back to England and cleanse the mother church and government, both of which had embraced moral and spiritual bankruptcy.

The Puritans built a covenant community where the laws of God, rather than man, would govern. They believed that the primary adversary of each individual was the self that yields to Satan's temptations. Puritan parents believed that their children belonged to God and that they would have to account to Him for their children's instruction. They viewed themselves as a community family. Every relationship strengthened or weakened the united family.

To help each other, they gave and received both advice and rebuke from fellow members with kindness. To belong to Christ was to belong to one another. They shared a common attitude of submitting cheerfully to authority and a willingness to serve each other. They had a stable, happy way of life, despite many trials. Their commitment to the community made them a covenant people.

Circumstances were difficult. Between April and December of their first year, two hundred members of their community died. Their death rate for several years was nearly 50 percent. Boatloads of new settlers arrived yearly with no supplies. Even with good harvests, winter always brought near-starvation. They met their adversities with faith and united strength. Unlike Jamestown two decades earlier, the Puritans maintained sound relations with the natives. They never doubted their future success in their New World colony. Their faith assured them that what God had planted, He would maintain.

The Puritan ethic generated another great American leader in addition to John Winthrop. Thomas Hooker was a humble, gifted, and compassionate spiritual leader. He asked permission of Governor Winthrop to divide the colony, and he moved his followers to present-day Connecticut. Combining the Pilgrims' Mayflower Compact, the Puritans' Christian charity, and his own belief in the ability of the common man to govern himself responsibly, Hooker drafted the Fundamental Orders of Connecticut for his followers. This document represented another step in the evolution of American self-rule. It introduced representative government in colonial America. The concept found its way into other colonial constitutions and eventually became part of the United States Constitution.

The American colonists were marching inexorably toward God's government—of the people, by the people, for the people. Of their many wise leaders, John Winthrop stood above the rest.

2.4 | John Winthrop, the "Puritan Moses"

INTERWOVEN in the history of the New World were great individuals raised by God's hand to guide her destiny. The great man in Puritan times was John Winthrop, the "Puritan Moses."[6] He was a rock of stability to this fledgling colony, equal to Nehemiah of the Old Testament. His importance to the Puritans parallels the influence of George Washington among America's Founding Fathers.

John Winthrop was a Cambridge-educated attorney and magistrate in Suffolk, England, a discreet and sober man who dressed in common clothing despite his wealth. He was known for his merciful judgments to lawbreakers. His towering conversion to Christ came during his teen years. He learned compassion and generosity of soul through adversity, losing his first two wives and seven of his children in death.

He became convinced that it was God's will for him to go to America and told his wife. He said: "I have assurance that my charge is of the Lord and that he hath called me to this work."[7] He and his fellow believers drew up their governing document, the Cambridge Agreement, and committed themselves to the New World venture.

Winthrop arrived in Massachusetts Bay in 1630 and found half the advance parties of the two previous years either dead or nearly so. He divided the colonists into work parties and required all, even the gentlemen who had accompanied them as business partners, to work. Although it would seem obvious that all would work toward common survival in difficult circumstances, this was not the elitist pattern of old England. Many gentlemen starved rather than work with their hands for their own support.

From Winthrop's single-handed leadership, the settlement resurrected itself. He labored with the community until there was not an idle person to be found in the entire colony. Women worked alongside the men. Fishing parties were organized, with competitions between the groups to stimulate effort.

With the first autumn, it became apparent that the colony's supplies would not last the winter. Governor Winthrop sent the ship *Lyon* and her captain back to England with a list of goods to purchase and instructions to sell his extensive land holdings in payment. By mid-February, the food supplies for the struggling colonists were exhausted. Winthrop set a day of fasting and distributed the last of the available cornmeal. That morning, the sails of the *Lyon* appeared on the horizon. She brought critical supplies, one of the most important of which was casks of lemon juice to prevent the dreaded and deadly scurvy.

It was John Winthrop's vision that unified and committed the group. His ability to organize saved the colony. He provided the leadership that kept them focused on their Christ-centered objectives. His unbounded love for his fellow colonists was obvious in his uncomplaining financial support of the colony and his merciful judgments during the decades he served as its governor. The Indians respected him, and the people followed him. "His justice was impartial, his wisdom excellently tempered . . . his courage made him dare to do right."[8]

John Winthrop, though little known today, was one of the great men who sustained the drive for freedom in a harsh but promising land.

2.5 | Life among the Puritans

THE PURITANS are often inaccurately portrayed as being dour and morose. They were not. They were genuine people who enjoyed life in the same ways we do today. The following insights and stories from the book *The Light and the Glory*, by Peter Marshall and David Manuel, describe their everyday lives.[12] The descriptions come from their many personal journals.

Puritan religious services, which were considered mandatory, were typically several hours long. A good minister was expected to speak for at least two hours. Sunday, the first day of the week, was marked with two meetings, each three or four hours long, with lunch in between. Time was kept by a large hourglass near the pulpit. The "tithing man," who was paid by the members, was responsible to turn the hourglass. His duties included bringing truant members to meetings. He was also charged to awaken sleeping members of the congregation with the aid of a long stick to which a sharp thorn had been attached.

As recorded in Obadiah Turner's journal of 1646, the tithing man spotted a Mr. Tomlins sleeping with much comfort during the meeting. Thrusting his staff behind Dame Ballard, he pricked the sleeper's hand. Tomlins sprang up, struck his hand forcefully against the wall, and cried aloud: "Curse ye, woodchuck!" in apparent response to the dream he was having. Turner records in his journal that he thought Tomlins would not soon sleep again in meetings.

***

Music was vital in the worship service, but no accompanying instruments were available. Congregational singing, while done in unison, took on a decidedly independent flair. Choirs consisted of participants who sang the psalms in a common meter as a deacon read one line at a time.

A story relates that one deacon, rising to lead the choir, found his eyesight failing him and apologized: "My eyes, indeed, are very blind."

The choir, assuming that he had begun, sang the line.

The deacon exclaimed: "I cannot see at all!"

The choir dutifully sang the line.

Frustrated, he cried out: "I really believe you are bewitched!"

This the choir also sang.

Loudly, the deacon declared: "The mischief's in you all!" and sat down in disgust. It is not recorded whether the choir sang that line.

***

A Puritan journalist wrote of the 1682 dedication dinner for the new Lynn, Massachusetts, meeting house, held in the largest place in town—a Mr. Hood's barn. Competing with the noisy chickens, the pastor, one Mr. Shepherd, lost his patience. "Mr. Shepherd's face did turn very red, and he catched up an apple and hurled it at the birds." A fowl fell floundering onto the banquet table, landed in the gravy bowl, and sprayed food on the faces and garments of the attendees. Some were not amused.

A Mr. Gerrish, attempting to gape and laugh at the same time, set his jaws so far open that they would not close again. One Mr. Rogers, knowing something of anatomy, had him sit on the floor. Rogers gave Gerrish a powerful blow and a sudden press to the jaws, which brought them back into working order. The journalist recorded that Gerrish did not talk much more that evening.

***

Despite their serious spiritual outlook and dour reputation, the Puritans brought laughter into their challenging lives. Perhaps this contributed to their inner strength and resilience.

2.6 | # The Puritans Receive Divine Assistance

GOD WATCHED over the Puritan colonies and sent them miracles. They were very much in need of them.

One illustrative story involves two ships at sea, one sailing to the Puritan colony in New England and the other bound for Barbados. The Barbados ship developed an unstoppable leak, and the crew abandoned to a lifeboat with plenty of food but little water. Eighteen days later, they had only a teaspoon of water per person per day. The Puritan ship, captained by Samuel Scarlet, was destitute of food but had ample water. When Scarlet's ship spied the lifeboat from the Barbados ship, crew members pleaded with the captain not to take the drifters aboard, saying that they would all starve. The captain replied: "I am resolved I will take them in, and I'll trust in God, who is able to deliver us all." With food from one ship and water from the other, they all arrived safely in New England a few days later.[9]

***

In the summer of 1646, a rain of caterpillars descended on the colonists. Black insects an inch and a half long arrived en masse and without warning during a great thundershower. An hour later, they covered everything. They ate the corn and peas and left the plants wasted. They fell on roads, leaving the cartwheels green from running over them.

The Puritans handled this situation as they did all others. They called a day of fasting, prayer, and "humiliation." Attendance at Sunday meetings had begun to slip, and some saw this plague as a warning from God. Shortly thereafter, the Lord took the worms away as suddenly as they had come, to the wonderment of the colonists.[10]

***

By 1665, prosperity had blessed the Puritans. Some had become lax in their covenant-keeping, especially among the younger generation. A massive Indian uprising jolted them back from apathy. The raids turned New England into a battleground for over a year. Fifteen hundred Indian braves, intent on driving the colonists from their continent, descended on scores of communities.

Individual instances of God's mercy surfaced during that year. One of those incidents involved Mary Rowlandson. When their community of Lancaster was attacked by Indians, she and her three children took refuge in the community safe house. The attackers set fire to it. Mary fled with her children, carrying her infant in her arms. Both she and the infant were shot and captured. They were taken with the roaming band of Indians as they traveled. She carried her infant through the snow as infection settled into their wounds, followed by violent fever.

After nine days, the baby died. Mary survived and related that "God was with me, in a wonderful manner, carrying me along and bearing up my spirit, [so] that it did not quite fail." Many of the women taken captive by the Indians either went mad or committed suicide. Twelve weeks later, shortly before the hostilities ended, she was miraculously released and found that her son, daughter, and husband were alive and safe.[11]

Even during calamity, God extends mercy to those who earnestly seek it.

2.7 | George Whitefield and the Great Awakening, 1734

THE MIRACLE of the Great Awakening prepared America to give birth to her inspired Constitution. This event, beginning in 1734, encompassed a tremendous outpouring of the Spirit of God on America and England.

This spiritual regeneration began in Northampton, Massachusetts, in the small parish led by Jonathan Edwards. It spread back to England, where it illuminated a young, devout Englishman named George Whitefield. He was a student at Oxford University and an associate of John Wesley, who founded the Methodist faith. In a moment of great truth, Whitefield turned his life over to God. This began an amazing thirty-three-year journey to teach people about Jesus Christ.

He preached, and revivals began in his wake. He came to America, where he taught groups of thousands and inspired other preachers, who did the same. Workmen shut their shops, farmers left their plows in the fields, and families came together to hear him preach of Christ. Crowds jammed the roads and streets in great throngs, raising immense clouds of dust as they came. Yet as he spoke, they stood perfectly still. Benjamin Franklin, his good friend, computed that, in an open space, Whitefield's voice could be heard by thirty thousand people. He sometimes spoke to groups of that size.

People began to change their lives. Towns became safe, psalms were heard in the streets, and the wayward repented. Those who had been heedless of religion came alive with the message brought by George Whitefield. He preached up and down the seaboard of the American colonies. He rode into the backwoods to bear his message. As he preached, even ministers who had grown complacent in their craft openly acknowledged their reconversion to Christ.

He kept a punishing schedule, sometimes preaching three and four times a day for two hours or more at a time. Year after year for over three decades, he preached a total of over eighteen thousand sermons. Finally, his lungs spent and his health gone, he returned to preach in Boston five months after the Boston Massacre. He died a month later after preaching one last, glorious sermon in New Hampshire.

George Whitefield was instrumental in stirring into action the spiritual unity of the thirteen colonies. He helped bring about the belief that, in the eyes of their Creator, all men were equal. He preached that geographical boundaries lost significance in the unity of God's purpose. In addition, he taught of action: that what one does results from conviction. Action would be badly needed in the coming War for Independence. George Whitefield pointed the way.

This quote piques the mind: "What was this Great Awakening? It was a deep awakening of a national desire to live a covenant life. It is a hunger so deeply ingrained in the American national psyche that it can never die, though it can go fast asleep. God reawakened that desire in the 1740s, and what He reawakened once, He can reawaken again!"[13]

Today's America is very much in need of another Great Awakening.

2.8 | British Oppression Builds

BRITISH OPPRESSION, and America's resistance to it, began 150 years before the Declaration of Independence was penned.

The British practiced watchful negligence in their political relationship with the colonies. Parliament made the laws, and the colonies governed themselves under state charters. The colonists tried to tread a path of neutrality and compliance when possible, but contention arose on occasion, in which the Americans proved themselves to be independent and headstrong. The British chafed at colonial resistance. The impression developed that Americans were uncooperative and willful.

America's churches began to advocate for British noninvolvement in colonial affairs. Word spread to England that the ministers were preaching revolution in America's churches. In time, the common citizens began to speak out against the Crown-appointed governors. One of the British governors wrote home to England: "If you ask an American who is his master, he will tell you he has none, nor any Governor, but Jesus Christ."[14]

Their resistance did not go unnoticed. In about 1685, England's King James II sent Sir Edmond Andros to impose the authority of the Crown in the Americas. Andros ordered all worship services replaced with Anglican services, the British state religion. He revoked the charters of all Crown colonies. Resentment flared, as the following example illustrates. British agents arrived after dark at the Hartford meetinghouse to collect Connecticut's charter. The cherished document was laid out on a table in the candlelit room. At the moment the document was to be handed over, the candles were suddenly snuffed out. A great hubbub ensued. When light was restored, the document was gone. Andros revoked the charter nonetheless, and the document was later found secreted in an old hollow tree.

The feeling grew among the colonists that resistance to tyranny was obedience to God. Even King James I had said that "a king . . . [ceases] to be a king, and degenerates into a tyrant, as soon as he leaves off rule according to his laws."[15] Parliament was violating the very charters it had agreed to. By all standards, James II had become a tyrant.

The situation was defused when James was overthrown in 1689 by William and Mary in England's Glorious Revolution. Sir Edmund Andros was apprehended trying to flee the American colonies disguised as a woman. The rights of the colonists as freeborn English citizens were restored, and contention temporarily dissipated. This bought an additional seventy years for the American colonies to mature in their preparations for freedom.

During the mid-1700s, the British and French fought a protracted war over control of the eastern North American continent. It was a costly endeavor. England was fighting the French around the world and could not raise sufficient troops at home. The colonists were required to fight, but they demanded a large wage to do so. England was forced to hire German Hessian soldiers, who later fought against Americans on colonial soil.

Parliament and King George III decided that Americans should pay the North American war costs through taxation. After all, the British reasoned, the Americans were the chief beneficiaries of the war.

This tax was a violation of every colonial charter. The American colonists rose in protest.

3

We the People

insure domestic Tranquility, provide for the common
and our Posterity, do ordain and establish this the

Section Three

℘

CONFLICT AND INDEPENDENCE

AMERICA was becoming prosperous. Cotton and tobacco sprang from her soil, and ships bearing manufactured American goods plied the seas back to England. She was also becoming important as her population and power advanced. Britain stood to capitalize on America's growth.

The war which lost America for the British began over taxation. America was a British colony, and Britain needed money to support its worldwide properties. To King George III, the issue was clear—the thirteen colonies would contribute to the mother country.

Taxation was only part of the conflict. The second issue was the lack of representation for those being taxed. The Americans were to forfeit their money without being given a voice in how it would be used. There was no promise that America's confiscated money would return to benefit the colonies. It was this combined abuse that pushed Americans into a wall of resistance against their British masters.

King George III was a myopic man who saw only that the colonies must be obedient to the throne. He sent tax collectors to America to raid its coffers and return the spoils to the king's treasury. Their corruption put the tax funds collected into the pockets of the collectors and their political cronies. This gave no benefit to King George. He and his ministers tightened the reins on the colonies, and resentment escalated. American sympathizers in the British Parliament warned the king that he was pushing the colonies into rebellion. The Americans pleaded for his benevolence. King George III would not listen.

His own people would not support his war. He could not raise the necessary enlistments and had to hire soldiers from other countries. Catherine of Russia refused to answer his request, and Frederick of Prussia curtly declined. The ruler of Holland touted the bravery of the Americans and pronounced the British request to purchase troops as detestable.

King George was on his own. Still, he moved forward into war with his own subjects. The results for the British Empire were tragic. By contrast, the ultimate effects for America were profoundly grand. Her natural leaders began to emerge. Among the first of these was Samuel Adams.

3.1 | Samuel Adams, Flame of the Revolutionary Fire

A CENTRAL FORCE exists in every movement, without which it would not survive. That force in revolutionary America was Samuel Adams. Without him, there might have been no American independence. He lit the flame and fanned it until it burst into the powerful fires of freedom.

Samuel Adams of Massachusetts was a kind, deeply religious man whose life was governed by unfailing integrity. His heart was in politics. With his instinctive understanding of the process, he was the political conscience of the patriot cause. He was unyielding and fully confident in the cause of liberty. He was quick to understand and calm in the clashes of the political world. Though he was of the upper middle class and Harvard-educated, he knew most of the fifteen thousand citizens of Boston by name, trade, and political preference. He accepted them as equals. His political positions were not tainted by personal ambition or self-interest.

English rule in the 1700s left the colonists largely in control of their own governments under Crown-appointed officials. In Massachusetts, there were two governing councils, the equivalent of our modern-day House of Representatives and Senate. They made and passed laws for the colony. Tariffs and import duties were paid to England, but only if the colonists could not evade them and the authorities enforced them (smuggling by American merchants was a respectable form of colonial enterprise).

In 1764, the British Parliament disregarded the provisions of the Massachusetts Bay Charter and imposed the Stamp Tax. Samuel Adams demanded that Parliament abide by the charter laws, which required colonial consent for taxation. Once Parliament started taxing, he reasoned, where would it stop? His message: "We have a charter. You will abide by it."

The American revolution thus began in May 1764 in Boston's Faneuil Hall, with Samuel Adams standing at the rostrum as its director. Through the next twelve years, he challenged every infringement of the Massachusetts charter, never letting any issue rest. He wearied each of the three successive governors with his unyielding tenacity. He railed at every injustice. He urged the colonists on when they grew tired and would have slid into apathy. Constantly recruiting those who could aid in the cause, he was the genius uniting the colonies into concerted action.

Initially, neither he nor his contemporaries had independence in mind. By 1774, he, along with his cousin John Adams, realized that there was no other option.

His powerful writing became the voice of the revolution, as well as its flame. He wrote voluminous essays, often under assumed names, as was common at the time. His articles appeared frequently in the weekly four-page periodicals of the day, especially the patriotic *Boston Gazette*. These colonial newspapers made the five-week voyage to England and informed the American sympathizers in influential British circles of progressive American resistance.

Samuel Adams did not keep a journal. He destroyed most of his correspondence to protect those mentioned within it from the proofs of treason, in case their cause failed. Hence, there is little written about him compared to his contemporaries.

He was the vortex of rebellion against tyranny. From him came the passion for freedom, igniting others who joined the cause.

3.2 | Rebellion Erupts

THE BRITISH seemed unable to understand or care about the issues important to American colonists.

Time and again they moved to irritate and increase conflict rather than resolve it. They were blind, unable to see anything but the demands of the Crown and Parliament. They turned deaf ears to the concerns of the governed. The English colonial governors, appointed by Parliament, were particularly obtuse. Some misrepresented colonial actions in their correspondence to their English counterparts. They made little attempt at compromise, and their authoritative position was clear: "This is how it is. Whether you like it or not, live with it." The ruling Britons seemed to believe that if they maintained a strong position, the Americans would eventually yield. They did not.

Massachusetts Bay, and particularly Boston, took the brunt of the British wrath. First came the Stamp Act in 1764. It required that any matter involving a piece of paper—such as business transactions, marriage licenses, and contracts—have a British stamp attached. The purchase of the stamp constituted a tax. The colonies responded by calling their first-ever Continental Congress in protest. Patriots absconded with all stamped paper and destroyed it, and the Stamp Act fell apart under rebellion.

The British retaliated in 1767 with the Townsend Acts, which imposed duties on imported goods. The colonists signed a nonconsumption agreement and boycotted goods on which these duties must be paid. This rebellion brought crisis again, and the British sent a thousand Redcoats to enforce the peace. Ultimately, all the Townsend Acts were repealed except the tax on tea. It remained as a symbol to the unruly colonials that the Crown believed it had the right to impose taxation.

In 1770, the presence of British troops in Boston led to tragedy in the Boston Massacre. It began as a street fight between colonials and Redcoats and ended with the British firing into the crowd. Three men were killed, and others were wounded. As a result, the Massachusetts colonists demanded the removal of troops from Boston.

An inflamed Samuel Adams initiated a writing campaign: the Committee of Correspondence. His purpose was to communicate with the other colonies concerning British actions in Massachusetts. This drew them together in the cause. From that time forward, the thirteen British colonies marched together toward what became their final destination—independence.

The infamous Boston Tea Party, in December 1773, resulted from the British tax on tea. The private British East India Company, a major contributor to the British treasury, was in debt and oversupplied with tea. Parliament had a solution: they would export the tea to America, where it would be sold at a cheaper price than Americans were paying for Dutch tea, even with the tax England would add. The Americans refused to yield. Their objection was not price, but taxation. They dumped all the tea aboard the ship *Dartmouth* into Boston harbor as a declarative act to Parliament: "You still don't understand. You cannot illegally tax us."

Other colonies reacted in similar ways to Britain's trampling of their rights, such as Virginia with its Virginia Resolves. Boston and her seaport, however, formed the central reactive force to British political injustice.

The pride and arrogance of the British ultimately cost them the richest prize imaginable—the North American continent. Outright war would soon follow.

3.3 | The Colonists Protest

T HE COLONISTS throughout the thirteen colonies resisted their British oppressors.[1]

Prior to the war, the colonists rebelled against the Stamp Act by refusing to transact any business using the embossed British paper bearing the stamp. They hung in effigy the officer in charge of selling the stamped paper. New Hampshire interred an empty coffin, labeled "Liberty is dead," then resurrected it, renamed it "Liberty's alive again!" and paraded the empty coffin through the streets. In Charleston, South Carolina, men gathered around the "Liberty Tree" and pledged to resist tyranny to the utmost. When the Carolinas later came under British occupation, British General Clinton cut the tree down and burned its parts. Patrick Henry of Virginia emerged as a powerful voice for independence. He spoke with such fervor that frightened old men begged him for moderation in his speech, lest there be retaliation.

Patriotic groups called the Sons of Liberty formed throughout the colonies to protest British oppression. The women formed groups they called the Daughters of Liberty. They refused English goods and made their own yarn and fabric. The entire 1770 class of Columbia College graduated in suits of homespun cloth in support of the colonial effort. Herbal teas were substituted for boycotted British tea.

After the war began, colonial involvement increased. The cloth woven by the Daughters of Liberty was made into clothing for the soldiers. The women maintained shops and farms, while the men went to war. Spinning groups met and competed to encourage faster production. The James Nixon family of Newport, Rhode Island, created 487 yards of fabric and 36 pairs of stockings in an eighteen-month period.

The statue of King George III on Bowling Green in New York City was pulled down, and the women recast the metal into bullets. Tallies were kept, and Ruth Marvin held the record for the 10,790 bullets she personally cast from the statue. Women donated their pewter dishes for bullets and tore their dresses into rag strips to make wadding for muskets. During battle, they reloaded muskets for their men. One elderly woman living near Lexington captured a squad of Redcoats and marched them at gunpoint into American hands.

Even children became involved. Cynthia Smith, about eleven years of age, gained entrance to a banquet hosting British General Cornwallis and demanded that he return Free 'n' Equal, her pet calf, which the British soldiers had stolen. She succeeded and was given a pair of silver shoe buckles in the bargain. The young daughter of Parson White of Windham, Massachusetts, gallantly contributed her pet lamb to the war effort. Through her tears, she gave it to the messengers taking food to starving colonists in Boston during the city's British occupation.

A group of young boys from Boston marched into the office of British General Gage to protest abuse by the Redcoats, who had destroyed their forts and skating ponds. When asked who had sent them, they replied: "Nobody sent us, sir, but your soldiers have insulted us, thrown down our forts, broken the ice on our pond, spoiled our coats, and we will not stand for it!" General Gage ordered his soldiers to desist and remarked to a junior officer: "Even the children here draw in the love of liberty with the very air they breathe."

Americans were determined to fight for freedom.

3.4 | The War for Independence Begins, 1775

UNINTENDED and unofficial war began at Lexington, Massachusetts, on April 19, 1775. As yet, there was no general to lead the American troops.

British regulars approached the seventy or so colonial militiamen waiting for them on Lexington Green, fifteen miles northwest of Boston. The "minutemen" had been alerted to the British advance by Paul Revere in his famous ride. The confrontation ended with eight patriots dead and ten wounded, several of whom later died due to lack of good medical care. The battle continued throughout the day as it moved to Concord. In their engagements, the British first experienced the frustration of sniper warfare conducted by the colonials. This battle method had been previously unknown to the regimented and highly visible Redcoats.

The experience of eighty-year-old Sam Whittemore offers a window into the involvement of common citizens. He prepared his personal arsenal of weapons, consisting of two pistols, a musket, and his old cavalry saber. After informing his wife that he was going to fight the British, he positioned himself behind a wall 150 yards from the road. His volley of shots aimed at a passing British column was so accurate that a unit of Redcoats was sent to destroy him. As they neared the wall, he dropped a Redcoat with his musket and, firing both pistols, took down two more. As he drew his saber, a ball hit him in the face. The British bayoneted him before leaving him for dead. But Sam Whittemore was not dead. With fourteen bayonet wounds and half his face gone, he lived to be ninety-six. He swore that, if given the chance, he would do it all again.[2]

The Redcoats under General Gage occupied Boston at that time. They were trapped in the city, surrounded on all land sides by the American colonials. The British chose to attack their rebellious rivals on Dorchester Heights on June 18, 1775. The colonials spent the night digging protective fortifications on nearby Breed's Hill. When daylight revealed the American entrenchments, the British attacked anyway and were mowed down in their first two assaults. The third attack succeeded and brought the Redcoats, with bayonets mounted, into the colonial trenches. The American defenders had exhausted their two rounds of ammunition each. Five hundred American patriots lost their lives. The British won this engagement, known as the Battle of Bunker Hill, but lost a thousand men. They were learning that these patriots were not cowards. They would fight.

In spite of these battles, most of the general colonial population in 1775 still hoped that hostilities would cease. They expected to resolve the issues and remain part of the British Empire. The spring of 1776 changed that. Thomas Paine published the booklet *Common Sense*, which advocated immediate independence. Individual states began to set up their governments outside the influence of England's Parliament. After all, they reasoned, King George had disowned them, so they were no longer British subjects.

For eight long years, the Revolutionary War drained the blood and resources of the American colonists. It became a purifying force for America. The war in Massachusetts drew the colonies together as a new nation began to emerge.

3.5 | Finding a Commander

As war began in June of 1775, The Continental Congress appointed a commander of the American revolutionary forces. At the urging of John Adams, that man was George Washington. His appointment initially surprised his contemporaries.

Washington had commanded troops during the French and Indian War. His somewhat limited and unimpressive services had ended fifteen years earlier. He was, however, very popular and a Southerner. The thirteen colonies were distrustful and suspicious of each other, and uniting them would be difficult. With mostly Northern soldiers, a commander from the South who could gain their respect would tie the colonial armies together.

There were others more qualified, yet Washington was the near-unanimous choice. Time proved the validity and inspiration of the congressional selection. Charles Lee, a professional soldier who was appointed second-in-command, later betrayed the Americans to the British. He was captured by them, and during his confinement, he offered to show the British how they could defeat the Americans. After his repatriation, he served dishonorably and was tried and suspended from the army.

General Horatio Gates, another professional soldier, had military qualifications and experience far superior to Washington's. After the war began, he worked behind Washington's back to try to oust him. He turned coward after his defeat at Camden and fled 150 miles on horseback from the battlefield. He was disgraced and investigated for his behavior.

Thomas Conway, an Irish-born professional military man who could have commanded the army, later instigated a plot to have Washington replaced, calling him inept and of "miserable talents." Thomas Mifflin, another potential candidate, joined Gates and Conway in a cabal to destroy Washington. Mifflin later became the quartermaster general in charge of supplies for Washington's troops. He was derelict and absent from his duties for long periods. Much of the responsibility for the deaths of two thousand men from starvation and freezing at Valley Forge lies with this conniving, irresponsible officer.

Well aware of his limitations, Washington discouraged his proposed appointment. He expressed his concerns to his wife, Martha, in a letter: "I have used every endeavor in my power to avoid this appointment . . . [it] being a trust too great for my capacity."[3] In his acceptance speech before Congress, he said: "I feel great distress from a consciousness that my abilities and military experience may not be equal to the extensive and important trust . . . I beg it may be remembered by every gentleman in the room that I this day declare with utmost sincerity, I do not think myself equal to the command I [am] honored with."[4]

At an offered salary of five hundred dollars a month (which he declined to accept at war's end), George Washington found himself "the commander of an unorganized military force to fight an undeclared war in behalf of a nation that did not yet exist."[5]

Time and circumstances proved the inspiration in Washington's selection as commander of the American army. His humility and excellent character held him steady, and his tenacity and determination never failed. Though he made mistakes, he learned from them and simply would not give up.

It was George Washington who held the army together through the great difficulties and hardships of eight battle-scarred years.

3.6 | George Washington, Revolutionary General

GEORGE WASHINGTON is rightly called the Father of our Country. Without him, there likely would have been no victory in war and no Constitution written. His dedicated and unselfish hand would have been absent as the first president of the United States.

Originally one of the wealthiest men in America, he yearned for life as a private citizen at Mount Vernon, his majestic estate in Virginia. However, when his country called, he went. After eight years on the battlefield and eight years as our first president, his neglected estate had deteriorated and much of his wealth was gone. He died less than three years after leaving office, struggling to meet expenses. As promised in the Declaration of Independence, he had pledged his life, his fortune, and his sacred honor to the cause of America. He gave all three.

He was six feet two inches, which was very tall by colonial standards, and weighed about 190 pounds. His hair was reddish-brown, and his eyes were blue-grey. His face was freckled and sun-beaten, with smallpox scars lightly visible. A few bad teeth showed when he smiled.

Thomas Jefferson describes Washington's character thus: "Never did nature and fortune combine more perfectly to make a man . . . His mind was great and powerful . . . No judgment was ever stronger. He was incapable of fear . . . never acting until every circumstance, every consideration . . . was weighed . . . His integrity was pure . . . he was, indeed, in every sense of the words, a wise, a good and a great man. [He was] the fittest man on earth for directing so great a contest under so great difficulties."[6] He had the bearing of a man accustomed to respect and to being obeyed, yet he was amiable and modest. He was revered by the men who followed him into battle, and his caring and concern for them was deep and genuine.

He became a military genius, though he was not born or trained as such. He adapted, he found creative ways to use his limited resources, and he sought counsel. He held to the course, never wavering, no matter the adversity. The force of his personality and integrity kept the Continental Army together through immense hardships.

Over and over, he gave credit to God for his success. He was very private about his beliefs, yet he mentioned God, His providence, and the Bible hundreds of times in his correspondence.

He received divine protection many times in his military endeavors, as one incident illustrates. In 1770, while surveying the Western wilderness, he met in council with the local Indians who had fought against him in the French and Indian War a decade before. One of their venerable chiefs related to Washington the prophecy he had given concerning the future general at that time: "A power mightier far than we shield[s] him from harm. He cannot die in battle . . . The Great Spirit protects that man, and guides his destinies—he will become the chief of nations, and a people yet unborn will hail him as the founder of a mighty empire."[7]

Such a description befits the man whose force of will became America's greatest weapon in her fight for freedom. Remove Washington from the Revolutionary War, and you alter its outcome.

3.7 | Writing the Declaration of Independence

T HOUGH WAR had begun, the Americans had not yet declared their independence from the mother country.

It was Thomas Jefferson whose mind and pen gave form to the document that changed the world. As members of the committee assigned to write the Declaration, he and John Adams discussed the assignment. Many years later, Adams related their conversation.

> Adams: "Jefferson proposed to me to make the draft. I said: I will not. You should do it."
>
> Jefferson: "Oh no! Why will you not? You ought to do it."
>
> Adams: "I will not!"
>
> Jefferson: "Why?"
>
> Adams: "Reasons enough."
>
> Jefferson: "What can be your reasons?"
>
> Adams: "Reason first—You are a Virginian, and a Virginian ought to appear at the head of this business. Reason second—I am obnoxious, suspected and unpopular. You are very much otherwise. Reason third—You can write ten times better than I can."
>
> Jefferson: "Well, if you are decided, I will do as well as I can."[8]

It had been a trying year for Thomas Jefferson, and he had not wanted to be in attendance at the Second Continental Congress. His beloved Virginia was drafting a new state constitution after their Crown-appointed governor had fled in the face of mounting hostilities. Jefferson wanted to be at home to participate in his home state politics.

In addition, his daughter and mother had recently died, and his wife was very ill. He needed to be at home.

The writing of the Declaration took seventeen days. During that time, Jefferson labored to express the sentiments of America which so perfectly aligned with the ancient freedom principles he had come to love in the Old Testament. His authorship of the Declaration would not be revealed for many months after its acceptance for fear of British retaliation. A good portion of the document's space is spent listing the grievances the colonists had with the British king. Most of the seventeen days, however, were spent on the opening paragraphs of the Declaration.

Not all the delegates felt courage and clarity of purpose as the conclusion of their convention drew near. At the last moment, John Dickinson, who would later draft the Articles of Confederation, spoke eloquently against independence. His attempts to deter the delegates fell largely on deaf ears.

One of the signers related that in the din of the last days of the convention debate, a mysterious man's voice was heard by several of the delegates. It loudly declared: "God has given America to be free!" No source for the voice could be found, and several took it as a sign that God wanted them to proceed to signing the document.[9]

The fifty-six delegates to the Continental Congress were now ready to sign the Declaration. With the future unrevealed, they could not know that fifteen of them would forfeit their fortunes and nine would lose their lives as a result of the War for Independence.

One of them, John Morton of Pennsylvania, died eight months after the signing from a sudden inflammatory infection. Among his last words to his family were his sentiments expressed to his future posterity: "Tell them they will live to ... acknowledge it [the signing] to have been the most glorious service that I ever rendered my country."[10]

3.8 | Thomas Jefferson, Author of the Declaration

IF WE ACCEPT the belief that history was changed by men who accomplished monumental things at critical times, Thomas Jefferson must stand as one on whom the doors of history hinged.

Born and educated in Virginia, it was said that he knew more about the law than those who scrutinized him in his bar exam. He spoke five languages and studied European history, the Greek and Roman classics, the Old and New Testaments, and the ancient Anglo-Saxons.

His universal proficiency was described by a stranger upon their meeting:

> *When he spoke of law, I thought he was a lawyer; when he talked about mechanics, I was sure he was an engineer; when he got into medicine, it was evident that he was a physician; when he discussed theology, I was convinced he must be a clergyman; when he talked of literature, I made up my mind that I had run against a college professor who knew everything.*[11]

His political accomplishments inspire awe. He revised Virginia's legal code and served as her governor and Congressman. He was not present when the Constitution was written due to his presence in Europe as the American ambassador to France. However, he influenced its principles through the trunks of books he sent James Madison to guide his thinking. Madison's genius, stimulated by Jefferson, guided the development of the Constitution.

Jefferson served as the first secretary of state under Washington. He resigned due to constant friction with Alexander Hamilton, whose policies he believed to be destructive. He served as vice-president under John Adams, then two terms as our third president, beginning in 1801. Upon the conclusion of his presidency, he gratefully retired to Monticello, his beloved home. He died at Monticello on July 4, 1826, exactly fifty years after the signing of the document he wrote—the Declaration of Independence.

Jefferson was a devoted family man who endured tragic losses, including the death of his wife, Martha, at the age of thirty-three after the birth of their sixth child. He never remarried, and only two of their daughters survived to adulthood. He had abandoned politics for private life, but after Martha's death he reentered politics. Our nation is fortunate to have had access to his political genius.

Jefferson has been one of the Founders most assailed by the enemies of America's liberty. An embittered political enemy defamed him during his presidency. Jefferson never responded publicly to the charges, though his family unequivocally and categorically refuted them. Some distortions continue today, perpetrated by those who "reinterpret" the lives of the deceased and famous. As one author said: "Though God cannot alter the past, historians can. [Concerning] our changing perceptions of great historical personalities . . . [who] are relentlessly 'reinterpreted' . . . it is doubtful whether many of these renowned characters . . . would even recognize themselves . . . in publications . . . today."[12]

The brilliant mind and eloquent pen of this great patriot live on today, through the Declaration of Independence.

3.9 | The Finished Declaration

WITH THE SIGNING of the Declaration of Independence, there was no turning back. Henry Knox, one of Washington's key generals who played a prominent part in the War for Independence, wrote: "The eyes of all America are upon us . . . As we play our part posterity will bless or curse us."[13]

The colonies had now entered a new stage. Not only were the eyes of all America upon her, but the eyes of all Europe as well. The Declaration was a monumental step, but without military victory it meant nothing. Immense effort and sacrifice would be required to give credibility to the Declaration.

The words of the Declaration of Independence were grand and sweeping. The heartfelt emotions of a fledging nation were laid bare for a doubtful world to see. The Declaration was signed on July 4, 1776, and released to the world on July 6. Newspapers throughout the colonies published it, and it was read in public squares throughout the thirteen colonies. On July 9, General Washington read the Declaration of Independence to his troops.

The opening and closing paragraphs of the Declaration of Independence offer great insight into America's heritage of freedom:

> *When in the Course of human Events, it becomes necessary for one People to dissolve the Political Bands which have connected them with another, and to assume . . . the separate and equal Station to which the Laws of Nature and of Nature's God entitle them, a decent Respect to the Opinions of Mankind requires that they should declare the causes which impel them to the Separation.*
>
> *We hold these Truths to be self-evident, that all Men are created equal, that they are endowed by their Creator with certain*

unalienable Rights, that among these are Life, Liberty and the pursuit of Happiness—That, to secure these Rights, Governments are instituted among Men, deriving their just Powers from the Consent of the Governed. That, whenever any Form of Government becomes destructive of these Ends, it is the Right of the People to alter or abolish it, and to institute new Government, laying its Foundations on such Principles, and organizing its Powers in such Form, as to them shall seem most likely to affect their Safety and Happiness . . .

In conclusion:

We, therefore, the representatives of the united States of America, in General Congress Assembled, appealing to the Supreme Judge of the World for the Rectitude of our Intentions, do, in the Name and by Authority of the good People of these Colonies, solemnly Publish and Declare, That these United Colonies are, and of Right ought to be, Free and Independent States; that they are absolved from all Allegiances to the British Crown . . . And for the support of this Declaration, with a firm Reliance on the Protection of divine Providence, we mutually pledge to each other our Lives, our Fortunes, and our sacred Honor.

Throughout the new nation, people cheered with unabashed joy. Church bells rang and cannon boomed. John Adams wrote to his beloved Abigail: "It is the will of heaven that the two countries should be sundered forever."[14]

Lives, fortunes, and sacred honor would now be required. America was free at last! What exactly was that freedom, and could she keep it?

3.10 | John Adams,
      | Voice of Freedom

MANY DYNAMIC individuals have spent their earlier years in the ranks of the unassuming. John Adams was among that group.

He was a simple, deeply religious man, plain in dress and without superficial social skills. He loved farming, good books, and long walks, which he said dispelled melancholy. Though he was ambitious, he was devoted to his wife, Abigail—his truest friend—and their four children. Two normally opposing habits of belief—a deep spirituality and independence in thought—resided comfortably in his mind. He was sensible and scholarly. He loved to talk and wished he could master the reserve of those like Washington, who kept their thoughts contained. He became a powerful orator who often infused his speeches with religious thought.

His rise to national prominence began as he turned forty. While serving as a local politician, he was elected to represent Massachusetts in the First Continental Congress. Delegates to the Congress would discuss the current political upheavals with England. Deep insecurity haunted him in facing this task. The natural political skills possessed by his cousin Samuel were absent in John. In his diary, he wrote: "We have not men fit for the times. We are deficient in genius, education, in travel, fortune—in everything. I feel unutterable anxiety."[15]

Yielding to his natural inclinations, he found his place in the Philadelphia convention. His sound opinions offered in support of American independence thrust him into national prominence. First viewed as a revolutionary for his foresight on American self-rule, he became the voice of independence. Washington's appointment as commander-in-chief of revolutionary forces was driven by John Adams. He predicted that Washington would become one of the most important people in the world.

Principles of integrity ruled his life. He defended British Captain Preston after the Boston Massacre of 1770, in which gunfire that erupted between British troops and a local mob left several Americans dead. In the minds of the prejudiced public, Preston had already been convicted. Adams took the case because he felt that the principles of justice must be applied, even for the enemy. Preston was acquitted in the trial, and Adams was not a popular man for having defended him.

Adams was instrumental in drafting the Declaration of Independence. He also largely authored the Massachusetts Constitution in 1780, which would have abolished slavery in Massachusetts had that provision been accepted. In the years prior to the Philadelphia Constitutional Convention, he was sent to represent the United States in France. He was then sent to England to negotiate the treaty that ended the Revolutionary War. Like so many of our Founders, he gave up the simple life of his beloved home for many years to serve his country.

John Adams became our first vice-president and second president, elected in 1796. By that time, political parties had formed opposing philosophies. Adams favored a strong federal government. This minority position turned him from office after one term. Bitter politics during the 1800 election defeated Adams and threatened to tear the government apart. Some politicians maneuvered to set aside the Constitution in an effort to put Adams back in office. They failed to do so. John's son, John Quincy Adams, later became our sixth president.

Despite political controversies, John Adams was a patriot and a formative influence on American freedoms.

3.11 | Embracing Independence

S OME DELEGATES wavered at signing the Declaration, and with good reason. Their signatures made them British traitors. If apprehended, they would be hung until unconscious, revived, quartered and disemboweled, then boiled in oil, which would be poured out upon the countryside so that their resting places would be unknown. Dire consequences awaited their families as well. One did not take this action lightly.

Noah Webster credited John Adams with having said to the potential signers of the Declaration:

> *Sink or swim, live or die, survive or perish, I give my hand and my heart to this vote . . . In the beginning we aimed not at independence. But there's a Divinity which shapes our ends . . .*

> *We may not live to the time when this Declaration shall be made good. We may die; die colonists; die slaves; die . . . ignominiously on the scaffold. Be it so, be it so. If it be the pleasure of Heaven that my country shall require the poor offering of my life, the victim shall be ready . . . But while I do live, let me have a country, or at least the hope of a country, and that a free country . . .*

> *But whatever may be our fate . . . this Declaration will stand. It may cost treasure, and it may cost blood; but it will . . . richly compensate for both. Through the thick gloom of the present, I see the brightness of the future . . . We shall make this a glorious, an immortal day . . . When we are in our graves our children will honor it . . . with thanksgiving . . . they will shed tears . . . of gratitude, and of joy . . .*

Sir, before God, I believe the hour is come. My judgment approves this measure, and my whole heart is in it. All that I have, all that I am, and all that I hope . . . I am now ready here to stake upon it; and I leave off as I begun, that live or die, survive or perish, I am for the Declaration. It is my living sentiment, and by the blessing of God it shall be my dying sentiment, Independence, now and Independence forever.[16]

John Witherspoon of New Jersey declared: "Gentlemen, New Jersey is ready to vote for independence. In our judgment, the country is not only ripe for independence, but we are in danger of becoming rotten for the want of it, if we delay any longer."[17]

Delaware delegate Cesar Rodney, home on an emergency, arose from his bed at 2 a.m. when summoned by an express rider to return to the drafting convention. He rode eleven treacherous hours through a raging storm to break the Delaware delegation's deadlock with his signature. Only a unanimous decision of the states would carry independence, and without Rodney's signature, the Declaration would have failed. His signature on the document prevented him from seeking help for his facial cancer in England and cost him his life.

On the day of signing, complete silence prevailed, with one exception. Colonel Benjamin Harrison of Virginia, a large and burly man, said to Elbridge Gerry of Massachusetts, who stood only five feet tall and weighed a hundred pounds: "I shall have a great advantage over you, Mr. Gerry, when we're all hung . . . from the size and weight of my body I shall die in a few minutes, but . . . you'll dance in the air for an hour or two before you die."[18]

Thus, liberty was carried into history on the backs of courageous men willing to give their all for its survival.

3.12 | Ringing for Liberty

WHEN THE Declaration of Independence was announced, bells rang throughout the thirteen colonies as word was carried abroad. A huge bronze bell, now known as the Liberty Bell, hung on the Pennsylvania State House, the scene of the signing. It first announced the breathtaking news that a new and independent country had been born.

Its elderly keeper was charged with ringing the bell for prominent funerals, elections, and state occasions. As the story is told, he employed the help of his young grandson on the day the Declaration of Independence was signed.

The following poem relates the anticipation of the people and their rejoicing when independence was announced:

There was tumult in the city, in the quaint old Quaker town,
And the streets were rife with people, pacing restless up and down;
People gathering at corners, where they whispered each to each,
And the sweat stood on their temples, with the earnestness of speech.

"Will they do it? Dare they do it? Who is speaking? What's the news?"
"What of Adams? What of Sherman? Oh, God grant they won't refuse!"
"Make some way, there! Let me nearer! I am stifling!" "Stifle, then!
When a nation's life's at hazard, we've no time to think of men!"

So they beat against the portal, man and woman, maid and child;
And the July sun in heaven on the scene looked down and smiled.
The same sun that saw the Spartan shed his patriot blood in vain,
Now beheld the soul of freedom all unconquer'd rise again.

See! See! The dense crowd quivers through all the lengthy line,
As the boy beside the portal looks forth to give the sign!

With his small hands upward lifted, breezes dallying with his hair,
Hark! With deep clean intonation, breaks his young voice on the air.

Hushed the people's swelling murmur, list the boy's exultant cry!
"Ring," he shouts, "Ring, Grandpa, ring, oh, ring for liberty!"
And straightway at the signal, the old bellman lifts his hand,
And sends the good news, making iron music through the land.

How they shouted! What rejoicing! How the old bell shook the air,
Till the clang of freedom ruffled the calm, gliding Delaware!
How the bonfires and the torches illumed the night's repose,
And from . . . flames like fabled Phoenix our glorious Liberty arose!

That old bell now is silent, and hushed its iron tongue,
But the spirit it awakened, still lives—forever young.
And when we greet the smiling sunlight, on the fourth of each July,
We'll ne'er forget the bellman, who twixt the earth and sky,
Rang out our Independence, which, please God, shall never die![19]

The Liberty Bell cracked fifty-nine years later while being rung to commemorate the funeral of John Marshall, fourth chief justice of the Supreme Court and signer of the Declaration of Independence. It stands today near Independence Hall in Philadelphia, a testament to the love of liberty that burns in the hearts of all American patriots.

3.13 | ### The Miracle of Jefferson and Adams

ONE FINAL STORY remains to be told about the Declaration of Independence.

John Adams and Thomas Jefferson were, respectively, the voice and pen of the Declaration of Independence. They met in the Congress of 1775 and became close political and personal friends. Although both were in Europe when the Constitution was drafted, each directly influenced its principles through their writings and influence on others.

In their later years, a vengeful political climate made enemies of the two former friends and allies. They disagreed over the French Revolution, which divided the American people. The bitterly contested 1800 presidential election ousted Adams in favor of Jefferson and left the two friends deeply divided.

Friends and family mourned the death of their friendship. Benjamin Rush, a signer of the Declaration of Independence and the physician general of the Revolutionary War, was the committed friend of both. He undertook the task of bringing the two great patriots back to the fold of friendship. Rush sent a letter to Adams which related a dream he had had of the reunion of the two old friends.

John Adams took the first conciliatory step and wrote to Jefferson. His letter was warmly received, and the two old men exchanged a series of letters. They reminisced on life, love of country, and their conviction of divine Providence in the work they had done. Each held a powerful belief in God and His benevolent destiny. Each believed in life beyond the grave in the presence of those they loved. Jefferson had lost his wife many years before. John Adams had the great fortune to spend many years with his beloved Abigail but lost her to death near the end of his life. He mourned her deeply, and Jefferson comforted him in his loss.

Both men died on the same day, July 4, 1826—the fiftieth anniversary of the signing of the Declaration of Independence. Thomas Jefferson breathed his last at his home in Monticello, Virginia, at 1:00 in the afternoon. Adams died at his farm in Braintree, Massachusetts, at 6:20 p.m. As the hour of Adams's death approached, a violent thunderstorm struck. It culminated in one resounding crash of thunder, followed immediately by a dazzling burst of sunlight. At that exact moment, John Adams left earth behind and entered the realm beyond life. In his final moments, he spoke from his semiconscious state and uttered the words: "Thomas Jefferson survives!"[20]

These two men, along with many powerful and committed others, had given heart and soul to the birth of free government under God's divine political plan. Joined in that cause, they were unified in this last evidence of divine sanction. Their deaths on the fiftieth anniversary of their great triumph testify of God's approval of their roles in the building of America.

The stewardship has passed to us. We face crisis in government, as they did. We face the need to restore virtue to government, as they did. We must stand and demand our freedoms, as they did.

They remained true to the cause. So must we. We must declare ourselves to heaven and restore our God-given liberty.

4

We the People

Section Four

— ☙ —

WAR AND VICTORY

THE DECLARATION OF INDEPENDENCE proclaimed freedom, and the Revolutionary War created it.

War was now a reality. With the exhilaration of independence came the need for troops, supplies, weapons, and leaders. America would need God's help in facing the greatest fighting force in the Western world.

Across America, the people prepared to fight. This included the ministers, who urged their parishioners to greater righteousness. They taught that repentance had become a war strategy. Without deserving God's help, they could not win. Many ministers joined the war effort and took their parishioners into battle with them.

Stephen Farrer of New Hampshire brought ninety-seven men of his congregation to join the colonial army at Boston. David Avery of Windsor, Vermont, marched with twenty-seven men to join Washington but preached as they traveled and garnered more along the way. Peter Muhlenberg of the Shenandoah Valley in Virginia preached his Sunday morning sermon on Ecclesiastes 3, then cast off his clerical robes to reveal his colonel's uniform underneath. "Now is the time to fight!" he thundered. The three hundred men who followed him that day became the famed 8th Virginia Regiment. Muhlenberg distinguished himself in battle, rose to the rank of brigadier general, and became the head of Washington's light infantry brigade.[1]

Of the twenty-one key battles of the war, the British won nine, the Americans won ten, and two were a draw. General Nathaniel Greene summed up the American genius: "We fight, get beat, rise, and fight again."[2]

The war would be long, requiring many, many miracles at God's hand to rescue unskilled men and leaders and to open doors for their escape from superior forces. With His help, victory would be the prize.

4.1 | America versus Britain: David and Goliath

A MERICA should have been quickly crushed in the Revolutionary War. In 1775, Great Britain was the most powerful nation on earth, with ten times the foot-to-the-ground manpower of the colonists and a marvelously equipped and skilled naval force. The Americans had no navy at all. The British had a strong currency, while the American dollar was inflated sky-high. Britain was a manufacturing center. America imported many of her needs and was hampered by naval war blockades. England's distinguished military leaders far surpassed the Americans' few experienced officers. British Redcoats were well trained and thoroughly equipped. The American Continental Army was a ragtag, undisciplined crew with weapons brought from home. There was little possibility of any outcome but total British victory.

Not all Americans united behind freedom. Tories, who wanted to continue under British rule, totaled about one-third of the colonial population. They sometimes joined the British effort to fight against American freedom. They were less than dependable, however, and were not well organized. Many eventually fled back to England or to Canada, and those who remained were not well received.

The Americans enjoyed some advantages, however. France sent troops and vessels to compensate for America's lack of naval forces. Geography worked in the Continental Army's favor as well. The territory was familiar, and communications and troops did not have to cross an ocean.

Further assistance to the Americans came in the form of Britons in the mother country who defended the American cause in the British Parliament. They believed that the war was unjust and helped to sway public opinion in England against it. This ultimately weakened the will of the British people and reduced military enlistments. Young Britons had little motivation to spend two months crossing the Atlantic in abysmal conditions below the ship's deck. Upon arrival, they would endure harsh weather, subsist on shoddy food, and risk death or disfigurement for a mediocre wage in an unpopular war.

Another unexpected benefit for the Americans came when experienced Europeans volunteered their expertise to the Continental Army. Benjamin Franklin sent Baron von Steuben, formerly of the Prussian army, from Europe, and Washington assigned him to mold a professional army from the ragtag soldiers America had to offer. Von Steuben wrote his own drill manual and trained Washington's officers. Discipline and the inevitable esteem it brings lifted the troops and unified the army. Entire regiments could now move quickly and efficiently. The time it took to reload and fire their weapons dropped dramatically, improving their chances of success in battle. Enlistments rose, and the dropout rate declined markedly.

America's will to win was her greatest strength. The Americans fought for their freedom, their homes, their wives and children, and the right to govern themselves. They were independent, rugged individuals infused with a spirit of national pride and the natural justice of God.

Just as David stood against the champion of the Philistines with only his sling and stones, the Americans faced the British with few men and weapons. Like David, they believed that they came "in the name of the Lord of Hosts" (1 Samuel 17:45) to fight their Goliath. Their faith in the rightness of their cause led them to believe that God would deliver them.

The Americans were stronger than they appeared.

4.2 | Miracle of the Cannon, 1776

HENRY KNOX, a gregarious, rotund, twenty-five-year-old Boston bookseller, entered the history books with fifty-eight pieces of artillery. His booming voice matched his love for booming cannon. He stepped into the Revolutionary War scene to become George Washington's chief of artillery.

The Continental Army needed cannon to defend Boston, and Knox knew where to find them. The defunct Fort Ticonderoga, near the Canadian border, housed abandoned French weaponry. However, winter weather and three hundred miles of rivers, lakes, and mountains separated the cannon and the army.

Few would have undertaken the task. The phenomenal delivery of the cannon to General Washington became a miracle story of the war with England.

Knox arrived at Fort Ticonderoga on December 5, 1775. He selected fifty-eight pieces of artillery, including three that weighed one thousand pounds each and one that weighed five thousand pounds. The first stage required that the cannon and mortars be loaded, with great difficulty, onto barges to be rowed across Lake George. Knox's men applied eight days of intense effort to the task. One boat sank, which required them to retrieve it and the artillery from the icy lake before they could proceed.

The second stage, in Albany, New York, required them to construct giant sleds to slide the weaponry across the snow. However, there was no snow. After a lengthy delay, it finally arrived in a three-foot blizzard. The caravan again moved forward.

Days later, the temperatures rose and the ground thawed, again delaying the troops. When the temperatures dropped again, the caravan pressed on over frozen ground to the ice-covered Hudson River. As the sleds dragged the heavy weaponry across, the ice gave way, and one of the largest cannon sank. Refusing to abandon it, Knox and his men retrieved it from the bottom of the river and traveled on.

The third stage of their incredible journey took them over the Berkshire Mountains, a range so tall that, Knox wrote, they could "almost have seen all the kingdoms of the earth."[3] Steep valleys, tumbled ridges, and lofty summits sorely taxed Knox and his men, who had no experience in such endeavors. When they reached the summit, the downhill grade was so steep that the teamsters who hauled the cannon initially refused to continue. They pressed on through sheer determination.

Word spread before them, and crowds lined the roadways as they completed their final, uneventful leg of the journey to Washington's camp.

Knox's plan succeeded brilliantly. Few men would have attempted the venture. Certainly, logic and experience would have spoken against it. Not one piece of artillery was lost during the two-month endeavor.

The cannon proved indispensible in the coming battle for Boston.

Henry Knox was a hero. He had given flesh to the biblical words of James, who spoke of small things accomplishing great events (James 3:3–5). His dedication to Washington and freedom carried the jovial Boston bookseller through eight years of faithful war service at Washington's side.

4.3 | The Battle for Boston, 1776

THE BATTLE for British-occupied Boston loomed large and worrisome for the new commander of the American forces.

While Henry Knox's arrival with the cannon from Ticonderoga gave the Americans hope, the British still occupied Boston. The Continental Army had very little gunpowder. Too many of Washington's troops were going home, taking their weapons with them.

The key to Boston's defense was Dorchester Hill. The patriot army needed to construct fortifications on the hilltop. This process would put them within weapon range and in plain sight of the enemy, who could blast them off the hill at any moment. Washington presented what seemed an unsolvable problem to his officers.

Junior officer and amateur engineer Rufus Putnam paid an unexpected visit to the tent of a senior officer. While there, he noticed a book on field operations. Opening it, he spied diagrams and a description for above-ground wooden fortifications called *chandeliers* by their French inventors. As effective as trenches, they could be constructed in parts and moved into place.

Putnam presented the information to Washington, who immediately ordered the construction of hundreds of chandeliers. He added his own twist—barrels of stones laid end-to-end in front of the fortifications, which could be released to mow down enemy troops as they climbed Dorchester Hill.

In order to put the fortifications into place unseen, the Americans began to bombard the enemy camp to create a diversion, using Henry Knox's cannon. Two days later, a heavy ground mist arose, blocking the enemy's view of the Dorchester summit, while the top of the hill remained clear and well lit by a nearly full moon. At the same time, an inland breeze carried the noise of the Americans' work away from the British, further preventing detection.

Eight hundred soldiers worked all night to place the newly built fortifications according to detailed plans drawn up by Henry Knox. Three hundred silent teams and drivers pulled the chandelier parts up the hill.

Miraculously, nothing went wrong. There were no advance warnings to the British, no innocent passersby to stumble onto the process, and no lowing oxen or broken carts.

At dawn, the British were stunned. Fortifications had appeared overnight out of nowhere. The chief British engineer called it "a most astonishing night's work" and speculated that it must have involved "between fifteen thousand and twenty thousand men."[4] British General Howe said in disgust: "These fellows have done more work in one night than I could make my army do in three months."[5]

British honor demanded an immediate attack against the firmly entrenched enemy. As the Redcoats waited for orders to advance, a violent storm struck unexpectedly. It approached hurricane velocity and drove the falling snow with horizontal force against the attackers. General Howe quickly abandoned the attack. He evacuated Boston a fortnight later, which left the city in the hands of the jubilant Americans. The miracle of Dorchester Hill had restored the city to patriot control.

Boston was the hometown of the liberty movement. When the British troops abandoned the city, they gave the American Revolution back its heart.

4.4 | The Miracle on Long Island, August 1776

CELEBRATION of the heady victory in Boston came to an abrupt end when Washington and the Continental Army, both inexperienced, were defeated on Long Island, New York. The Americans lost over a thousand men, while British casualties numbered less than a hundred.

Trapped on the northwestern shores of Brooklyn, Washington and his men faced the distinct possibility of being surrounded and captured by the British. American independence would be shattered, and the war would end in immediate defeat. The situation seemed hopeless.

The American Continentals faced an army of twenty thousand British troops, backed by four hundred ships, the largest naval fleet ever to sail against an enemy in Western history. Washington had no ships and barely nine thousand American troops, many of whom had just endured their first war engagement.

Washington retreated to the East River to carry out his only hope—evacuation. Anticipating his move, the British sent their five fastest warships up the East River to cut off the American escape. Ferocious winds arose and blew the British ships back downriver, so the British waited for morning, when they intended to attack the American forces.

Washington then attempted the unthinkable: to evacuate his nine thousand troops across the East River to Manhattan in one night, in every possible conveyance and in plain sight of the enemy.

The general instructed his men to set decoy campfires to prevent detection. At first, the raucous winds that had hampered the British earlier in the day stormed against the Americans. Miraculously, an hour later, the winds shifted dramatically in the Americans' favor, and the secret ferry operation proceeded.

As night ended, a substantial number of troops had not yet escaped the enemy shore. Divine intervention again directed the elements. An unusual fog, so dense that a man could not be seen six yards away, descended upon the East River, concealing the American evacuation. The Brooklyn area, occupied by the British, experienced no fog at all, but the British sentries could see nothing beyond the river. The fog held into the morning well after the sun rose. An hour after the last man, followed by General Washington, had cleared the opposite shore, the fog lifted.

The evacuation, a resounding success, was accomplished without the loss of a single man.

The vacating American army was out of reach and in full view of their bewildered and frustrated British opponents. The escape of the Continental Army seemed inconceivable. British General James Grant later wrote of the evacuation: "We cannot yet account for their precipitate retreat."[6]

The miraculous event had been foretold in a sermon three months earlier by the Reverend John Witherspoon, president of what is now Princeton University, who had signed the Declaration of Independence representing New Jersey. He had asserted that God "overrules all his creatures, and all their actions. Thus we are told, that 'fire, hail, snow, vapour and stormy wind, fulfill his word,' in the course of nature."[7] Washington had also declared that victory would come if "the finger of Providence is in it, to blind the eyes of our enemies."[8]

The Continental Army was safe. Hope surged, and the American cause lived to fight again. The army's benefactor was the divine hand employed to direct the elements. Other miracles were soon to follow.

4.5 | The Miracles at Trenton and Princeton, 1776

AFTER EXPERIENCING several miracles, General Washington was now in need of another.

His troops had escaped Long Island with the British in pursuit. The morale of the American colonists was low. Many of his men had left the army, and enlistment terms for three thousand more would expire soon. The army was chronically short on supplies and ammunition, yet Congress was locked in internal squabbles that left it inattentive, uncooperative, and neglectful of the troops. Washington determined to strike a bold move against the Redcoats quartered at Trenton, New Jersey, in hopes that a victory would embolden his troops and strengthen their weakened morale.

In the predawn hours of December 26, three columns of colonial troops assembled to cross the Delaware. Washington's plan was to mount a surprise attack on the fifteen hundred Hessian mercenaries quartered at Trenton who fought for the British.

As the Americans began their crossing, a violent storm with alternating hail, rain, and snow struck. Two of the three columns were unable to embark. The third column, led by Washington himself, was delayed. With only one of the three columns able to participate, the element of surprise became vitally important.

The troops marched to Trenton as daylight approached, fearful of discovery. The weather again favored their endeavor. The enemy was unaware of their advance, trusting that no attack would come in such horrific weather. Surely, if the enemy approached, their sentries would alert them.

Just after 8 a.m., the Continentals attacked with the violent storm at their backs. Their opponents were caught completely by surprise. With the storm slashing their faces, they floundered. House-to-house fighting lasted only forty-five minutes, and one thousand Hessian soldiers were taken prisoner. With astonishment, Washington found that his troops had sustained only four wounded in the fighting and two who froze to death on the march from the river.

The engagement was far from over. As the Americans left the area, five thousand British troops followed in pursuit to squash Washington's success. Rising temperatures turned the main roads into muddy swamps, and the Redcoats were forced to camp for the night. Again, Washington left decoys with lighted campfires to mask their departure and through the night led thousands of troops—with their baggage, animals, wagons, and cannon—around the enemy on obscure, frozen roads. The Continental Army next mounted an attack on the British at Princeton. Again, they were victorious.

Although these were minor battles, their success buoyed American hearts. The fear of defeat that had gripped the former colonies began to lift. Hope, mixed with a spirit of unity, flowed through the thirteen American states.

Three weeks before the Battle of Trenton, the Congress of the Confederation had called for a national Day of Fasting and Repentance, urging Americans to implore almighty God to forgive them of their sins. As a nation, they pleaded for God's help in the war effort.

This event is reminiscent of the Pilgrims in 1621, who called a day of fasting and prayer to offer their repentance as a means to relieve the drought that was destroying their crops. Just as God had answered the Pilgrims, He answered the pleas of Washington and his men.

With battles won, many of the troops extended their enlistments to remain with Washington. Several long years of fighting remained, but the American states were learning to pull together. They also learned that, as a united group, God would bless their efforts and grant them victory.

4.6 | Valley Forge: Crucible of Freedom, 1777

W ASHINGTON's exhausted troops marched into their winter quarters at Valley Forge in December of 1777.

This became their great testing ground—their refiner's fire—and the final resting place for one-fourth of Washington's army.[9] Men died there from starvation, disease, and freezing temperatures during the most trying time in the American War for Independence.

Only fifteen miles away from the discouraged Americans lay Philadelphia, the seat of government, now occupied by the British. The Continental Army had been walloped at Brandywine as it attempted to prevent Philadelphia's fall.

For shelter, Washington instructed the men to build log huts without windows and floors. Only after the last hut was built did he abandon his own ragged field tent for the stone house nearby, where his wife, Martha, joined him for the winter.

Temperatures fell to six degrees to torment the soldiers. They slept on the dirt floors, many without blankets. Their shirts and pants were in tatters, and a thousand had no shoes. Their feet and legs froze and turned black.

The Congressional Board of War was responsible for sending supplies to the troops, but it was negligent. Under the ineffective Articles of Confederation, states could not be forced to contribute war funds, and few contributed their fair share. Politicians spent their energies in bickering, intrigue, and jealousy rather than support of the troops. Consequently, Washington's men froze and starved. They died from diseases such as smallpox, influenza, camp fever, and typhus, all made worse by their poor living conditions. Some defected to the British, who had food and clothing.

The army subsisted largely on fire cakes, which were a mixture of flour and water baked on a griddle. By February, the entire army had only twenty-five barrels of flour left with which to provide even that meager fare.[10] Had the Continental Army received adequate funds, quartermasters could have purchased the food available in the area. Because the Americans had no money, the locals sold their goods to the enemy instead, who paid well.

Washington visited the troops daily. His deep empathy for their misery gave a fatherly air to his efforts to minister to them. His wife, Martha, was likewise tireless in her exertions to give the men relief. She would often pray with and for the suffering men.

The general spent his days writing imploring letters to the Congressional Board, pleading for supplies. He said of this time: "No history . . . can furnish an instance of an army's suffering such . . . as ours has done, and bearing [it] with the same patience and fortitude. To see men without clothes to cover their nakedness, without blankets to lie on, without shoes, by which their marches might be traced by the blood from their feet, and almost as often without provisions . . . submitting . . . without a murmur is a mark of patience and obedience which . . . can scarce be paralleled."[11]

Their endurance under extreme hardship became the miracle of Valley Forge. The men stayed with General Washington because they believed in him. Those whom the general trusted throughout the remainder of the war had proved themselves at Valley Forge.

This great trial was the crucible of freedom. From iron, God forged the refined steel of the revolutionary cause.

4.7 | Miraculous River Crossings, 1781

REPEATEDLY, God sent miracles to the Americans through the weather.

The Continental Army soundly defeated the British at Cowpens, South Carolina, in January of 1781. After the battle, the army headed for safety in Virginia. Their march led them for two hundred miles through the Carolinas. Winter had arrived, leaving the men with many icy rivers to cross. British General Cornwallis and his Redcoats followed the Continental Army in hot pursuit.

Cornwallis headed for the fords at the Catawba River and arrived at dusk, just hours after the Americans had crossed. Too late to ford his troops that night, Cornwallis planned to cross at first light. However, when morning came, water levels had swelled to flood stage, making the river impassable. He was forced to wait for two days.

Both armies thrust forward through North Carolina toward the Yadkin River, but the Continentals arrived first. Water levels allowed their horsemen to cross in the dark, and the foot soldiers followed at first light. The British arrived just hours later, with the Continental Army in plain sight across the river. Flood waters had again risen to levels impassible for the British.

In a rapid march, Cornwallis took his men down the banks of the Yadkin and located a passable ford in the river. This shortened the distance between the two forces. Both armies raced for the Dan River, which bordered Virginia, as they skirmished along the way.

The two armies jockeyed and pursued each other for four weeks. The Americans marched up to thirty miles a day with only six hours of sleep every other night. As a result, they reached the Dan River first. This time, the water levels made passage possible only by boat, but advance parties had procured every available craft. By midnight, all the Americans were safely on land in Virginia.

The British, still only hours behind, were stranded yet again. Pursuit was impossible, as all the boats were on the other side of the river. The frustrated Cornwallis abandoned the chase. Years later, Sir Henry Clinton, second-in-command of the British forces, referred to the rising waters as near-miraculous.

Again and again, God sent the Continental Army a means to escape. His aid came in part because of the virtue of America's men. The standards of conduct for the Continental Army were set high. Attendance at Sunday worship services was strongly encouraged, and no swearing was allowed.

Washington's demeanor set the example for his men. When one of his officers uttered an oath during a meal the staff was eating together in New York City, the general loudly dropped his fork on the table. In the ensuing silence, he said: "I thought that we all supposed ourselves gentlemen." The story passed through the ranks, and no swearing occurred in his presence again.[12]

Washington held himself, his officers, and his troops to a high moral standard, and God rewarded them for it. The divine hand of Providence commanded the elements and the circumstances. America needed His help to defeat the British.

4.8 | British Surrender at Yorktown, 1781

THE BRITISH had grown tired of the war. Antiwar sentiment in England was building. Both armies were exhausted, but the Americans simply refused to admit defeat. The Continental Army consistently rose to fight again and again. The British lost heart and began to make critical mistakes, one of which was tardiness. It defeated the British at Yorktown.

While minor battles played out across the southern United States, the northern battlefields had been silent but tense. Washington used this silence to strike what would be the final blow of the war. He marched into Virginia to trap the Redcoats on the Yorktown peninsula. A series of miracles accompanied him.

General Cornwallis had brought his Redcoats to Chesapeake Bay for evacuation by the British fleet. British Admiral Graves, who was to rescue the British forces, dawdled, allowing the French fleet, which had come to assist the Americans, to sail into Chesapeake Bay one day before their British rivals.

The British were defeated in the ensuing battle. The French, archrivals to the British, handed them their only serious defeat in 350 years of British naval superiority. Admiral Graves withdrew his fleet to New York for repairs, leaving Cornwallis and his men stranded.

The Americans, under Alexander Hamilton, backed the British against the Atlantic coast as they waited for the return of Admiral Graves. Cornwallis could not know that God's hand had struck the British navy. As Graves prepared to sail to Cornwallis's defense, a violent thunderstorm arose. The storm slammed one ship into another, which forced a halt to repair the damage.

Grasping at straws, Cornwallis drew upon the strategies he had learned from General Washington. He tried to evacuate his troops under cover of night across the York River, where they could escape. The British, however, were not the beneficiaries of divine assistance. Rather than being favored by the elements, they were overcome by them. A sudden, violent storm arose when only a third of the army had crossed, making it impossible to continue. Cornwallis had no option left but surrender.

The British defeat came none too soon. The Americans were bone-tired and ready to be done. They had outlasted the British through sheer fortitude and divine Providence. Had the British navy arrived a day earlier, the Battle of Yorktown might have recorded a different victor.

Effectively, the war was over, although two years passed before all battles ended and a peace treaty was signed in Paris in 1783. Despite his yearning for home, Washington's honor kept him on duty until formal peace was concluded and the British left the continent.

God had intervened over and over to assure victory to a ragtag American army. Through the years, General Washington retold the story of Yorktown, always acknowledging that "the interposing hand of Heaven, in the various instances of . . . this operation, has been most conspicuous and remarkable."[13]

With God's help and their refusal to give up, the Americans had defeated the greatest military power in the Western world.

4.9 | The Failure of Offensive War

AMID THE improbable victories, one theatre of war failed miserably for the Americans in every respect. During their only offensive campaign, the attempt to conquer Canada early in the war, everything went wrong.

In late 1775, two American armies, harassed by misfortune, marched toward Quebec, Canada. The campaign was delayed, pushing it into the winter months. Orders directing the two divisions became confused.

Weather, which later came so often to the Americans' defense, worked against them. Roads were alternately icy and frozen or nearly impassible with deep mud. Torrential rains created treacherous rivers and rapids. When snow came, it turned an already dangerous route into a nightmare.

Short supplies plagued the troops, and the men were left for days without food. When their food supplies gave out completely, the men ate the company dogs, then the shaving soap, lip salve, leather boots, and finally the cartridge boxes. Nothing muted their raging hunger.

Their boats, made of green wood, often leaked, which ruined their provisions and ammunition. Lives were lost when the boats capsized.

Inaccurate maps led four companies into a quagmire of swamps. The men wandered aimlessly, lost in frozen wastes, for three days and nights with nothing to eat. Many died from sheer exhaustion, unable to take another step.

The element of surprise was destroyed when the British received advance notice of the impending attack. When the American troops arrived, the enemy was prepared.

In preparation for the attack, the Americans split into two forces. The first column quickly came under fire, and General Montgomery and all his senior officers were killed almost immediately. Leadership fell to the commissary (supply) officer, who promptly ordered retreat. The commanding officer of the second column, General Benedict Arnold, was seriously wounded, and his troops surrendered. Tragically, within a matter of minutes, the weeks of grueling sacrifice and agony ended in a complete fiasco. The entire expedition produced nothing to benefit the American cause.

The forcible American annexation of British Canada was not in God's plan. He supports defensive wars. Those who enter into a covenant relationship with him, as the Americans had done, are expected to defend themselves. They are not to be the aggressors, as was the case in this offensive campaign.

God instructs us to make war with good advice (Proverbs 20:18). The Canadian campaign was not sound. It was not a necessary step to gain independence. It was directed by the Congress of the Confederation, not by Washington and his generals. The Congress wanted to woo the French Canadians into an alliance against their British neighbors and bring French support into the American war effort. While France did eventually help the Americans, this campaign did not prove an effective means to obtain an ally.

America had no reason for war with Canada beyond the fact that it was under British control. It was inappropriate for the newly independent colonies to have conducted this campaign. The failure of the American invasion of Canada would suggest that God supports defensive war only.

4.10 | The General Retires

THE BATTLE OF YORKTOWN secured the American victory, and the peace treaty was signed in April of 1783. Washington remained on duty for an additional eight months until all the British troops had departed. Then he began his return home.

Ben Tallmadge, the general's chief of intelligence, describes Washington's farewell to his officers on December 4, 1783, at Fraunce's Tavern in lower Manhattan, New York. Washington's senior officers, who had been with him either from the beginning or since Valley Forge, gathered, dressed in their best uniforms. A heaviness settled over the group as they waited.

Washington arrived, fighting to control his emotions. He said: "With a heart full of love and gratitude, I now take leave of you. I most devoutly wish that your latter days may be as prosperous and happy as your former ones have been glorious and honorable." With moist eyes, he asked: "I cannot come to each of you, but shall feel obliged if each of you will come and take me by the hand." Henry Knox, who had retrieved the cannon from Fort Ticonderoga, came first—silently, as tears streamed from his eyes. One by one, the rest shook Washington's hand and departed.

Tallmadge wrote:

> *Such a scene of sorrow and weeping I had never before witnessed . . . Not a word was uttered to break the solemn silence . . . or to interrupt the tenderness of the interesting scene. The simple thought that we were then about to part from the man who had conducted us through a long and bloody war, and under whose conduct the glory and independence of our country had been achieved, and that we should see his face no more in this world, seemed to me [to be] utterly unsupportable.*[14]

Washington then rode to Philadelphia to settle accounts with James Milligan, comptroller of the treasury. He was reimbursed for his expenses as recorded in his detailed accounts. Ever willing to sacrifice for his country, he refused the eight years' accumulation of his generous salary. He later offered to serve without salary for his two presidential terms, but Congress declined.[15] Washington's absence from Mount Vernon during the war had drained his personal wealth. His absence during his presidential terms left the estate in decline. As a result, he was in financial duress at the end of his life.[16]

Washington finally proceeded to Annapolis to resign his commission before the Confederation Congress. Restraining his emotions, he said:

> *I consider it an indispensable duty to close this last solemn act of my official life by commending the interests of our dearest country to the protection of Almighty God, and of those who have superintendence of them to His holy keeping. Having now finished the work assigned to me, I retire from the great theatre of action, and bidding affectionate farewell to this august body under whose orders I have so long acted, I here offer my commission and take my leave of all the employments of public life.[17]*

He could not have known that much of his public life remained ahead of him. He wanted only to return to his family and his beloved Mount Vernon.

5

We the People

Section Five

― ☙ ―

WRITING THE CHARTER OF FREEDOM

THE TIME was fast approaching to write the Constitution. With the help of a benevolent, watchful God and His many miracles, America was now free of British domination. No foreign troops marched across her soil. No foreign leaders dictated her allegiance. No foreign monies bought her soul, although she was deep in debt for her war efforts. She had set her course for sovereignty.

Leaders had arisen and proven their mettle through diligence, tenacity, and sacrifice. Men such as Thomas Jefferson and James Madison had absorbed the wisdom of nations, peoples, and movements. They were poised to embody those principles in a new, original form of self-governance.

The European world waited, watched, salivated. If this virgin country's reach for freedom floundered—and the leaders of Europe surely believed it would—other nations, crouched like wolves, waited to tear her asunder.

America was a vast and pristine prize. Conquest had failed to win her. War had failed to keep her. Now, surely, they believed, freedom itself would deliver her to her enemies. It was only a matter of time. How could a people so naïve of the political process, with its intrigues, cabals, and conspiracies, find its way to greatness?

Like a ship tossed upon tumultuous waves as it sought a peaceful harbor, the American ship of state faced an arduous course. Nations require rules, and rules are drafted by men appointed to create them. America's task now was to supply the men to create those rules.

In time, she would reach the safe harbor of sound government. Trial and error, the dual winds of inexperience, would hold sway for a time. But the process had begun.

5.1 | The Articles of Confederation

THE UNITED STATES did not move smoothly from the Declaration of Independence to the Constitution. A way-station stood between the two: the Articles of Confederation. The central government the colonists created was an ineffective vehicle for freedom. In fact, the Articles came close to costing the fledgling republic its independence.

Because the American colonists were determined to have no more dictators and tyrants, the nation first established a governing system too weak to be effective. While too much government is oppressive, so is too little. A fine line determines the balance between excess and famine. The Articles did not have the proper balance of self-sufficiency and interdependence that good government requires.

A major failing of the Articles was that they were toothless. They lacked the ability to enforce policies or punish the uncooperative. Congressional authority amounted to pleading for action, rather than compelling it when necessary. This had created serious problems during the Revolutionary War. States had ignored their obligation to fund the troops on the battlefield. As a result, Washington's men had suffered without food or clothing, and many had died. Only the states of Pennsylvania and New York had fully discharged their fiscal obligations during the conflict.

The Articles of Confederation did not operate under majority rule. Because they required unanimous consent to accomplish any national business, one dissenting state could block the decisions of the rest and hold the others hostage to its demands. Effectively, public policy under the Articles of Confederation was based on minority rule determined by the most stubborn state. The consequences paralyzed the political process.

Many other weaknesses overshadowed the Articles of Confederation. Under them, the states could not be compelled to pay taxes to support the federal government, and it had no authority to regulate commerce between states. Treaties with other nations could not be enforced, leaving foreign countries disinclined to form alliances with the new nation.

The authority voice in the United States—its governing document—was thus nearly powerless. A government without authority is incapable of governing. Serious contention resulted, and the states began to fight bitterly among themselves, as factions are wont to do when no superintending authority provides security and stability. Each state tried to exert its authority above the rest. In these circumstances, the fledgling nation floundered.

Massachusetts had contributed far more than her share of men to the Continental Army. When no funds to pay the troops were available after hostilities ended, a rebellion that approached civil war broke out in that state. Known as Shay's Rebellion, the unrest cast a pall on the national complexion and sent state leaders into flurries of anxiety. Some worried that European enemies would attack the weakened and disjointed United States. Others feared a desperation-driven return to the monarchy of the past, led by those who might snatch at any form of government that appeared to be stable. The worth of good government was becoming apparent by the want of it.

The new nation urgently needed a more sure foundation. Fortunately, God's hand steadied the ship of state until a better system of government emerged for a free and independent people.

5.2 | Verging on Economic Collapse

AFTER THE WAR, the United States of America, under the Articles of Confederation, moved uncomfortably close to bankruptcy. Unbridled freedom paired with economic instability moved the country away from the pursuit of happiness instead of toward it. The economic nightmare of inflation faced the thirteen former colonies.

War requires a chest filled with gold, and the colonies had none. Without cash to fund the protracted conflict, only two options remained. One was to tax the populace. This was not possible, because the Articles of Confederation were so weak that the Congress of the Confederation could not enforce taxation. The only remaining source of funds was to print paper money.

Printing paper money was the path to economic downfall. Since paper currency has no intrinsic value, it is worthless unless backed by solid assets—usually gold or silver. Adding more money simply made each dollar worth less. The people had to use more money to purchase what they needed. Inflation was the result.[1]

Rather than high prices causing inflation, high prices resulted from it. A cycle of unending price increases began to destroy the colonial economy. The prosperity and well-being of all citizens of the country were in jeopardy.

When prices rose abruptly, some states began price-fixing. This inevitably produced shortages which led to black markets, bribery, corruption, and a loss of confidence in the government. When the value of a colonial dollar bill went below one copper cent, even the government refused them in payment.

An epidemic of spending ensued. Goods could cost much more tomorrow, so people hurried to buy what they wanted right away. The poor and those on fixed incomes were caught in an economic vise.

Individual states attempted to remedy the situation. Some states passed laws that required merchants to take worthless money in payment for goods and services. Rather than accept the currency, some merchants and businesses closed their doors.

Colonial society shuddered under the weight of spiraling inflation. Former friends became enemies, and employees and employers distrusted each other. The aftereffects left the governed contemptuous of their government.

George Washington lamented the times in a letter to James Madison: "No day was ever more clouded than the present . . . we are fast verging to anarchy and confusion . . . What stronger evidence can be given of the want of energy in our government than these disorders? . . . A liberal and energetic constitution, well guarded and closely watched to prevent encroachments, might restore us."[2]

Alexander Hamilton, who would become Washington's Secretary of the Treasury in a few short years, decried the state of affairs as having reached "almost the last stage of national humiliation."[3]

The core problem was the lack of a workable government. A critical need existed for a political system that would unite the thirteen colonies into an indivisible nation. A workable economy would follow political stability and bolster the prosperity of all thirteen states.

A sound government system was badly needed, and soon.

5.3 | The States Agree to Meet

WITH GREAT DIFFICULTY, George Washington, Alexander Hamilton, and others eventually induced the states to meet to resolve the weaknesses in the Articles of Confederation.

The wary, obstinate states, locked into mutual suspicion, had to be pushed into conference. Past attempts to amend the Articles had failed because the system required a unanimous vote. One state always objected. None of the necessary adjustments to the system ever took place.

Finally, Washington found a way to bring about agreement on the need for change. Virginia and Maryland both contested fishing rights on the Potomac River and Chesapeake Bay. Washington invited them to Mount Vernon to discuss the situation. Relations became cordial, and Virginia recommended a trade conference to revise the Articles of Confederation.

Only five states sent delegates to the resulting Annapolis conference. Without a majority, no business could be accomplished. The process had begun, however. In early 1787, the Congress of the Confederation issued an official invitation to all the states to meet in convention to revise the Articles of Confederation to create a federal government capable of preserving the Union.

Twelve of the thirteen states sent delegates to the convention. Rhode Island did not. Dubbed "Rogue Island" for her recalcitrant attitude, she was an intractable state, stubbornly focused on her own concerns. All through the drafting and ratification processes, she ignored the Constitution and refused to attend the Convention. The rest of the states pressed on without her, ratified the Constitution, and began to treat her as a foreign entity. When faced with the possibility of tariffs being assessed against her and foreign ambassadors required of her, Rhode Island finally ratified the Constitution and came into the Union.

Some of the great voices in the revolutionary cause were absent from the Constitutional Convention. Jefferson was in France and John Adams was in England, both serving as American ambassadors. However, both men provided dynamic input to the process. Adams wrote a treatise entitled *A Defense of the Constitutions of Government of the United States,* which circulated throughout the thirteen former colonies. Thomas Jefferson mentored James Madison, sending him trunks of carefully selected books to read. When Madison spoke, he spoke for himself and Jefferson, and Jefferson's depth of wisdom and research would have been sorely missed had James Madison not been such a diligent, discerning pupil. Madison's advance study added clarity to the process. His expertise gave direction when it was sorely needed throughout the Convention. Because of this, we refer to Madison as the Father of the Constitution.

Patrick Henry's soaring oratory and Samuel Adams's core commitment to independence were voluntarily absent from the Convention. Not all the leaders of the day approved of the plan to improve their political system. Some feared the possibilities of the Convention, and Henry and Adams were among that number. Samuel Adams later changed his mind about the evolution of the Articles of Confederation into the Constitution. Patrick Henry did not, and he raised a strident opposing voice through the end of the ratification process.

All was ready. The birth process of the document had begun. The primary influence to shape the Constitution would come from James Madison Jr. of Virginia.

5.4 | James Madison, Father of the Constitution

JAMES MADISON of Virginia was the mastermind of the Constitution. He encouraged and guided the process, forcefully argued its principles, and persuasively explained it in the Federalist Papers afterwards.

Only five feet four inches tall, Madison was difficult to see and harder still to hear when he stood to address the Convention. His soft, cultured voice barely carried to the other delegates assembled at the Philadelphia State House in 1787, and they cried out for him to speak up when he addressed the group.

He was agile, energetic, and muscular, with clear blue eyes and receding hair. He was, by habit, well dressed and precisely groomed. Physical limitations had prevented his service during the Revolutionary War in spite of his strong desire to serve. Although one of the youngest delegates at the Constitutional Convention, he was one of those best schooled in the Old Testament. Years of Hebrew study allowed Madison to read the Old Testament in its original language. Under Madison's influence, the government of ancient Israel figured prominently in the finished Constitution.

James Madison was part of the early political scene in Virginia. He spent his life in politics both before and after American independence was declared. He formed strong friendships with George Washington and Thomas Jefferson. As he helped draft Virginia's state constitution, he developed strong feelings about freedom of religion and encouraged it thereafter.

Madison was passionate about rights and constitutional freedoms. Cool, forceful argument was his trademark. His ability to reason was based on deep study and thorough preparation. His agile mind could connect facts and draw conclusions with lightning speed, allowing him to approach any political concept with confidence. He waited tenaciously for the right moment to speak and then presented his precise and well-reasoned arguments as if they had just occurred to him. Few could stand against his crisp logic.

It was Madison's great gift to know the political process. To actually bring about a new, original form of government would be very difficult, and Madison understood that. In communication with a friend beforehand, he wrote: "The nearer the crisis approaches, the more I tremble for the issue."[4] He did not despair, however. The matter was too important for despair.

He was present every day for every hour of the Convention. He sat front and center, where he took copious notes, which he transcribed each night into legible form. The grueling process took its toll on him, both physically and mentally. His notes were largely ignored until they surfaced thirty years later. Without them, we would know little about the Convention or the arguments and discussions that took place. With Madison's notes, we can follow the reasoning process of the delegates. This helps clarify their intent when differences of opinion arise concerning important provisions of the Constitution.

In an assembly of great American statesmen, James Madison was, by most accounts, the most able political leader at the Constitutional Convention. His abilities and contributions led to his election as the fourth president of the United States.

5.5 | The Miracle at Philadelphia

SEEMINGLY insurmountable challenges faced the fifty-five men who proposed to write the Constitution. It is a miracle that they succeeded.

The original purpose of the Convention was to rewrite the Articles of Confederation. When a movement to create a new constitution emerged, many balked. It took time to resolve the matter. So much disunity existed among the thirteen states that some talked of forming three separate nations: New England, the middle states, and the South. Most of the states were already treating the others as foreign nations. Seven were printing their own money, and nine had their own navies. State legislatures attempted to draw more power unto themselves, a policy made possible by the weak Articles of Confederation.

To get the states to agree to a convention and then to actually attend it had been a monumental task. Now they had to write the document, which would require immense effort to reach agreement. It then needed to be put into a form acceptable to the Congress of the Confederation. Finally, it must win ratification in at least nine states to become effective. Any states not ratifying would stand outside the new nation, so the delegates profoundly hoped that all thirteen would ratify the document.

This was a multi-step process, with each step presenting new chances for failure. Each delegate faced the possibility that he would return home politically bankrupt. If the nation failed in this endeavor, it faced national and international humiliation, because there would be little hope of calling another convention.

On many critical issues, two or more groups had to agree. Some had faith that the common man could govern himself, including James Madison and George Mason. Others, such as Gouverneur Morris and Elbridge Gerry, distrusted the common man and believed that he would be too easily deceived.

The needs of large states versus small states and the suspicions of the small states toward the larger had to be reconciled. At one point during the Convention, Gunning Bedford of Delaware addressed the delegates of Massachusetts, Pennsylvania, and Virginia and said: "I do not, gentlemen, trust you!"[5]

The Northern and Southern states also suspected and disliked each other. They had very different needs. Those in the North were fishermen and sailors, while planters dominated the South. They also disagreed on future expansion. Seacoast states were unconcerned, but those bordering new territories regarded expansion as a vital issue.

The matter of slavery divided the Convention as well, although not necessarily along predictable lines. Some Southerners, though they held slaves, deplored the practice and greatly desired its abolition. Some Northerners profited from the slave trade and wanted the practice to continue. Also at odds were those who favored a strong central government and those who favored the strong rights of the state.

John Adams dreaded the consequences of these differences. He wrote from England: "Without the utmost caution on both sides and the most considerate forbearance with one another and prudent condescension on both sides, they [the differences] will certainly prove fatal."[6]

The assignment was monumental, but the fifty-five men who attended the Constitutional Convention proved equal to the task.

5.6 | Setting the Rules

RULES FOR ANY endeavor can make or break its success. It was critical that the Constitutional Convention choose its operating guidelines carefully.

The process began well with the selection of George Washington as its president. Universally regarded as the greatest man in America, he was firm, courteous, and inflexible in positive ways. Washington was deeply invested in the constitutional process. His presence kept the Constitutional Convention together, just as it had kept a straggling, ill-conditioned army together through eight years of war. When he approved a measure, delegates reported that his face showed it.

Yet it was hard to tell what Washington thought and impossible to inquire. He was uncommonly reserved. The story is told that Alexander Hamilton bet Gouverneur Morris that he would not dare to greet George Washington with a slap on the back. Brassy and self-assured, Morris entered a drawing room a few days later, laid a hand on Washington's shoulder, and boomed: "Well, general!" Washington said nothing, but Morris knew at once that he had made a mistake. He stated afterward that he was ready to sink through the floor.[7]

Each state was allowed one vote in the convention, and a majority of the delegates from each state had to be in agreement. Each delegate could speak only twice on any topic. All remarks were addressed to the president, rather than to other delegates. Frequent unrecorded opinion polls allowed a delegate to change his position without fear of embarrassment when the proceedings later became public.

The Convention functioned as two distinct bodies. During discussion, all delegates constituted an informal Committee of the Whole, with Nathaniel Gorham as president. When an official vote was to be taken, they became a formal Convention, with Washington presiding. Switching between the two allowed for open debate in the

Committee of the Whole during the decision-making process. Only the final vote of the Convention was officially recorded, so the group could hold free discussions before their decisions became permanent.

Strict rules of secrecy were in operation. It would have been unsettling if misinformation had prematurely leaked to those outside the Convention. No copies of notes from the meetings were allowed without permission. Sentries guarded the doors, and the windows were kept tightly shuttered, even in the oppressive summer heat.

William Pierce of Georgia related that at the close of one day's afternoon meeting, a paper with notes about the day's proceedings was found on the floor and given to George Washington. The next day, on adjournment, Washington rose and stated: "I am sorry . . . that some one member . . . has been so neglectful . . . as to drop . . . a copy of [his] proceedings . . . I must entreat gentlemen to be more careful, lest our transcriptions get into the newspapers and disturb the public repose by premature speculations. I know not whose paper it is, but . . . let him who owns it take it." Washington left the hall "with a dignity so severe that every person seemed alarmed." Pierce was doubly so, as he could not find his copy of the same paper. (He found it afterward in a spare coat.) He later stated: "It is something remarkable that no person ever owned the paper."[8]

5.7 | Men of the Constitution

M ANY WOVE the brilliant tapestry of American political supremacy. Without their personalities, character strengths, and even their weaknesses, our national foundation would have been diminished. Here are the stories of some, including the three who chose to not sign the completed Constitution.

Alexander Hamilton served as Washington's private secretary during the war and distinguished himself at the Battle of Yorktown. An ambitious man, he married into one of New York's most powerful families. He best diagnosed the shortcomings of the Articles of Confederation and the need for a new Constitution. Sadly, during the Convention he had no voting voice. The other two New York delegates angrily abandoned the Convention in its first month. No majority vote was possible, so New York and Alexander Hamilton were officially mute. He drifted in and out of the Convention's proceedings after the plan he proposed was ignored but returned at critical junctures to give input. He later served as Washington's Secretary of the Treasury for two terms.

His death in 1804 in a duel with Aaron Burr, his bitter personal and political enemy, was a tragedy. Hamilton tried to avoid the duel, but Burr challenged his integrity publicly and mercilessly. No longer able to avoid it, he decided not to fire in the duel, put his personal effects in order, and knowingly faced his death. He died of his wound a day later, at the age of forty-nine.

Tall, handsome Edmund Randolph of Virginia served as Washington's aide-de-camp during the war, as his attorney, and as Virginia's governor during the Constitutional Convention. He presented, though he did not substantially author, the Fifteen Virginia Resolves. The Resolves formed the core of the future Constitution and the starting point for debate in the Convention. In the end, he refused to sign the Constitution but changed his position eighteen months later when the Bill of Rights was added. Washington appointed him the first United States attorney general.

Not all who drafted the Constitution were popular men—a few tested the patience of the other delegates. One such was Elbridge Gerry of Massachusetts. His nervous, obstinate temperament often led him to risk the important for the trivial. A contemporary called him a "Grumbletonian"[9] who objected to anything he did not himself propose. He ultimately refused to sign the Constitution and actively worked to defeat its ratification. He later became vice-president under James Madison and died of heart failure while in office.

George Mason, sixty-two, silver-haired, and owner of a large estate bordering George Washington's, was boldly patriotic. He authored the Virginia constitution. Thomas Jefferson called him "a man of the first order of wisdom . . . of expansive mind [and] profound judgment."[10] An aristocrat who had great faith in the common man, he feared a powerful central government and favored giving strong rights to the states. He cautioned other delegates who leaned toward rule by aristocratic privilege to beware, for their children would someday be among the common people. Though he held slaves, he was an ardent abolitionist. He chose not to sign the Constitution because of its lack of a Bill of Rights.

Each of the fifty-five delegates brought power and insight to the Convention process. Without them, the miracle at Philadelphia might not have come about.

5.8 | Two Plans—and a Third

LATE ARRIVALS delayed the opening of the Convention. As they waited, the Virginia delegation put pen to paper and drafted the Fifteen Virginia Resolves, which became the starting point for debate.

The Resolves stunned the delegates. It became obvious that the objective of the Convention was not a revision of the Articles of Confederation, but the creation of a new system of government.

The Resolves called for two branches of the legislature. Legislative powers would be derived from the people, and majority vote would determine action. A single executive could be removed through impeachment when necessary. A central court with a system of lesser federal courts formed the judicial branch. These points, in large part, became our Constitution.

After two weeks of heated deliberation, the small states introduced the New Jersey plan, which was a version of the Articles of Confederation. The power in government would be derived from the states rather than the people. A small majority would control the sole legislature. The new plan proposed more than one chief executive, and those executives and the legislators could be removed by the states. Little individual freedom was possible under this plan. A few leaders would be overly powerful, and the state legislatures would have ample opportunity to abuse their power.

Three days later, Alexander Hamilton rose abruptly and presented a third plan of his own creation. Believing that it was dangerous to tread unknown waters, he proposed a return to the British system, which featured a dual legislature. Senators would be chosen for life, and Representatives of the House would be chosen by the people. He promoted a single executive, chosen for life by the states, with absolute veto power over all legislation (in other words, a monarch). State governors would be appointed by the central government.

The acceptance of Hamilton's plan would have given the United States a king. This was not America's destiny. If a just man is king, there is little danger. The central authority a king provides makes for simple, effective government. However, the power available to a monarch frequently attracts those who will abuse that power. When, inevitably, the people suffer under oppressive government and wish to depose their king, they can rarely accomplish it without bloodshed.

After Hamilton's proposal, the room was silent. No discussion and no support ensued.

The following day, in the Convention, James Madison pleaded for a constitution that would last through the ages. He declared that only the Virginia plan could stand the test of time. The vote that followed defeated the New Jersey plan. Consensus had been reached.

Hamilton departed several days later and returned only occasionally.

Throughout the process, delegates made every attempt to achieve unity through complete consensus. A unanimous vote was far preferable to majority rule. The state-by-state fight for ratification would follow, and greater unity in the drafting process would be more likely to encourage ratification.

Still, three key topics required compromise: slavery, regulation of commerce between the states, and representation in Congress. No unanimous vote was possible on these topics. Compromise and majority rule were the only alternative.

Looming ahead of the delegates was the great test of the Convention—the crisis period that would test the mettle of all involved.

5.9 | The Great Compromise

Several matters before the Constitutional Convention were divisive, but one topic threatened to tear it asunder.

The subject of determining representation in Congress had the potential to send the delegates home as failures. Its roots lay in the division of power between the large and small states. Without agreement on this issue, there would be no final document. This crisis was Mount Vesuvius erupting among the fifty-five men who deliberated in Philadelphia that sultry summer.

The larger states demanded representation by population, which would favor their size. The smaller states, considering the large states potential bullies, refused to accept anything but one vote per state, which would grant them power equal to that of the large states.

Georgia's delegates argued that if representation was determined by population, Virginia would have sixteen times more representatives than Georgia. Virginia argued that if each state had one vote, a person from Georgia would have sixteen times more representation than a Virginian.

For weeks, the arguments flew back and forth as tempers mounted and frustration grew. The delegates would debate the topic until it became volatile and then set it aside to deal with less controversial matters. Later they would take it up again, only to reignite the same quarrels. Washington and others at the Convention despaired of ever finding resolution to the crisis.

Throughout the conflict, one voice offered a different solution. That voice belonged to Roger Sherman of Connecticut. John Adams described him as being "honest as an angel." Jefferson once said of him: "That is Mr. Sherman of Connecticut, who never said a foolish thing in his life." The story was told of Sherman being asked to make a speech at the opening of a new bridge. He walked out onto the bridge, turned, and came back. He then gave his speech: "I don't see but it stands steady." That was all he said.

An experienced politician, his political philosophy was: "When you are in a minority, talk; when you are in the majority, vote."[11]

Sherman proposed different representation for each branch of Congress. He suggested that the states have equal representation in the Senate, with representation apportioned in the House by population. Because both houses must agree on legislation before it became law and each had veto power over the other, neither group could coerce the other.

He proposed the plan three times during the heated debates before the other delegates finally understood and accepted it. Their reluctant agreement came not because all the delegates embraced it, but because it was the only solution available. This became known as The Great Compromise.

The smaller states were elated with it, and the larger states were chagrined. With no other option available, however, they accepted their losses and moved on.

The crisis had passed. The pages of history would later recognize the brilliance of the Great Compromise that made union possible.

5.10 | What about a President?

THE ISSUE of the nation's chief executive was one of the most important matters of discussion in Philadelphia. The delegates agreed that they did not want the English system. They had fought an eight-year war to be free of tyrannical monarchy. The time had come to decide what kind of executive they would have and how many there would be. In addition, they must determine what powers the executive should have and what to do if he began to assume too much authority.

James Wilson of Pennsylvania championed the cause of a single executive—a position of "energy, dispatch, and responsibility"[12] to preside over a strong central government. A native of Scotland with a heavy Scottish brogue, he wore his round spectacles hooked into his powdered wig to keep them in place. He was a deep and independent thinker whose ideas occasionally produced stormy debates at the Pennsylvania State House that summer. He had served faithfully in Congress and was influential in colonial banking and money matters. He later pronounced the newly drafted Constitution "the best form of government which has ever been offered to the world."[13] He is sometimes called the unsung hero of the Constitutional Convention. Shortly after it ended, he was burned in effigy by those who opposed his politics.

Wilson's proposal of a single executive induced a sudden, lengthy silence in the Convention, followed by strenuous opposition. Its resemblance to the English system alarmed many.

Edmund Randolph of Virginia touted a plan for three executives. He believed that the American people would never have confidence in any one man and called the one-executive plan a "fetus of monarchy."[14] Besides, he argued, any single executive would favor his own part of the country, whereas three executives, drawn from differing regions, would not.

The presidential veto, or executive negative, was another source of contention. It posed great potential for political abuse and private extortion. Political opponents and cronies alike could persuade a president to manipulate the political process, line their pockets with silver, or strike at enemies through his use of veto power.

Benjamin Franklin pushed for a single executive without salary, saying: "There is scarce a king in a hundred who would not . . . follow the example of Pharaoh, get first all the people's money [and] . . . lands and then make them and their children servants forever."[15] His position received little support. Few believed that any competent individual would donate the time and effort necessary to guide the nation.

It took a long time for the delegates to embrace the term *president* for their future executive. It took still longer to agree on his election. The delegates cast more than sixty ballots in mid-July before reaching agreement. Washington was in despair, and two of the three New York delegates, Robert Yates and John Lansing, departed the Convention in disgust, never to return.

The delegates eventually determined that one native-born American, elected for four years, would preside over the country, and they assigned to him six carefully controlled and limited responsibilities.

A path for leadership was set.

5.11 | Admitting New Territories

T HE DELEGATES understood that new states would enter the Union in the future, so they laid careful plans for those events.

Several of the thirteen states occupied areas much larger than they do today. Virginia, both Carolinas, and Georgia, for instance, stretched from the Atlantic coast to the Mississippi River. Ultimately, all these states ceded their western lands to the Union to rid themselves of the need to administer and defend them.

In addition, as the delegates met, the Congress of the Confederation was enacting the Northwest Ordinance, bringing vast new territory into the United States of America. How to handle this expansion was a matter of concern. Pressing decisions had to be made to determine whether new territories would enter the Union on an equal basis with the existing thirteen states.

Delegates from the Eastern seaboard were uninterested in the Western issue of new territories. Gouverneur Morris of Pennsylvania, who expected war with Spain over control of the Western territories and the Mississippi River, strongly campaigned against equal admission of Western states. The central and Southern states, however, were very interested. They wished to retain navigation rights on the Mississippi River.

Some delegates thought it suicidal to encourage settlement of the West. Others were already involved in serious speculation and investment in the region. One promoter had obtained a grant of five million acres in the West, the largest in United States history. Among his investors were several members of the Constitutional Convention. Residents of the existing states were already flowing into the new lands, and the states they formed would be powers to reckon with in the future. This was of great concern to some delegates.

Independent of the Convention, the Confederation Congress struggled to determine how to divide the six and a half million square miles of land coming into the Union through the Northwest Ordinance. It settled on not less than three and not more than five territories. Each could apply for statehood when its population reached sixty thousand.

James Wilson championed equal admission for Western territories. He believed that unequal admission would foster jealousy between the old and new states and eventually tear them apart. Settlers of new states would have the same state pride as those in the current ones, he asserted, and would never accept admission on any basis except full equality.

The Convention ultimately accepted new states as equal with the original thirteen, as long as a new state was not formed within an existing one. The decision came none too soon, for America stood poised to more than double her size.

At the heart of the matter was the issue of property ownership. To Americans, property was freedom—both a position and responsibility in society, and a voice in local affairs. Anyone with drive and ambition could work his way into property. In fact, not owning property was considered a sign of laziness. But property was not just what a man owned. It included his opinions, the free use of his faculties, and the safety and liberty of his person. Even his life was his property, to do with as he pleased.

5.12 | Finishing the Document

GRADUALLY, the Convention resolved issues such as the balance of power between state and central governments, the existence of a standing army, and the ratification process.

The major matter of a unicameral versus a bicameral Congress—one legislative house or two—was more easily settled than expected. Most delegates favored the bicameral model. As a result, the United States has both a Senate and a House of Representatives.

Now it was time to put the Constitution in its final form. By ballot, the delegates chose five men for the Committee of Style and Arrangement to organize four months of decisions into one commanding presentation of the whole. This major task required four days for completion.

The committee selected Dr. William Johnson of Connecticut as its chairman. Johnson, the president of Columbia College, was a popular man with all factions. Every day since his arrival in Philadelphia, he had been present at the Convention. Respected for his disarmingly quiet demeanor and his readiness to share ideas without being tedious, he could calm the din of debate without offending.

Others on the committee included James Madison of Virginia, Alexander Hamilton of New York, Rufus King of Massachusetts, and Gouverneur Morris of Pennsylvania.

Madison, the guiding light and driving force of the Convention, brought to the committee his knowledge of political science. Hamilton, with his quick and powerful pen, was later instrumental in bringing about the ratification of the Constitution because of his eloquent and persuasive writings in the Federalist Papers. Some called King the most eloquent man in America, a superb orator with no equal, and one of the most prominent men of his age. He had originally opposed drafting a constitution but changed his mind during the Convention and became a strong proponent.

The man whose hand actually put pen to paper was Morris. Very tall and brassy by nature, he sported a wooden leg from a youthful riding accident—a feature that did not diminish his popularity with the ladies. A devoted patriot, he understood human nature. He had made himself heard at the Convention, for he was outspoken, opinionated, and given to abrupt and explosive declarations. By the accounts of other delegates, however, he was never foolish or tedious.

Gouverneur Morris later explained that putting historical facts together required more than scholarship. Judgment and skill were needed, and Morris had both a keen brain and the gift of harmony in form. He felt that one should clothe the written skeleton with "muscles . . . [of] symmetry, strength, and grace"—the best preparation for writing history, then, being to read Shakespeare.[16]

Once the committee had finished its work, the Constitution of the United States was ready to receive the signatures of its creators. One man's voice would offer the final stamp of approval. That man was Benjamin Franklin.

5.13 | Benjamin Franklin

BENJAMIN FRANKLIN raised a powerful voice in favor of the Constitution.

The men who laid the foundation of the American government were the finest men God had available. Twenty-eight served in the Confederation Congress under the Articles of Confederation. Thirty-one were lawyers, nineteen were former army officers, five served as college presidents or professors, and nine were foreign-born, having experienced repressive government firsthand. They ranged in age from twenty-six to eighty-one and came from all walks of life and economic levels.

One who stood above the rest was Benjamin Franklin. This diversely gifted Philadelphia citizen was universally loved and respected by his native Pennsylvanians, and his accomplishments were laudable. The fifteenth of seventeen children from a poor family, he was largely self-taught. Although he fit into a world of men who had graduated from the finest universities, he had only two years of formal schooling.

As an author, he wrote the popular *Poor Richard's Almanac*. It was so filled with humor that some call it America's first joke book. As a scientist, he described sunspots, magnetic attraction, and the origin of the common cold. He organized the first American expedition to the Arctic. His prolific inventions included bifocal eyeglasses, daylight savings time, and the glass harmonica. He spoke five languages, held the largest private library in America, and developed the first fire insurance company in the colonies.

His genius also extended to politics. Early success in the printing industry left him financially able to retire in his forties to devote his life to his country. As postmaster general of the colonies, he moved in circles of wide influence. He worked to promote colonial unity decades before others saw the need. He preferred that British conduct toward its colonies would "savor of fatherly tenderness and affection [rather] than of masterly harshness and severity."[17]

During the most contentious debates of the Constitutional Convention, Franklin submitted a plea to the delegates for God's help. "The longer I live the more convincing proofs I see . . . that God governs in the affairs of men . . . I . . . believe that, without His concurring aid, we shall succeed in this political building no better than the builders of Babel."[18] His reminders of God's watchfulness calmed the troubled proceedings.

For eleven years, he worked in London to reconcile the growing bitterness between Britain and the American colonies. His return to America coincided with the eruption of war at Lexington and Concord in 1775. Home for only a year, he returned to Paris to seek French aid for the needy Continental Army. He did not return to the United States until 1782.

He served for three years as Pennsylvania's governor and signed both the Declaration of Independence and the Constitution. His last public act, weeks before he died at the age of eighty-four, was a plea for the repeal of slavery, which he loathed.

Franklin has been maligned in the modern popular press. Those who degrade his character use the fictitious reports generated by jealous political associates of his day. As with all popular, successful men, his success invited envy from lesser men.

The life, writings, and desires of this great patriot stand as a testament to his moral character. He was a brilliant man, a great patriot, and a great American.

5.14 | Signatures and a Bill of Rights

T HE LONG-ANTICIPATED MOMENT had arrived. Fifty-five delegates had participated to create the United States Constitution. On September 17, 1787, forty-one were present to sign it. Three abstained.

The document was read aloud. Benjamin Franklin, eighty-one years old at the time, rose to address George Washington and the other delegates:

> *I confess that there are several parts of this Constitution which I do not at present approve . . . But I am not sure I shall never approve them . . . I consent, Sir, to this Constitution because I expect no better and because I am not sure that it is not the best. The opinions I have had of its errors, I sacrifice to the public good. I have never whispered of them abroad. Within these walls they were born, and here they shall die . . . In these sentiments, sir, I agree to this Constitution.*[19]

As the moment for signing drew near, any who disagreed had one last opportunity to speak. To do so, they had to defy the approval of giants such as Franklin and Washington who had validated the political contract. Each delegate represented his home state, in which powerful factions opposed the Constitution.

Mixed emotions ranged throughout the group. Some demanded that a second convention be held. Others believed that the necessary minimum of nine ratifying states would never be reached, which would create chaos. Still others asserted that the delegates had to be unanimous in signing the Constitution to encourage ratification by Congress and the states.

The lack of a bill of rights loomed large in the Constitutional Convention. Eight states had bills of rights. George Mason had broached the topic in the convention a week before. Now the issue arose again and divided the signers. Most felt no need for a Bill of Rights. The text of the Constitution mentioned individual rights hundreds of times, assuring their protection. It described the responsibilities of the different branches of government clearly, making it illegal for them to usurp personal freedoms. Some delegates believed that listing inalienable rights might open the door to future distortions and misinterpretations and make a bill of rights a possible liability. And, finally, any listing of rights might unintentionally omit some, which would then be presumed forfeited.

In the end, three delegates—Elbridge Gerry of Pennsylvania and George Mason and Edmund Randolph of Virginia—did not sign the document. All three believed that, in its present form, it did not sufficiently guarantee individual rights. Without those guarantees specifically enumerated, they would abstain. All three requested a second convention. The delegates voted no.

The signing process proceeded. At shortly past three o'clock, the delegates arranged themselves by states in geographical order, from northernmost New Hampshire to southernmost Georgia. All twelve states present during the debates recorded signatures from their representatives. As each approving delegate stepped to the table to affix his signature, the great Constitution of the United States became a reality.

The document would now go to the Confederation Congress for acceptance. Upon its approval, the Constitution would go to each of the thirteen states for ratification. Time would reveal whether Congress, the states, and the people would accept it.

6

We the People

SOUTH CAROLINA

THE
ORIGINAL THIRTEEN
STATES

Section Six

——————————— ⚬⚬ ———————————

THE FIGHT FOR RATIFICATION

T HE CONSTITUTION was complete. The delegates had resolutely stuck to their task for six and sometimes seven hours a day, six days a week, for four months. They took only one recess, a ten-day period in late July, while the five-man Committee of Detail brought preliminary order to the proceedings.

The signing event was emotional. The delegates helped the elderly Benjamin Franklin to the signing table. Tears welled up in his eyes as he wrote his signature. After all had signed, they went to dinner at the City Tavern. Thereafter, they bade each other farewell and returned to their respective states to await the actions of the Congress of the Confederation.

Across the colonies, newspapers came alive with the news. Published everywhere, the new Constitution created a stir unlike anything colonial America had ever seen. The country was unprepared for the proposed new government. Convention delegates had minded their tongues well, and little was known about its features. Most people expected an amended Articles of Confederation, but they were given a new entity altogether. Some felt apprehensive about the document and the secrecy that surrounded its creation.

The discussion and heated debates from the Pennsylvania State House now began again with greater fervor in the public square. Public opinion waxed strong and suspicious. Why had some delegates not signed? Was the central government too strong? Why were individual rights not clearly stated in a Bill of Rights? Some were outraged because the new government seemed uncomfortably close to the British model. Feelings ran so strong that some delegates feared reprisals for their support of the Constitution.

Acting quickly and unanimously, the Confederation Congress voted to accept the Constitution after only eight days of debate. This raised concern among those who feared that the matter was being handled too hastily.

The Constitution now moved to the individual states for acceptance. Ratification would be a long and hard-fought process.

6.1 | The Federalist Papers

THE NEW CONSTITUTION created alarm and angst in the public, which boded ill for ratification. With the nation thoroughly agitated, someone needed to step forward and explain the document and the individual liberties it promised.

Alexander Hamilton's home state of New York was a hotbed of opposition to the Constitution that could set the trend for the rest of the country. It would be a challenge to promote ratification, but he rose to the occasion.

Hamilton enlisted the help of James Madison and John Jay, a nondelegate who strongly favored the Constitution. They agreed to share the writing effort in a series of newspaper articles to explain the new government. The articles were published in the six New York newspapers under a pseudonym, a common practice of the day. Their fictitious author, named "Publius" after a noted Roman orator, answered the criticisms lobbed at the Constitution and explained its benefits.

The three men who wrote the articles each had an area of expertise. Alexander Hamilton, the lawyer, naturally inclined toward economics and the judiciary. John Jay was a skilled diplomat and understood foreign policy. James Madison handled the rest. Among them, they understood the details of the Constitution—why it worked and how. As a team, they could effectively present the virtues of the proposed government.

In what became known as the Federalist Papers, "Publius" clarified the balance of powers. He explained the division of responsibilities between state and federal governments. He touted the organization and efficiency of the new government. He also described the checks and balances that put chains on human lusts for power to prevent a return to monarchy.

"Publius" provided four weekly articles from October of 1787 to May of 1788. John Jay fell ill after contributing five articles and was unable to continue, so the workload increased for the remaining two authors. Hamilton wrote fifty-one of the eighty-five articles, and Madison contributed the rest. The 175,000 words they penned during eight months constitute another miracle in bringing forth the Constitution.[1] Thomas Jefferson considered the Federalist Papers to be "the best commentary on the principles of government . . . ever written."[2]

Hamilton, Madison, and Jay intended the Federalist Papers to offer transparency in government to the common man. Their goal was to reveal the *why* of the Constitution, not just the *what*. Transparency is an essential element of representative government. Without it, the people cannot be sure their representatives are passing sound laws that they have studied and understand. They may find themselves bound by unknown laws over which they have no control. The Constitution, which gives power to the people, was drafted to prevent this kind of tyranny. Its creators recognized that a true government of the people must always be transparent.

The Federalist Papers had a powerful impact at the time of their publication and in the centuries since. They clarify the Constitution and offer a clear portrait of the Founders' original intent. They have been translated into dozens of languages. Leaders of nations around the world have studied them and patterned their own constitutions after that of the United States.

Centuries ago, settlers came to America to establish their dream of a "city on a hill" dedicated to principled government. Our original Constitution is that government. The Federalist Papers illuminated it.

6.2 | In Pennsylvania

MANY POWERFUL INDIVIDUALS throughout the thirteen states opposed the Constitution. It appeared at first that they dominated the decision.

Opponents to the Constitution had no organized plan. They simply worked upon people's fears of what might happen. They spotlighted what they deemed the unproven principles of the Constitution and the secrecy of its formative Convention. Much was made of supposed favoritism toward one part of the country over another. They lamented the lack of complete independence of the individual states. The detractors railed against the power of the president and vice-president. They expressed fear of the federal powers of taxation.

Pennsylvania provided the first and worst of the opposition. Its popular state constitution provided for a one-chamber legislature, annual elections, and a president chosen by the legislature. For eleven years, intense party disputes had raged for and against Pennsylvania's system and its shortcomings. Now a different federal system was being proposed. Some welcomed the differences. Others feared them.

Those against ratification were called Antifederalists. They tried to stop ratification by preventing the state assembly from calling for a ratification convention. Nineteen legislative members who opposed the Constitution locked themselves in their lodgings and refused to attend the legislative session to vote on the issue. With insufficient members in attendance at the legislature, no convention could be called. Surging crowds of Federalists, who favored the Constitution, broke through the locked doors and carried two Antifederalist members, white-faced with rage, to the assembly. With a working quorum now present, the vote for a state ratification convention carried.

Opponents continued to foment fear. The pro-Constitution Federalists spoke with logic and common sense through James Wilson, a delegate to the Constitutional Convention known for his deep, thoughtful opinions. His skillful presentation of the facts spoke plainly. He pointed out that opposition to the proposed Constitution came from those who profited by the current system. He reminded those who opposed federal powers that they had favored a unified central government eleven years earlier when the Declaration of Independence was signed. He explained that a union of the states was not possible unless each state surrendered some of its sovereign rights to the central government.

One of his opponents in the debates was Elbridge Gerry of Massachusetts, who had refused to sign the Constitution. He was invited unofficially to Pennsylvania's ratification convention to argue against the Constitution. When his efforts were unsuccessful, he departed resentfully.

The convention lasted five weeks. Wilson spoke day after day as he tirelessly defended and explained the new "federal liberty" at hand. Despite the fervor of the opposition, the vote on December 12, 1787, carried for the Constitution by a margin of 46 to 23.

In the fracas that followed, Antifederalists rushed James Wilson with clubs and knocked him to the ground. An old soldier threw himself between Wilson and the clubs to take the blows.

Pennsylvania was the first to call its convention but not the first to ratify. Delaware garnered that honor with a unanimous vote for ratification six days earlier. New Jersey ratified four days after Pennsylvania. Georgia ratified on January 2, followed on January 9 by Connecticut.

Five states had ratified the Constitution. With eight left to persuade, much work remained to move toward full adoption.

6.3 | In Massachusetts

THREE HUNDRED fifty-five delegates attended the ratification proceedings in Boston. The great patriot Samuel Adams posed powerful opposition to the federal Constitution. The Federalists represented a solid force for ratification.

The state legislature initially favored the Constitution. Then Elbridge Gerry, unelected to the convention, inserted his list of objections. With his prejudice staining the issue, ratification became more difficult.

The early debate focused on the farmers of Massachusetts, most of whom opposed the Constitution because they distrusted the wealthy, who favored it. An impressive voice swayed the decision—that of a common farmer, Jonathan Smith. He related that he was a simple man not used to public speaking. He had come to value good government by suffering from the lack of it. Of the Constitution, he said:

> *I got a copy of it and read it over and over . . . [I] had learnt something of the checks and balances of power and I found them all there . . . I formed my own opinion, and was pleased with this Constitution. Some gentlemen think that our liberty and property are not safe in the hands of moneyed men, and men of learning. I am not of that mind. These . . . men are all embarked in the same cause with us, and we must all swim or sink together. There is a time to sow and to reap . . . We sent our men to the federal convention . . . [and] now is the time to reap the fruit of our labor. And if we don't do it now, I am afraid we shall never have another opportunity.*[3]

As in Pennsylvania, the Antifederalists were ill managed, wordy, and excitable. The Federalists were logical, organized, and respectful of all opinions. As debate progressed, Samuel Adams changed his mind and joined his powerful voice to the Federalist cause. His opinion carried great weight. He realized the dangers: the vote would be cast only once, and much rested on its outcome, but politics could easily defeat ratification. To carry the day, the Federalists would need the influence of Governor John Hancock, who was absent.

To soothe most objections, Samuel Adams compiled a list of proposed amendments to assure individual rights. This he gave to Hancock, who presented it as his own creation. The ambitious governor appeared to be the source of genius.

After six days of heated discussion, the crucial vote was taken on February 6, 1788. Massachusetts became the sixth state to ratify, by a slim margin of 187 to 168. One delegate to the convention who changed his vote to favor ratification so angered his constituents that he had to move from his community.

Leading Antifederalists now pledged their support to the new government. A celebration in the streets followed. The ratification drive developed further momentum when Maryland and South Carolina voted to enter the Union during the spring of 1788.

Surely the hand of God was present throughout this process. Massachusetts was critical to the acceptance effort. Had any of the large states failed to ratify, the Constitution could have been lost.

6.4 | In Virginia

ASSEMBLED IN RICHMOND, Virginia's ratification convention went through the Constitution one clause at a time. Among the delegates were fourteen Kentuckians, whose territory was then part of Virginia and who had ridden through the Indian lands of Virginia's western territory. They sat in the rear of the convention with guns hanging from their belts. Four ultimately voted for ratification.

George Washington offered written support from Mount Vernon, while James Madison and George Wythe, America's leading law professor, led the contest for ratification. Wythe had attended the Constitutional Convention but left early because of family illness.

Imposing forces stood against ratification. The most formidable was the eloquent, inflammable Patrick Henry, notable for his "Give me liberty, or give me death!" speech in 1775. Tall and thin but broken in health at age fifty-two, he kept his audiences riveted for hours with his magical oratory and was one of the great voices of revolutionary America. In impassioned moments, he would twirl his ill-fitting brown wig several times around his head. His influence was so powerful that he could undo an hour's worth of previous oratory with a shake of his head. "Whither is the spirit of America gone?" he thundered. "Whither is the genius of America fled?"[4]

The Federalists warned of dire consequences if ratification failed. Henry rebutted them with his argument that no unrest had touched Virginia under the Articles of Confederation. He discoursed on the dreadful absurdity of entering into an unacceptable government on the promise that it would be rendered acceptable by a bill of rights. The new system was "pregnant" with immense dangers. The Kentuckians could lose navigation rights on the Mississippi. Prosperity would sour.

In one burst of ardent elocution, Henry envisioned angels on high in review of America's future. At that exact moment and without warning, a major storm struck. Lightning blazed, thunder crashed, and rain pounded the windows. As doors slammed like the roar of musketry, the meeting adjourned. It was a memorable moment.

The answering voice to Patrick Henry came from James Madison, a powerful orator in his own right. To Patrick Henry's emotion, he returned logic—careful, measured, and brilliant.

Governor Edmund Randolph, who had refused to sign the document originally, changed his vote to favor ratification when he saw that a bill of rights would become a reality. Henry accused him of seeking favors. Governor Randolph flamed back in his own defense at this challenge to his honor.

Virginia ratified the Constitution on June 25, 1788, by a vote of 89 to 79, including twenty submissions for a future bill of rights. Patrick Henry submitted his own proposed amendments to the Virginia legislature, and they were similar to those ultimately submitted by the state.

Prefacing the vote, Henry pledged to be a peaceful citizen if he was found in the minority. That night, at an Antifederalist rally protesting ratification, he made good on his promise by sending the wrathful crowds home.

Virginia expected to be the ninth of the nine states needed to bring the Constitution to life, but New Hampshire had preempted her by ratifying four days earlier. New York had been watching the proceedings and waited in the wings for Virginia's decision. When Virginia ratified, New York followed her lead.

With eleven ratifications, the Constitution drew breath and became a certainty. Only two states remained outside the new nation. Would the vote be unanimous?

6.5 | Waiting and Celebration

NINE had been the magic number. Without ratifying votes from nine state conventions, the United States would remain under the feeble Articles of Confederation and would almost certainly fail.

But America was not to be built on a majority. She would be united—a unanimous nation.

In July 1788, New York joined the Union. She did not come lightly or pleasantly, but she did come. Her opposing forces were led by Robert Yates and John Lansing, her former delegates to the Constitutional Convention, who had abandoned it early in bitter protest. Opposition forces in Albany rioted in the streets and burned a copy of the Constitution. The indefatigable Alexander Hamilton fueled the pro-Constitution effort and turned the tide for ratification.

North Carolina and Rhode Island eventually ratified to make the vote unanimous.

In retrospect, the process had been arduous. The public did not know of the long and bitter debates during the four months of the Constitutional Convention—moments such as July 1787, when the vote on legislative representation had failed yet again: five states for, five against, two not voting, and Georgia's vote split.

The people lived the uncertainty of waiting, as reported by the *Pennsylvania Gazette*:

> *The states neglect their roads and canals till they see whether those necessary improvements will not become the objects of a national government. Trading and manufacturing companies suspend their voyages and manufactures till they see how far their commerce will be protected and promoted by a national system of commercial regulations. The lawful usurer locks up or buries his specie till he sees whether the new frame of government will deliver him from the curse . . . of paper money and tender laws.*[5]

When the Constitution was finally unveiled, the *Pennsylvania Packet* published it, four pages long, with no other news. In bold type, the title read: "WE, THE PEOPLE OF THE UNITED STATES OF AMERICA . . ."[6]

In the wait for ratification, contention had been rife. Political opposites had battled to the vote before the public eye in the larger states. For ten long months, the nation had held its collective breath in suspense.

Now it was done. A new government had been born.

The delegates marveled that they had achieved a government so perfect from so much discord. General Washington analyzed the ratification process and found it good. "It has called forth . . . new light upon the science of government. It has given the rights of man a full and fair discussion, and explained them in so clear and forcible a manner as cannot fail to make a lasting impression."[7]

It was time to rejoice! Every state celebrated. Parades were held with uniformed military platoons in full dress. Bands played original music. A full-sized frigate was pulled down the streets of New York City by five teams of horses. Heralds trumpeted, foreign emissaries rode in open carriages, and Indians smoked peace pipes. Speeches were made, oxen were roasted, and a great many toasts were tipped to the glorious Union.

What an effort it had been! The Convention, the agreement on form and principle, the affixing of signatures, and the tumult of ratification— all had been a miracle.

Benjamin Rush said it most succinctly: "'Tis done. We have become a nation."[8]

Section Seven

───────── ભ ─────────

BASIC GOVERNING PRINCIPLES

OUR FOUNDING FATHERS embraced sound principles in drafting the Constitution. The principles were not new. They had existed with God from the beginning of time. Moses had them. The ancient Anglo-Saxons, under their chieftains Hengist and Horsa, also had them.

That so many of the Founders understood these truths is startling. Names of authors such as Locke, Cicero, Polybius, Adam Smith, and Montesquieu rolled from their tongues with ease. We would not expect to find fifty-five men from such different backgrounds and occupations who were so well versed in the great political classics. They were all prompted to search out wisdom from the masters of political thought.

The Founders ranged from frontiersmen to affluent planters, from those with backwoods home-schooling to those educated at the greatest universities. The union of these men at this place and time, with their penetrating insights in politics and human nature, is evidence of God's hand in America's development. They occupied a continent inhabited just decades before by native tribes. God surely brought them together for His purposes. Their dedicated efforts manifested God's involvement. The intelligence and integrity of these men was astounding.

The Founders were nearly unanimous in their belief and practice of Christianity. They promised to give their lives, their fortunes, and their sacred honor for freedom, and they did. The love of liberty inspires good people to sacrifice priceless things to obtain it. These men and their families put America's liberty before their own interests and safety.

The greatness of our Constitution unfolds before us as we investigate its underlying principles. Our desire to protect and restore it will grow in concert with our understanding.

7.1 | Is the Constitution Outdated?

S OME SAY that our Constitution no longer works. They call it unwieldy and outdated—a simple document for a simpler time. They say that it is not effective in our modern, sophisticated world of instant communication and rapid worldwide travel.

Our Constitution is not outdated. It is profoundly more than a statement of political rules. It is a document of human nature—a statement of man's universal tendency to usurp and abuse power when given the opportunity.

History confirms the human tendency to abuse authority. The world has always contained individuals who want power. Some want it for worthwhile things. They reason that with power, they could bring about much good. This may be the case initially, but the annals of history are filled with tales of those who began with honor and ended in corruption. Others began with dishonorable intentions and carried their desires to ends that caused misery and heartache for others.

Lord Acton of Britain expressed it best: "Power tends to corrupt, and absolute power corrupts absolutely."[1] In our modern world, we would probably say: "Give someone an inch, and he'll take a mile"—of our freedoms.

Our Founding Fathers were optimists but also realists. They recognized the human thirst for power—that all humans have both strengths and weaknesses. In the words of James Madison: "As there is a degree of depravity in mankind which requires a certain . . . distrust, so there are other qualities in human nature which justify . . . esteem and confidence."[2] The intent of our inspired Founders was to create a government that encouraged the virtues in those who lead while restricting their vices.

The Constitution places limits on these tendencies through the application of checks and balances. It distributes power among the branches of government so that no one branch is given more than a limited and carefully controlled amount. This is the brilliance of the Constitution: while it creates rules of political operation, it also sets rules of human conduct.

Those who want power often accuse the Constitution of being slow and antiquated. For those in a hurry to get and use power, it is indeed slow, and for a very good purpose.

The original Constitution of the United States, as it came from the pen of the Founding Fathers, was a rich, perfectly balanced document that controlled the use of power. Its parts were crafted to create a marvelous working whole that distributed power rather than centering it in one individual or group. This distribution of power among government branches is part of the great genius of the Constitution and is known as the balance of power. Time proved this government structure to be both simple and durable.

Some have unwisely tried to readjust the Constitution's balance of power. The Constitution as it stands today is an altered version, changed over time by unwise constitutional amendments and inappropriate Supreme Court decisions. Only with great thought, caution, and care should one alter such a carefully balanced entity. An investment of time and prolonged deliberation is required: if this changes, what will happen to that? Those who want a government that increases freedoms, protection, and prosperity must be sure of the results of their actions before proceeding.

There are times when the race goes to the turtle. This is one of them.

7.2 | Rights, Duties, and Government

OUR GOVERNMENT operates on the basic principle of inalienable rights. We all have rights given to us by God. They are inalienable because He gives them to us. They do not come from government or from man. They are ours because we are children of a divine God who loves us.

We instinctively know what these rights are, although we may be at a loss to name them all. We have the right to govern ourselves through personal choices, to obtain and keep property, and to have privacy when we choose. We have the right to speak, to gather together, and to receive accurate information that is untainted by another's bias. We are entitled to improve our lot in life and to be treated fairly. We have the right to use the bounty of the earth, to keep and enjoy the fruits of our labors, and to beget our own kind. We have the right to protect ourselves and to possess the tools that afford us that protection.

Rights, however, require a force to safeguard them, for there are some who would take our rights from us. That protective force is government. Government, therefore, is about power. As George Washington put it: "Government is not reason, it is not eloquence—it is force. Like fire, it is a dangerous servant and a fearful master."[3] Without the power of a government that will ensure our rights, we might as well have none. That which cannot be enforced is no better than a request for the unscrupulous to ignore.

Workable government is an essential part of any society. With too little government, citizens are victims of anarchy. With too much government or without good government, they are the victims of its opposite: tyranny.

The Founding Fathers knew the results of both. They set their course for that perfect central point between the two unwelcome extremes of anarchy and tyranny. They wanted government with enough power to protect its citizens but enough restraint to prevent abuse.

It is important to remember that every right has a corresponding duty. If we have the right to protect ourselves, everyone else has the same right. If we wish to own and retain property, we have the duty to allow others the same right. If we are allowed to speak freely, be treated fairly, and have privacy, we have the responsibility to allow others the same privileges.

Not only are we duty-bound to give others their rights, but we are also required to see that our government protects them, just as we expect it to protect us. A right implies action, and a duty requires restraint.

So it becomes the duty of government not only to protect our rights, but to require all of us to perform our duties. If rights are violated, government must extract justice from those who commit the violations. It must compel them to honor their future duties. In addition, government must see that justice prevails and compensation is made for violations.

We have the responsibility to consider and value not just our rights, but also our duties. To do less is to lose our balance.

7.3 | Vertical Powers and Local Government

G OOD GOVERNMENT keeps the greatest power close to the people it serves. It separates power vertically, with families as the foundation and the federal government at the uppermost point. Our Founders, particularly Thomas Jefferson, learned this from the Bible.[4]

In the Old Testament, Jethro offered his son-in-law Moses a plan to organize Israel into manageable units. He suggested grouping families by tens, fifties, hundreds, thousands, and so on. Each group was to have a leader with assisting councils (Deuteronomy 1:13–15).

Using this system, Moses organized three million people and could receive the opinions of every single person. When a consensus or vote was needed, the leaders of ten polled their families and passed the information to the leaders of fifty. Those leaders compiled the votes and sent them to the leaders of hundreds, and so on to the top. Every person was heard, and justice flowed smoothly.

America's adaptation of this system of vertical powers also features the family as the basic unit. After the family comes the city, the county, the state, and finally the national government. Each jurisdiction has its own responsibilities and authority.

The closer governmental power rests to the people, the more freedom they have—for several reasons. Organizing a large group leaves little room for individuality. Manageability requires conformity, which is the opposite of individual freedom. This is the danger of a strong national government. When power rests at the federal level, individual rights cannot be considered because individuality cannot be accommodated. Variations in the rules create disorder. The Founders left power with the states to bring control closer to the people and allow them greater individual freedom.

Regional differences illustrate this principle well. A small, densely populated seaboard state with a maritime and manufacturing economy needs different laws and policies than a large, sparsely populated, and mountainous state with industries that center on lumber, ranching, and mining. When states are forced to keep the same standards, they will spend time, money, and energy on unnecessary programs.

Individuals make a difference within smaller groups. One voice in a vast group may be lost. That same voice in a smaller group can change a course of action. Local changes can transmit to states, which then carry the message to the national level. States can join together for greater solidarity when working with the federal government.

When a government passes laws, it must also enforce them. Local government is more likely to enforce laws fairly among its citizens. Therefore, local government must be strong and honest to protect local citizens. When laws are fair and uniformly enforced, most people voluntarily comply. When they are unfairly drafted or enforced, people rebel.

Citizens are the core of our system of self-rule and elected representatives. They must be well informed. Wise laws do not come from ignorant or misinformed people. Free speech and a free press are essential to self-rule. Information given to the people will guide them in their decisions, so that information must be accurate, fair, and complete.

God's pattern of self-rule flows upward from the family to the federal level. This keeps government close to the people for their safety and protection.

7.4 | Who Is in Charge: State versus Federal

THE STATE and federal governments have different responsibilities under the Constitution. Our liberty depends on maintaining the balance between these two forces. A strong federal government allows little freedom for the people. Strong state governments allow greater freedom.

Under the original Constitution, the states are the power centers of government, with responsibility for the internal workings of their territories. They tax and regulate commerce. States establish court systems and punish crimes. They provide schools, roads, waterways, and more. They solve problems and take responsibility to ensure the quality of life in the towns, cities, and counties within their borders.

The states are not appendages or auxiliaries of the federal government. They are sovereign units, acting independently according to their state constitutions. They follow the limited federal laws but are otherwise self-governing.

The federal government handles all external matters for the country, such as international affairs and policies that involve all the states. The Founders carefully identified twenty areas in which the federal government would assist the states, including, for instance, defense, immigration, coining money, and a national postal system. The federal government was given no authority outside those twenty powers. It could not intrude in state or individual affairs.

With the federal government, through Congress and the president, presiding over external affairs and cities and counties responsible for local matters, the states have authority over everything else. They are to customize policies for their citizens on a broad range of important topics.

State governments were designated to protect the people from federal abuse. It was intended that any federal requests be carried out by the states or in cooperation with the states. If a request was foolish, the states could refuse to carry it out. They could put chains on a heavy-handed federal government.

National government is far removed from the people, which increases the potential for abuse of power. State governments were intended to prevent the federal government from infringing on the personal affairs of their citizens. Of course, the state can also misuse power, just as all governments can. But because state government is closer to the people, it is easier for them to see and stop political chicanery. The people can supervise state authority and adjust where necessary.

Today, federal control of state affairs is rampant, as feared by our Founding Fathers. State governments have little authority and are weak. Their hands are tied by federal requirements, and they are dazzled by the possibility of federal funding. Divested of the powers that our Founders intended them to wield, they can no longer protect us.

Thomas Jefferson warned of this possibility over two hundred years ago: "When all government . . . shall be drawn to Washington as the center of all power, it will render powerless the checks provided (for our safety) . . . and (the government) will become as venal and oppressive as the government from which we separated."[5]

We have ignored Jefferson's warning about ceding power to Washington. We now live with the results. To regain our liberties, we must return power to the states, where we can better oversee our elected officials.

7.5 | Horizontal Powers

GOVERNMENT is about power. Because power tends to corrupt, the Founders tried to divide power so that no part of the system had too much. They divided it vertically, to flow from the family to the city, county, state, and federal governments. They also divided power horizontally between the three branches of the federal government: legislative, executive, and judicial.

John Adams first saw the benefits of this horizontal division of power. Great political minds had written about it for centuries, but John Adams put horizontal power into practice in the Massachusetts state constitution. Later, he encouraged it for the federal Constitution. His proposal, unpopular at first, gained approval as people understood it better.

Horizontal power divides authority between Congress, the president, and the court system. The legislative branch creates law, the executive branch administers law, and the judicial branch assures that laws are properly enforced.

Under the original Constitution, each of these three branches remained separate and distinct. Each branch acted only within its assigned responsibilities. Checks and balances were built into the system to ensure that it flowed uniformly. One defiant branch could not overwhelm the others, and they could not combine powers.

These checks and balances are the genius of the United States government. This inventive arrangement maintained the delicate balance between the three branches of federal government. Power was distributed evenly and safely so that no branch of the government could abuse its authority.

Our Founders knew that the system would come under assault. Inevitably, power-hungry leaders would try to usurp power. The Framers were students of human nature as well as of political thought. They built the American system to withstand such leaders. As William Grayson, an early patriot, stated: "Power ought to have checks and limitations as to prevent bad men from abusing it. It ought to be granted on a supposition that men will be bad, for it may be eventually so."[6]

Principled men of good character drafted the rules of United States government. A limited number of rules were necessary to maintain freedom and prosperity. Once established, it was essential that they be followed. The people's task was to understand the rules and be sure that their leaders obeyed them.

The greatest responsibility of government is to preserve liberty through four simple principles concerning our duties as citizens. First, government must insist that we perform our duties. Second, it must not create new duties or eliminate existing ones. Third, government must punish those who refuse to perform their duties. Finally, it must punish *only* those who refuse to perform their duties. When government acts within these limitations, it protects life, liberty, and property.

The rules of good government have been undermined in America because we have not insisted that the rules be kept. Our understanding of the purposes of government has been warped. Our current governmental structure is unbalanced. The executive and judicial branches are bloated, and Congress has failed to control the gluttony. Every American pays for this imbalance through excessive taxes, oppressive regulations, and diminished prosperity.

To bring prosperity back to America, we must restore the principles of our original Constitution and insist that each branch of government follow the rules of good government.

7.6 | Equality: What It Is and What It Isn't

THE DECLARATION OF INDEPENDENCE states that people are equal. This equality falls into three categories: we are equal before God, equal before the law and the courts, and equal in the justice that we should receive.

Many do not understand equality. They believe in the equality of *things*—of incomes and outcomes. About the French philosopher Jean-Jacques Rousseau, who declared men's rights to be equal in every way, John Adams wrote from France: "That all men are born to equal rights is true . . . But to teach that all men are born with equal powers and faculties, to equal influence in society, to equal property and advantages through life, is as gross a fraud . . . as ever was practiced."[7]

Because we misunderstand equality, we—the people and our elected officials—focus on giving equal *things* through government. This requires taking goods from some and giving them to others. This redistribution of wealth includes two factors that invest the federal government with inappropriate power. First, the government decides who has too much and takes what it deems proper from them. Second, the government decides who has too little and gives to them what it deems appropriate. It carries out this redistribution without individual evaluation of what is needed or helpful and without requiring corresponding effort from the recipient.

Federal agencies administer this "raze and rise" program. Government, whose responsibility it is to prevent injustice, thus becomes the agent of injustice. It unjustly takes, and it unjustly gives. Some lose their goods. Others become dependent on handouts. Government teaches the recipients that they cannot or need not provide for themselves.

Our federal government was not assigned to provide goods, but to protect us while we provide our own goods. The assignment to assist the less fortunate, when necessary, was given to the states, not the federal government.

The Lord provides for the poor in His own way—a superior way. He admonishes us to give voluntarily of our substance for their care. Any other means involves compulsion, and God does not compel. He is a God of perfect fairness and personal choice. He instructs us to give freely to those in need—the widows, the fatherless, the poor, and the sick. His intent is to sustain individuals and families through difficult times as they work to regain self-sufficiency.

United States President Grover Cleveland addressed this issue: "The friendliness and charity of our countrymen can always be relied upon to relieve their fellow-citizens in misfortune. This has been repeatedly . . . demonstrated. Federal aid . . . encourages the expectation of paternal care . . . and weakens the sturdiness of our national character."[8]

Many well-meaning individuals believe that charity means ensuring that all have equal things. No group of people will ever have equal things. Through luck, talent, or superior effort, some will always have more than others.

We are responsible to provide for our less-fortunate fellow beings. Government should not intervene by taking from us goods we have rightfully earned. This is the antithesis of equality, the very principle the Founders attempted to uphold in our Constitution.

7.7 | Freedom and Morality Intertwined

MORALITY AND VIRTUE are indispensible to liberty, which is freedom rightfully used. Listen to the words of the Founding Fathers:

John Adams: "Our Constitution was made only for a moral . . . people. It is wholly inadequate to the government of any other."[9]

Benjamin Franklin: "Only a virtuous people are capable of freedom. As nations become corrupt . . . they have more need of masters."[10]

Virtue and integrity define our moral code—our beliefs of right and wrong. Without those beliefs, concepts of good and evil do not exist. There is no incentive to treat others fairly, to obey law, or to tell the truth. Dishonor becomes irrelevant. A person without virtue can justify any self-serving scheme if there is no punishment for it. An immoral person will rob, steal, or even take life if it can be done without consequence.

Through our moral beliefs, we care about others and value their well-being. Our moral beliefs make us tender at the pain of another, and we take care not to prolong or increase it. We are inclined to give and desire good for others. Our morality makes us want liberty for all of us and not just for ourselves.

Good government is not possible among people who do not understand right and wrong. Anarchy would reign, and there would be no freedom, no justice, no protection, and no rights. The "law of the jungle" would prevail. No sane, thinking person would advocate such a world.

Freedom, morality, and virtue are synonymous ideas. The more moral we are, the less law we need and the more free we are. If most people are honest in their dealings, fewer laws are needed to control theft. If most financial institutions are fair and upright with their customers, only basic oversight is necessary. If most manufacturers act with integrity and offer their goods at fair prices, few regulations are needed to protect consumers.

The Founders' political rules made morality and the basic knowledge of religious principles central to society. They wrote and discussed this copiously for decades. The Framers could not and would not conceive of government without the constant influence of God and virtue. Our collective belief in God is the source of our virtue. We are moral when we follow God's laws. If we do not follow God's laws, political forces will step in to fill that vacuum and impose laws upon us. William Penn, founder of colonial Pennsylvania, explained: "Men will either be governed by God, or ruled by tyrants."[11]

Calvin Coolidge, United States president, wrote: "We do not need more law, we need more religion."[12] Elsewhere, he reiterated: "Our government rests upon religion . . . There is no way . . . we can substitute the authority of law for the virtue of men . . . Peace, justice, humanity, charity—these cannot be legislated into being."[13]

If we wish for greater freedom, it makes sense to strive for greater morality and virtue. Dedicated church leaders of all denominations the world over address our current problems in society with calls for greater virtue.

Speaking of God's law, Proverbs 29:18 tells us: "[H]e that keepeth the law, happy is he." Not only are we happier when we keep God's law, but we require less of man's law.

$$7.8 \quad \Big| \quad \text{Separating Church and State}$$

W E HEAR it often. "Eliminate all references to God and religion in the public square. We must have separation of church and state!" Holidays are renamed, biblical inscriptions removed, and public prayers prohibited. This "search and desist" mission leaves practicing Christians dismayed to see religious artifacts and rituals forbidden and then abolished altogether.

The United States Constitution never mentions either the words or the concept of separation of church and state. The concept has been invented by our popular political culture. The phrase "separation of church and state" was first used by Thomas Jefferson in an 1802 letter and again by James Madison. Neither used that phrase as it is interpreted today.

What the Constitution does say is in the First Amendment: "Congress shall make no law respecting the establishment of religion, or prohibiting the free exercise thereof." No laws can be made that interfere with the establishment or practice of religion. The position taken today is exactly opposite to that of our governing document and the Founding Fathers. Rather than keeping government out of religion, today's application declares that we must keep religion out of government.

The Founders would be dismayed by what we have done with the issue of church and state. Their concern was to prevent any one religion from becoming entrenched as a state-sponsored religion, as had occurred in England and other European countries. When the national government sanctioned one church, all others were persecuted. Under governmental control, the favored church became inseparably tangled in political issues. Religion was no longer about God but about government, and political intrigues appeared to be sanctioned by God. This unholy union of church and state fostered abuse and spiritual degeneracy.

The federal government's position on religion and morality is found in the Northwest Ordinance, which brought 260,000 square miles into United States territory. It was passed by the Congress of the Confederation in 1787, the same year the Constitution was written. Its third article reads: "Religion, morality, and knowledge being necessary to good government and the happiness of mankind, schools and the means of education shall forever be encouraged." Religious and moral values were an integral part of school curricula at the time. The Congress intended these teachings to continue.

The basic religious beliefs encouraged by the Founders were part of all major religions. They were summarized by Benjamin Franklin in a letter to Ezra Stiles, president of Yale University: "Here is my creed. I believe in one God, the Creator of the universe. That he governs it by his providence. That he ought to be worshipped. That the most acceptable service we render to him is in doing good to his other children. That the soul of man is immortal and will be treated with justice in another life respecting his conduct in this. These I take to be the fundamental points in all sound religion."[14]

These beliefs are the foundation of right and wrong, good and evil. They continue to be taught in some form in most major religions today. No people in a free society can maintain a successful government without them. Our society has seriously misunderstood this issue.

7.9 | The Golden Rule in Government

F EW PEOPLE think to apply the Golden Rule to government, yet our Founding Fathers esteemed this ancient universal principle and built the Constitution around it.

"Therefore all things whatsoever ye would that men should do to you, do ye even so to them" (Matthew 7:12). On a personal level, this law teaches us to work for that which brings good to others and not to exercise control over our fellow beings. On a governmental level, it does the same, for the Golden Rule substantiates the concept of inalienable rights of all men—that all are entitled to life, liberty, and the right to possess goods secured through their honest labor. Every major religion has its version of the Golden Rule.

In political action, the Golden Rule becomes the premier law of a democratic republic. Under self-rule, no supreme authority exists except God—no favored bloodline or consecrated monarchy. Power is vested in the people themselves, who are all of equal importance.

This law decrees that no government—monarchy, oligarchy, democracy, or a blend of the three—should do to its people what they, ethically speaking, would not want to have happen to themselves. No government is authorized to be more important or privileged than its citizens are. The source of governmental power is the people, and the servant cannot rise above his master. By this key, we can judge the fairness of any law. If the law can do what the people cannot do, it is wrong. If the law exempts some lawbreakers from punishment, it is wrong. Law should apply equally to all.

Those we select as our representatives have two fundamental responsibilities. First, they must make, amend, and repeal laws. Second, they must judge those accused of breaking the laws. The Golden Rule, applied appropriately, assures that both of these processes will proceed fairly.

The Golden Rule also identifies appropriate penalties. We can see the fairness of God's legal system by looking at God's laws to ancient Israel. Lawbreakers were dealt with according to how they dealt with their victims. Compensation went to the victim, not to the government or the courts. A thief had to replace the stolen item several times over. This provided justice and discouraged further stealing. If a person's wrongdoing cost another his eye or limb, and if the perpetrator refused to offer acceptable compensation, that same consequence could be imposed on him. If he willfully took a life, his own life was taken.

Government is force and power, as George Washington stated, so it is easy for government to take advantage and work beyond its legitimate bounds. Men tend to usurp power under the corrupting influence of authority. The process may begin innocently and even kindly, but rarely does the thirst for power or the control arising from power lead to anything but oppression.

Some believe that government cannot operate on virtuous principles. Experience and reason disagree. Good government has no alternative but to abide by the Golden Rule. The Lord gave us this law as a yardstick to measure the actions of people in relation to their fellow beings. We are wise to use it as a measurement of fair and honest government as well. The Golden Rule governs us personally. It should also govern us politically.

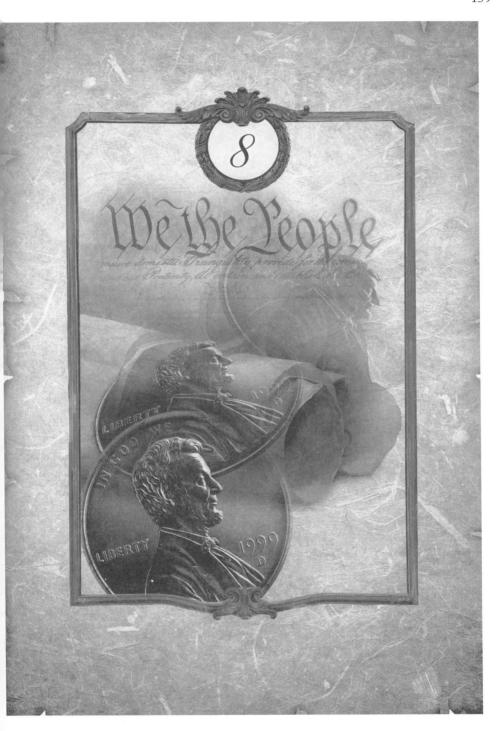

8

We the People

*insure domestic Tranquility, provide for the common
and our Posterity, all ensure and established by the...*

Section Eight

❧

ECONOMIC FREEDOM

PLENTIFUL JOBS, a robust economy, and prosperous citizens are the result of a free market. Economic freedom and political freedom are twin pillars. Free government succeeds only with a free marketplace in which to operate, and an uninhibited market is impossible without free, limited government. Either both give freedom, or both take it away.

The economy works when government provides overall structure and then leaves the market open to regulate itself. This is the free enterprise system, or free agency in economics. Differences in wealth will always be part of the system, as some have greater talent, more luck, or a stronger drive to work than others. However, under economic liberty, all, including the poor, have opportunities to rise.

America's economic greatness developed when people worked, saved, and practiced thrift and frugality. Government placed a protective umbrella of sound economic principles over the nation which allowed open competition to set prices and make goods available with little government intervention. Prosperity in the marketplace was the result, and the United States grew to become a dominant force in the world.

Gradually, we have abandoned this successful system. We have allowed ourselves to be convinced that the government owes us goods and knows better than we do what is best for us. As one instance, we have given up money with intrinsic value for paper. Now we watch as our dollars succumb to inflation. We have become a welfare state. We have far less freedom and far less prosperity than we had in the past.

We are still the greatest nation on earth. We are strong, and as a people we value freedom. We have the capability to cast off the economic shackles that have slowed our progress. We have the past to show us the future. A vibrant, booming economy awaits us if we are willing to understand and bring back the economic principles we once embraced.

Our first step—and it is always the first step—is to understand the problem. In our discussion of money, property, and regulation, we can begin to discover a better way.

8.1 | Appropriate Government in Economics

Our Founding Fathers received a gift in 1776 in the form of a newly published set of books called *The Wealth of Nations,* by Adam Smith. This Scottish professor introduced an original free-enterprise system for the marketplace. Our Framers believed that it offered economic freedom to parallel our new political freedom. Under free enterprise, America flourished and became the world leader in prosperity.

Free enterprise features a marketplace of individual choice and little government intervention. Open competition improves the number and quality of goods and sets their price. The supply of goods is based on demand for them. If demand and supply remain high, the commerce in goods will naturally bring about the purpose of business, which is to make a profit.

Four basic laws guide economic freedom. First, we have the freedom to try. America is a land of creative entrepreneurs who conceive an idea and bring it to reality. New products emerge to meet people's needs. Next, we have the freedoms to buy and to sell in a healthy free market that offers various goods from limitless sources. This merchandising creates a robust, self-propelled economy. Finally, we have the freedom to fail.[1] Failure is part of the learning process. It often teaches us more than success and paves the way for future achievements.

The greatest threat to free enterprise is excessive government control through regulations, which ought to be kept to a minimum. Regulation is necessary in only four areas. First, we need government to prevent criminal invasion of the market, so that we may participate economically without being either forbidden or forced. Second, government must prevent fraud by those who would push false products, services, or information on the public. Third, we rely on government to prevent monopolies, in which businesses join together to destroy competition and fix prices. Finally, we need government to prevent debauchery, or the exploitation of vices which injure society.[2] This includes gambling, drugs, pornography, and prostitution, along with other ills.

America changed direction in the early 1900s. The manipulation by unprincipled individuals created disruptions in the free market, and government stepped in to control the resultant problems. Their regulations brought more disruptions. New rounds of regulatory intervention, each introduced to correct the dislocations of the previous round, further displaced the markets. Today, we continue to "fix" the problems of too much regulation by adding more regulations.

Our nation, once the poster child for economic freedom, ranks high in government interference in the marketplace. Millions of regulations strangle businesses and strip profits, with thousands of new regulations to control trade, wages, working conditions, and environmental issues introduced yearly.[3] Government even decrees what light bulbs we can purchase. These regulations substantially raise the prices of our goods and spell death to economic vitality. The current American economy is proof that markets can be managed into apathy and regulated to death.

The temptation to "fix" the marketplace by controlling it is as old as government itself. Every government in the history of our planet that has attempted control of the marketplace has failed. More rules cannot solve the problems caused by too many rules. Rather, they result in a stagnant economy, high taxes, and a shortage of jobs. A return to minimally regulated commerce will restore vitality in the free market.

8.2 | Owning Property

GOD COMMANDED that we subdue the earth to have dominion over it. We do that when we own and manage property. This right to obtain and keep personal property—such as personal effects, homes and land, means for food production, salaries, and even our lives—and depend on its use for our personal security is important to happiness and prosperity. Our Founding Fathers recognized that freedom and property ownership are intertwined inalienable rights. When we cannot own property, we have no freedom because we cannot control our circumstances. When we have no freedom, we cannot own property.

Property ownership holds us accountable for that property. When a community owns property jointly, no one is ultimately responsible. The settlers of Jamestown and the early Pilgrims learned how disastrous that could be. No one made sure that the crops were grown, harvested, and stored for winter. Few people invested their wholehearted efforts when they would not fully benefit from their own work. However, when individual stewardship was assigned, people worked hard. This is human nature—we work best for what we keep. This is inborn in each of us.

Abraham Lincoln said: "Property is the fruit of labor; property is desirable; it is a positive good in the world. That some should be rich shows that others may become rich, and, hence, is just encouragement to industry and enterprise."[4] Some will work harder and some will be lucky, but it is God's plan that each of us work to provide for ourselves. It is also His plan that we keep what we earn.

Despotic governments do not always seize property but can exercise control through excessive taxation and heavy regulations. Property taxes, vehicle registrations, and zoning restrictions are examples of control by government. Business licenses and manufacturing regulations restrict what was once a free economy. Government agencies, such as those to protect the environment or ensure worker safety, often overextend their reach. Regulations act as laws but are not voted on by our elected representatives. These examples of excessive control shackle our right to own and use property.

Government programs to oversee this control are paid for through taxation and are expensive. They drain the wages of the common people and drive the cost of goods upward. Regulatory costs push businesses out of the marketplace, and jobs are lost. Taxes and excessive regulations create a large poverty class.

Some government is necessary, of course. It must be limited, close to the people, and carefully supervised. When we understand the intent of government and get involved in the process at some level, we can supervise. This helps us secure laws that work to our best interests.

Originally, our system of free government was known as a democratic republic. Political systems that control and confiscate property—socialism and communism, both of which violate constitutional and divine law—are the opposite of a democratic republic. Dishonesty always characterizes these systems. The benefits of government control never equal the freedom and prosperity that are lost. Our wise Founders warned that if government began to control the property of its citizens, either through regulation or outright seizure, freedom would fall.

Unfettered property ownership is both a responsibility and an inalienable right. We must return that right to our society.

8.3 | The Gold and Silver Standard

GOLD AND SILVER give us prosperity in more ways than the obvious. The federal government is responsible to create a national economy that unifies the states. Without a national fiscal base, each state would function as an independent nation. When the economy falters, freedoms falter, because citizens lose their ability to provide for themselves. With a strong and united economic base, personal freedoms are protected.

The Constitution places the United States on a gold and silver standard by requiring states to pay their debts with these precious metals. This requires that the entire economy be based on a gold and silver standard. These precious metals were selected as the basis for our money because they are universally available and valued by all societies, hold their worth over time, and are nonperishable. This part of the Constitution is routinely ignored.

Centuries ago, precious metals were the world's currency. Coins were heavy to carry, so they were deposited with those who became the first bankers. Paper receipts were given to the depositors, who could return at any time and exchange them for their gold. Over time, people came to use the receipts indefinitely as though they were gold, and few returned to exchange them. Paper money was born.

Bankers soon learned that they could give out more paper receipts than the gold they had stored, so they began making loans using the paper receipts. The receipts were deceptive, because only a fraction of the money loaned out actually had gold to back it, but no one knew. A banker could collect interest by creating loans for many times the amount of gold that he actually held. Bankers became very wealthy through this process and thus very influential.

This system, known as fractional banking, is standard practice today worldwide. Though firmly entrenched in the business world, it raises ethical questions. Just as with fraudulent investments, it seems morally indefensible to lend out for interest funds that one does not actually have.

So long as United States currency was backed by precious metals, it maintained its value. Paper money symbolized actual worth, and a paper bill could be redeemed for its equivalent in precious metals. However, beginning in 1933 and continuing for some forty years afterward, the United States abandoned the gold and silver standard by stages.

Nothing of any worth backs our paper currency today, and paper money has no intrinsic value. A dollar is worth only the paper and ink used to print it. It is given as compensation for the effort and time of every worker in America, but in an economic crisis its buying power can dwindle to nothing.

Furthermore, because the currency is only paper and has nothing of worth to back it, more can be printed for the national government at will. The printing of additional money is a routine process for the federal government today, despite the fact that the Constitution does not give government the right to do so. This excess printing of paper money causes inflation.

Both fractional banking and the demise of the gold and silver standard hurt the pocketbooks of the average American daily. We are less prosperous because our government has allowed both of these fiscally irresponsible practices. Our dysfunctional economic system is even more worrisome when we consider the inflation that results from unsecured, essentially worthless paper money.

8.4 | Inflation

INFLATION is a national and worldwide concern. It causes our dollars to buy less, so we must use more of them for what we need. Our standard of living drops, and financial worries destroy our peace of mind.

This problem is not new; inflation helped bring down the Roman Empire and plagued ancient China. It has played havoc with nations around the world for millennia, and it jeopardized the new United States of America under the Articles of Confederation.

Most people think that inflation is caused by increased prices. The opposite is true—the rise in prices is caused by inflation. The real cause of inflation is the addition of more money into the economy without an increase of things to buy with it. This unbalances the economy, and inflation is the result.

To illustrate, if there are one million things to purchase and one million dollars in the marketplace, each item will cost an average of one dollar. If we add an additional one million dollars into the economy without increasing the number of things to buy, the average cost of each item will rise to two dollars. Because there are no additional goods to compete for a consumer's dollars, the merchant will charge more and the consumer will pay more, both simply because they can. Add another million dollars, and the average cost will rise to three dollars per item, and so on. This is inflation—adding money to the economy that is not balanced by adding things to purchase with it.

Our current government routinely adds money into the marketplace to pay for programs and goods it cannot afford. Government habitually outspends its budget and prints money to cover its excesses. Every time it does so, prices rise through inflation, and ordinary citizens struggle with the side effects. Family budgets suffer because the federal government does not control its spending.

Everyone must balance income with obligations and wants. The federal government had to budget itself when we lived under the gold and silver standard. It could add money into the economy only by buying more precious metals to back it. Now that it does not have to secure paper dollars with precious metals, the government ignores budgeting and prints paper money freely. Prices rise when this money is added into the marketplace, although the increases take time. The federal government is only slightly affected by the increase because it spends its money before inflation registers.

This access to free-and-easy money created out of nothing leads to a fiscally irresponsible mindset in leadership. Government officials become frivolous with national funds. Because most Americans do not understand the cause of inflation, there is limited outcry over this inflation cycle that gradually takes away our earning power. Through tax dollars, the uneducated public pays for our government's irresponsibility. Eventually, political corruption dominates the system, oppressive laws are passed, and liberty dies.

Every nation that has followed this path since the beginning of recorded history has fallen. Most of them never again rose to past glory. The United States has traveled far along this path. There is still time to change course, if we hurry. A return to the gold and silver standard is essential.

9

We the People

_____ ❧ _____

THE CONSTITUTION: MAKING THE LAWS

OUR CONSTITUTION began as an inspired document written by inspired men. Adhering to it made the United States the most prosperous nation in modern history. Since then, unprincipled men have found ways to stretch, balloon, and distort the Constitution into its present altered form.

Today, its checks and balances have been rendered all but useless. Laws are drafted by unauthorized groups and are not approved by our elected representatives. We suffer from regulatory overload. The balance of power is tilted recklessly, and Congress has become a full-time career. All this has occurred because each new amendment to the Constitution supersedes all those before it and changes the very core of our government. Judicial decisions interpreting the Constitution also affect all others that follow.

To understand exactly how our Constitution has been changed and how we have lost our liberty, we must compare the original Constitution and the altered Constitution and identify the differences between the inspired document and the modern, impaired replacement.

The Founders' political plan considered the power to make laws the most significant part of the government machine. Congress was the central power plant for the entire system: the House and the Senate received exclusive power to draft laws for the United States. They were to monitor the entire system and pass new laws when needed.

The Framers wrote the Constitution in simple language so that citizens could study it in preparation for selecting and supervising their elected representatives. The three horizontal branches of government—Congress, the president, and the courts—would pore over it in detail. This simple, easily understood four-page document is a gift to us from the Framers. It supported America through her period of greatest prosperity.

The following pages begin with the Preamble and describe Article I of the Constitution, which details the procedures for the Legislature—the only body authorized to create laws. The original Constitution is explained first, followed by the changes that have altered our Constitution and the freedoms that we have lost because of those changes.

9.1 | The Preamble to the United States Constitution

OUR CHARTER of freedom begins with a mission statement:

"We the People of the United States, in Order to form a more perfect Union, establish Justice, insure domestic Tranquility, provide for the common defense, promote the general Welfare, and secure the blessings of Liberty to ourselves and our Posterity, do ordain and establish this Constitution for the United States of America."

The original Constitution defines the people as the source of power. Thomas Jefferson explained: "I consider the people who constitute a society or nation as the source of all authority in that nation."[1] We delegate our authority to those we elect to represent us in Congress, and they write our laws. If we disapprove of their actions, we replace them in the voting booth.

Our claims to the right of self-government are as follows:

- We choose to form a more perfect Union in which we, as a collective group, decide what is best for us. If we allow others, unelected by us, to govern us, we will have little recourse if they violate our best interests.

- We choose to establish justice by forming laws that will be enforced uniformly and equally among us. If left unchecked, graft and greed will take control over justice.

- We choose to ensure domestic tranquility because happy families form the core of good government. Laws and government greatly affect family stability.

- We choose to provide for the common defense because others may try to take what is rightfully ours. We claim the right to protect ourselves from their encroachments. This must include the right to possess weapons of defense.

- We choose to promote the general welfare. The lessons of history prove that people flourish when they are free to earn their own way, keep what they earn, and provide for themselves. We choose to help those less fortunate, but only until they can again supply their own needs.

- We choose to secure the blessings of liberty to ourselves and our posterity. We choose to build a society in which we and our children prosper. Happiness requires freedom; misery comes from control, regimentation, and loss of agency. We claim the right to form and maintain a government that gives us freedom.

Our Founding Fathers crafted a government in which "We the People" take charge of our laws. Our elected representatives will act on our behalf if we elect them wisely and supervise them.

Nowhere in our system do we find authority to make and enforce laws through anybody but our elected Congress. Laws made by presidential executive orders and administrative agencies are unconstitutional in the original Constitution. When laws are drafted by unelected people who are not responsive to us, we lose our right to self-government.

We are important in the governing process as we evaluate and redirect our system. Jefferson said: "We owe [it] . . . to ourselves . . . to pursue . . . laws self imposed . . . and even when the government of [our] choice shall manifest a tendency to degeneracy . . . reform its aberrations, recall it to original and legitimate principles, and restrain it within the rightful limits of self government."[2] As the holders of governing power, we choose to control the process through supervision and the ballot box.

9.2 | The Brilliance of Balanced Government

BALANCE is essential in forming good government. Under the Constitution, power is split between three separate entities: Congress, the president, and the Judiciary, each with its separate and distinct functions that must not interfere with the work of the other two branches.

Congress creates laws—that is its purpose. Our bicameral Congress has two arms. One arm, the House of Representatives, is elected by the people so that it represents the peoples' wishes and answers to them. The other arm is the Senate. Under the original Constitution, Senators were appointed by state legislatures, so they were accountable to and served the interests of the states who appointed them.

Under this original system, the needs of the two governed bodies—the people and states—would be satisfied by any laws enacted. The House and Senate had to agree on a law before it could be passed. This maintained balance and control by limiting the power of each legislative arm.

The chief executive oversees the process and vetoes any law that does not benefit the entire country. He coordinates unity among the states and interacts with foreign countries. He is neither the master nor the servant of Congress—he presides as the nation's chief magistrate and its mediator to the world.

From the lowest courts to the Supreme Court, the judicial system guarantees that laws remain true to the original Constitution and prevents any branch from seizing power. Its role is that of guardian, making certain that the rules are strictly obeyed.

This form of government had never been seen in the modern world. It combined the strengths of the three main types of government and avoided their weaknesses. When people follow the rules and supervise, our original system was as foolproof as men could make it. It was not a volatile, easily manipulated democracy prone to majority tyranny, although the House operates by the voice of the people. It was not an oligarchy, a system ruled by the wealthy upper class, although the Senate would likely include those individuals. The Senate drew on the knowledge and experience of the wealthy and influential but avoided their self-interested rule. The new government was not a monarchy, although it had a president. One executive allows speedy decision making, but selecting a president through the electoral college would avert the indifference common in kingships. Combining all three, this American government was delicately balanced but sturdy. It would last for centuries if moral people chose wise, ethical leaders to carry on the true success formula.

The Constitution is a document of human nature more than of politics. It acknowledges that men will naturally usurp or draw power to themselves and places roadblocks to prevent them from doing so. Essentially, these constitutional restrictions act as chains to restrain men's desire for power.

Because government was limited, the Founding Fathers anticipated that Congress would sit only part-time. Government would flow smoothly with minimal effort and little intrusion, given the superb balance of power and checks to safeguard authority.

The original plan worked beautifully for the first 130 years. Though the balance of our original Constitution has now been dangerously altered, it can be restored. We can begin that exciting process and see it through to completion.

9.3 | The House of Representatives

IF THE PEOPLE are the source of power in government, they must be heard. The Founding Fathers had confidence in the common people and gave them substantial authority—an unusual move for a government to make. No other government in modern history has shown such faith in its ordinary citizens.

The House of Representatives is elected by majority vote of the people, so it is the branch of government that answers to them. According to the Great Compromise made during the Constitutional Convention, the number of Representatives a state has in the House is determined by the population of each state. A national census taken every decade determines accurate representation for the House. As new states were added and population grew throughout the country, a cap of 435 members was set for the House. Originally, a Congressman represented thirty thousand people, but today each represents about five hundred thousand. The need to determine representation by population eventually brought about the "three-fifths rule" concerning slaves, which will be explained in the next subsection.

The House has great power because it initiates all laws dealing with money. The Senate and the president can veto any bill generated in the House, and the Senate can originate bills that do not deal with finances, but only the House can initiate revenue laws. The Framers expected the people to supervise their money closely, so members of the House serve for only two years. The flexibility of the short term allows the people to register their assent or discontent quickly and when needed. James Madison explained that the more power an elected official has, the shorter his term should be. The people's branch of Congress, the House, also commences any impeachment proceedings against the chief executive or federal judges. Centuries of abuse stood between the common people and their rulers, so the Constitution gave the House the right to oust unfair leaders. This right of citizens is one of the checks of power found in the Constitution that halts an unscrupulous leader who might perform illegal activities, embezzle authority, or perpetuate fraud on the people.

The Founders debated setting requirements on voters who would choose representatives to Congress. They decided that anyone who could vote for his state officers would qualify to vote for federal officers. Therefore, each state was put in charge of this right. The Founders feared that a voting requirement such as property ownership, a monetary payment, or a required educational level would divide the people. Nearly two hundred years later, in 1964, the Twenty-fourth Amendment to the Constitution clarified this by declaring even a minimal poll tax unconstitutional.

As a point of interest, members of Congress cannot be arrested when the Legislature is in session except in the case of a few serious charges. This is to prevent political enemies from arresting a valuable member of the opposing party on trivial charges to affect a vote in Congress. The Founders had seen a great deal of political chicanery and moved to eliminate it in America.

Government of the people, by the people, and for the people was an exciting new concept. The House of Representatives helped make that a reality.

| 9.4 | Slavery and the Three-Fifths Rule |

REPRESENTATION in the House of Representatives was affected by slavery in the South. The delegates solved this divisive moral and economic issue through compromise.

Americans did not choose slavery. The British forced the practice on Jamestown in 1619. Slavery was not new, nor was it fundamentally a racial issue. Most past nations had practiced it, enslaving those that they conquered in war regardless of their race.

The Constitution provided a twenty-year transition period in preparation to end slavery. This was wise for several reasons. In 1787, the Southern economy depended on slaves to harvest cotton and tobacco, but many Americans favored abolition. Vermont outlawed slavery in 1777. Jefferson proposed manumission (freedom) for slaves in the Virginia legislature in 1779, but the bill was rejected.

Several factors complicated manumission. For one, Southern plantations mortgaged to British banks had used slaves as collateral on loans. For another, most whites refused to perform slave work in the South, so the economy would collapse without slaves. Thirdly, many state manumission laws split up slave families, so some remained in slavery to keep their families intact. Finally, few slaves had the skills necessary to survive outside the system.

Views on slavery were not regional. Many slaveholders deplored slavery and railed against "this infernal traffic." George Mason, a slave owner, urgently favored abolition, saying that "every master of slaves... bring[s] the judgment of God on a country."[3] Yet Northerners who profited through slave transportation saw the issue as purely economic and resisted abolition. Some of these Northerners held slaves.

Most of the Founders, from both South and North, wanted to abolish slavery. Georgia and the Carolinas, however, were adamant that they would exit the Union and form their own country if the Constitution freed slaves. If the United States had been divided into two nations, slavery would have continued indefinitely in the South. The only hope of ridding America of slavery came in the compromise that kept the Union intact.

The compromise had two aspects. First, the Southern states feared Northern control of their seaboard navigation rights, so they traded the future of slavery to gain constitutional protection for them. Second, the importing of slaves would be allowed for twenty years, until 1808, after which Congress would abolish it. Until then, slaves would be counted for representation and taxation purposes, with five slaves equaling three whites.

This three-fifths rule has been badly misunderstood. It was not a value judgment about the worth of human beings, as some insist. It was a simple accounting technique to establish representation. The South had many slaves, and if each slave had received the same representation as a white person, the Southern states would have had disproportionate power in the Union.

Major changes sometimes hinge on comparatively small events. Such was the case with slavery. As America moved toward the 1808 date to begin emancipation set in the Constitution, the cotton gin was born. Cotton could now be processed rapidly, so the race began for more cotton, delivered faster. Within a few years, 70 percent of the world's cotton was exported from the American South.[4] Plantation owners did not intend to free their labor force when there was a fortune to be made in American cotton. So the manumission of slaves was abandoned, and freedom for slaves waited another sixty years. Only blood and the ravages of civil war would resolve this issue.

9.5 | The Senate under the Original Constitution

U NDER THE ORIGINAL CONSTITUTION, the United States Senate, our second arm of Congress, was a unique American invention.

Such chambers in other countries, if they existed, consisted of the clergy of the state church, the wealthy, and those seated for life or by heredity ties.

In the United States, Senators were originally appointed by their state legislatures. They worked for the states and reported back to them often. Failure to do so meant recall. A Senator did his state's bidding, and his state legislators watched to be sure he did.

Each state has two Senators who serve for six years. One-third of the Senate's members are reelected every other year, so that the main body has continuity and stability. Senators were intended to exercise sound judgment and be respectable, experienced, and mature. Their assignment was to link the state and federal governments and subdue the more numerous and tumultuous House.

The appointment of Senators offers several benefits. State legislators may select the most able men with knowledge of public interests. The Founders feared redistribution of wealth by the federal government, as they had seen this practice defeat other nations. They designed the Senate to help block that practice. The Founders also feared the development of power coalitions between one legislative branch and the executive. To prevent this, they placed checks on each branch.

The Founders intended the states to prevent a greedy federal government from abusing the people. To do this, states must remain independent and not become servants of the national government. Vigorous, healthy state governments could work together to block the encroachment of federal control. This important check on power would help the federal government keep its balance and remain fair.

The Senate is presided over by the vice-president, who votes only to break a tie. This helps him unify the states and involves him in national matters in case he has to succeed the president. The Senate and House each select their own officers and set their own rules, including policies to expel misbehaving members. Because one branch could "go rogue" and disrupt the system, each is required to keep the other informed of its doings.

The critical power of impeachment is shared between the House and Senate. The House brings charges, while the Senate conducts the trial and passes judgment. In a presidential trial, the chief justice of the Supreme Court presides. This puts the highest judicial authority on the bench rather than the vice-president, which would be an obvious conflict of interest. All Senate members are placed under oath, and a two-thirds majority brings conviction.

Members from either branch are paid by the federal government and cannot hold other government positions while in office. Immunity from interrogation allows all members safety to speak freely in general sessions. Both branches must publish their proceedings for public viewing.

The Constitution carefully assigns equal power and control among the people and the states, the two power centers of government in a democratic republic. The construction of the legislative branch of the United States government under the original Constitution was exceptional—well balanced and wisely conceived.

Most unfortunately, the altered Constitution changed the rules and destroyed the limitations of power built into the original document. The Seventeenth Amendment, passed in 1913, made the change.

9.6 | Upending the Constitution: The Seventeenth Amendment

SEVERAL HARMFUL CHANGES have been made to our charter of freedom, but none as harsh as the Seventeenth Amendment, which destroyed many of its checks and balances.

Under the original Constitution, power remained balanced between the states and the people. The House represented the people, and the Senate represented the states. Both worked together under the federal "umbrella," which managed international affairs and overall concerns. The states kept the federal government in check and kept government close to the people.

The Seventeenth Amendment changed the selection process for Senators, so they are now elected by the people. Because a body answers to those who put it in power, the Senate now serves the people, not the states. The states have been left with no voice in the legislative process, so laws are passed that ignore the requirements and authority of the states, which govern regionally. The people now have power over both branches. The Legislature has lost its balance.

The Framers intended the Senate to prevent the people from voting themselves largess, or overly generous benefits. When laws were passed, Senators were to assure that needs of the states were respected. With the state legislatures silenced at the federal level, Senators soon learned they could "buy" reelection with gifts of social programs, welfare, and works projects. Under the original Constitution, this would not have been possible. The states would have prevented excess by instructing their Senators to veto wasteful or unnecessary projects.

Under the altered Constitution, Senators now compete with Representatives to create federal programs that bring money to their states. These programs, which frequently favor one state over another, and the burgeoning bureaucracies and regulations they create are entrenched under the executive wing, which presides over this largess.

Higher taxes were necessary to pay for the programs Congressional members created to buy their reelection. The Sixteenth Amendment, passed in 1913 as well, allowed the federal government to pay for these programs by directly taxing people's income, properties, and goods purchased. Government was no longer small, close to the people, or fair.

Why was the Seventeenth Amendment passed?

The states were partly to blame. Several state legislatures bickered over potential appointees, leaving seats in the Senate vacant for months. Others openly corrupted the system by appointing unscrupulous, self-serving individuals, eventually resulting in scandals. Our Founders repeatedly emphasized that honest, wise men must be elected to government to prevent these problems.

It is better to keep a vigilant eye on elected state officials and correct the problem at its root than to disable the entire system, which is what the Seventeenth Amendment did. The solution was worse than the problem it was supposed to correct. Certainly, dishonesty operates at the state level as well as the federal. However, misused power at the state level is easier for the people to detect and rectify.

To regain our past prosperity, we must first return power to the states by making Senators responsible to state legislators. This will restore the checks and balances that gave our federal system its balance.

9.7 | What Congress Does: Taxation and the Sixteenth Amendment

THE ORIGINAL Constitution gave only twenty powers to Congress, one of which was the power to tax. The altered Constitution has dramatically expanded both the number of powers and taxation.

Government must compel taxation to meet its obligations. However, taxation can become a vehicle for serious government abuse. Any government has an insatiable appetite for money and will overspend if allowed to do so.

The original Constitution structured taxation to benefit the citizens. Government was to remain small and taxes minimal. The Framers expected indirect taxes on imported, exported, and manufactured goods to cover its normal operating expenses. In wartime or emergencies, as a last resort, temporary direct taxes on persons and property might be necessary. The assessment for each state was based on its population, and each state legislature determined how to collect it. The Founders settled on this as the fairest way to directly tax the people. State involvement limited the potential for federal abuse of taxation.

The laws on taxation have changed, to our detriment. The Sixteenth Amendment (1913) altered the entire landscape of American society. It gave Congress the power to collect direct taxes on any income from any source. Taxes assessed by income violated constitutional instructions. The graduated income tax was driven by political mischief and the desire to "soak the rich."

Did the Sixteenth Amendment soak the rich? No. Loopholes and exemptions allowed the wealthy to sidestep taxes. The poor, with little or no income, paid correspondingly little in taxes. So the burden of taxation was—and still is—carried by the middle class.

This violation of the original Constitution meant that most citizens could no longer keep all that they legitimately earned for the benefit of their own families. It removed revenue from the people and the states and put it into the hands of the federal government, which used it to fund bureaucracies whose aim was to ensure that taxes are fully paid. Today, we are submerged in tax regulations that violate privacy and invade businesses, restricting freedoms. The states should have stood firm to prevent this, but the impending passage of the Seventeenth Amendment two months later left the states voiceless in the federal government.

The Founders insisted that federal funds be used to benefit all, not just some of the people. The Supreme Court's pivotal 1936 *United States versus Butler* decision dissolved these restraints and allowed the federal government to spend tax funds for anything it deemed pertinent to the national welfare. This unleashed a wide variety of social programs and projects. In effect, the federal government received a credit card with no limit and little supervision. Government could now put its hands directly into the pockets of its citizens for any reason it chose. Today's massive federal debt has been the result.

In the public square, many debate how much income tax we should pay. The real issue is that direct taxes and government authorization to spend citizen funds at will have destroyed the careful balance of the Founders' republic.

It is the job of our elected Representatives to prevent this abuse of taxation and ours to see that they do so or are removed from office.

Excessive taxation and rampant government spending impoverish every one of us daily. A return to the original Constitution would restore American prosperity.

9.8 | What Congress Does: Regulating Money

ANOTHER of the twenty powers of Congress under the original Constitution is the responsibility to coin and regulate money. When this is properly done, no inflation results. The value of money remains stable when the government controls the money supply and backs it with gold or silver. If the amount of money in the marketplace is balanced with the amount of goods and services available for purchase, no inflation occurs. If this law were still honored, goods would cost the same today as they did fifty years ago. We would be thriving families in a prosperous nation.

The United States followed sound money principles, despite bumps in the self-correcting system, until 1913, when Congress turned our money system over to a private banking group. Called the Federal Reserve Bank, it manages our money and our economy for the profit of its own executives and shareholders.

The idea of a privately owned United States central bank dates back to Alexander Hamilton. Twice before in our history, for terms of twenty years each, such a bank has existed. President Andrew Jackson, elected in 1828, refused to extend the second bank's charter because he believed that it constituted a monopoly. Later, credit given too freely caused banking disruptions and prompted national calls for monetary reform. Congress voted the Federal Reserve Bank into law, along with "flexible currency"—paper money with no actual gold and silver to back it. This legislation was intended to stabilize the economy, but history proves that it did the opposite. Boom-and-bust cycles, severe inflation, recessions and depressions, and federal debt have increased.

Today, the Federal Reserve still prints our paper money with no assets to back it. It then charges us interest on the face value of the money. To illustrate, it spends perhaps a hundred dollars to print one million dollars in paper money. It then charges interest for loans on the million dollars it fabricated as if it actually possesses precious metal worth that amount. This interest, added to interest on other fabricated debt, comprises much of our national debt. Then, through fractional banking, it loans this fabricated money, and much more, and collects interest on that as well. While the money loaned by banks may be fabricated, the assets required from borrowers as loan collateral are real and will be forfeited if the loan defaults. This situation seems to bear out Andrew Jackson's opinion of the central bank system.

The Founding Fathers knew that similar plans had created economic chaos in Europe. They warned against the very practices seen in the Federal Reserve today. Jefferson said: "If the American people ever allow the banks to control the issuance of their currency . . . first by inflation and then by deflation . . . the banks . . . will deprive the people of all property until their children will wake up homeless on the continent their fathers occupied."[5]

Our nation can be free of debt, inflation, and economic crises if Congress will exercise its constitutional responsibilities and if the people will be prudent with their money and carefully watch what Congress spends. Control of our money supply should be returned to Congress, as our original Constitution stipulated. The power to abolish the Federal Reserve is included in the legislation that created it.[6] Our families will benefit if we urge Congress to do so.

9.9 | What Congress Does: Spending

T HE CONSTITUTION gives Congress the power to coin and regulate our money and to spend it. The Constitution's general welfare clause approves tax monies for "the general welfare" of the United States.

Debates about the meaning of this clause arose from the start. The writings of the Founders show us their original intent: public funds were to be used only to benefit the entire body of Americans, not merely groups of the people. Within a few years, President Washington's treasury secretary, Alexander Hamilton, pushed for a reinterpretation of this clause. He wanted federal spending for matters outside the twenty powers allotted to Congress. This would have been a fundamental change from limited government to wide federal powers.

The Supreme Court's *Butler* case put Hamilton's interpretation into law 135 years later. Government funds could now be addressed to subgroups of the people.

Because government does not generate its own income, in order for it to give to one group, it must take from another—those who labored for their goods. This public generosity to one requires violation of the rights of another. Even those who are generous by choice do not willingly part with what they have worked to earn when they are coerced.

Government thus becomes the aggressor. Rather than protecting rights, it violates them in a system of organized injustice that abuses freedom, prosperity, and peace. Social programs, government giveaways, and entitlement programs to small groups breed resentment among overtaxed citizens who might otherwise have donated freely out of true charity.

As stated by Frederic Bastiat in *The Law,* subsidies, guaranteed jobs and profits, welfare, free credits, social programs, and public works always plunder the people—what Bastiat calls "legal plunder."[7] America has adopted this policy to allow government to become our caregiver.

Today, massive bureaucracies oversee government's legal plunder. The idea that government may not do anything which its citizens cannot do also fell by the wayside. Common citizens cannot forcibly take the goods of others, so government should not have that ability either. Government is there to protect the rights of all its citizens, yet it cannot do so when it takes from some to give to others.

This concept that government is not our caretaker was illustrated by an experience of the famous frontiersman Davy Crockett, who spent nearly a decade in Congress. A constituent challenged his vote to provide a large government subsidy to assist a neighborhood razed by fire, pointing out that the Constitution did not allow Congress to spend the people's money for charity. Crockett recognized and embraced the truth of this concept and later voted against a similar allotment. He explained in the Legislature that he had the right to give his own money but not the funds of others. He offered a week's salary to the needy individual under consideration, invited others to follow suit, and urged that the appropriation be defeated. It was, but no other Legislators matched his offer.[8]

This is the concept of limited federal government. When compassionate aid or programs are needed, they are to originate at the individual, local, or state level where they can be supervised and adjusted. At the federal level, control will be lost.

9.10 | What Congress Does: Borrowing and Bankruptcy

TWO OTHER POWERS that deal with money fall to Congress: developing national bankruptcy laws, and borrowing money on behalf of the nation if necessary. Our Founders hoped that future Americans would avoid debt, with some leeway during wartime. Jefferson stated that "buying nothing without the money in our pockets to pay for it would make our country one of the happiest on earth."[9] He strongly opposed a debt that would carry through the generations, which he believed to be immoral.

When Congress turned our monetary system over to a third party in 1913, the spending glut and financial chaos began. Our nation is currently in unrelenting debt that saps our prosperity and energy. The Founders would be heartsick to see the state of our finances. If debt is bondage, our modern society is in chains. The only people profiting from the national debt are bankers, politicians, and recipients of what Congress spends. When a nation dramatically overspends, it goes bankrupt. America is dangerously close to that ugly reality. To avoid economic collapse, we must stop our financial hemorrhage.

Our elected legislators—the members of Congress—created this problem, and they must fix it. Several things can be done to avert national bankruptcy.

First, the massive spending must stop. We have come to expect many forms of financial assistance from the federal government. That is not its responsibility. Citizens can learn to take care of themselves. When and where necessary, private and charitable sectors and the state should provide needed assistance. Government giveaway and social programs are expensive, unfair, wasteful, and ineffective, and they must be discontinued.

Second, we can demand that our elected Representatives restore fiscal soundness. Both political parties are to blame. If they do not stop spending and repair the damage, we need to replace them in the voting booth.

Third, we can relieve much of our massive debt by releasing the Federal Reserve as our unnecessary middle man. More than half of our federal debt is interest we owe on money fabricated by these international bankers. Firing them and becoming our own banker again would eliminate this interest and cut our national debt by more than half. This step would be challenging, but no other course of action will give us back our prosperity. We need God's help to make this happen.

Fourth, we can eliminate fractional banking in America, which allows all banks to fabricate money and loan it out multiple times. Ideas such as the suggested Monetary Reform Act provide a means to end fractional banking and erase a substantial portion of our debt.[10]

As an additional possibility, Thomas Jefferson paid debts from the Revolutionary War during his tenure as president with the sale of public lands. Over one-third of America's land mass today is held by the federal government. Principled men can adapt this possibility to our current situation and generate the funds necessary to pay down our debt.

Other valid ideas will be discovered. Combined with disciplined budget practices, we could dramatically stabilize our economy.

It is our constitutional birthright to enjoy a sound economy and a stable money system. Our personal actions can help. Each of us can discipline ourselves, eliminate personal debt, and demand legislative accountability. We can petition God's help to reduce our indebtedness. We need not do this alone.

9.11 | What Congress Does: The Hotly Contested Commerce Clause

O NE OF THE FREEDOMS granted to United States citizens is the right to do business together. While effective government can aid that process, the states had drafted trade policies that hampered their neighbors under the ineffective Articles of Confederation. The entire commercial system floundered. The Framers consequently set the regulation of commerce as one of the twenty powers of Congress. The commerce clause in the Constitution allows federal involvement only in trade with other nations and among the states.

Two original theories existed on the interpretation of the commerce clause in the Constitution. Alexander Hamilton believed that this clause expanded federal power, while James Madison declared that it restricted and controlled it.

The Supreme Court has sided with Hamilton and expanded the definition of *commerce* to include every kind of movement of people or things, "whether or not profit is the motive." This also includes anything that will sooner or later involve an act of transportation, including every means by which people, objects, or communications of any kind move from state to state.[11] This intentionally broad interpretation puts government in control over almost every action of businesses and citizens in the United States.

Federal regulation began with consolidation of the railroads into a vast interstate system in 1866, and control of the rates followed. Control moved to all transportation systems—gas and oil pipelines, aviation, and communication by wire and radio. Next, federal control moved into manufacture of transportation devices, such as automobiles. Human labor and working conditions came under federal domination. Price regulations and control of electricity and telephone services ensued.

In direct violation of the Constitution, the federal government then stepped into the states' role to regulate commerce within state boundaries. Today, the federal government regulates labor policies and working conditions of even small local businesses and goods produced on small local farms that will be consumed onsite. This is a major usurpation of power.

Some believe regulation is necessary. The problem is that there is no stopping place: once begun, the momentum of regulation eventually envelops everything. The stated objectives are always protection and fairness, but control is always the end result. An endless cycle of regulations to fix regulations suffocates free enterprise. And, as always, what regulation is necessary is always best handled by state or local governments that can adapt the regulations to fit the situation.

History proves that businesses work best when government stands aside. Necessary controls and safety procedures should come from the individual states and the private sector, which looks to its own welfare by protecting its consumers. Such a course is more effective in the long run and maintains liberty. Problems inevitably arise, but the free market can resolve them in less-invasive ways. Suppressing free enterprise with regulations enforced by bureaucracies and taxation stifles personal and national prosperity. And because it is difficult to get rid of entrenched regulations, personal freedoms remain diminished.

Historians say that forty centuries of federal control, covering thirty countries on six world continents, have proven the universal failure of federal control in the marketplace.[12] Isn't it about time we listen?

9.12 | ## What Congress Does: War Powers and National Lands

A S PART of its twenty powers, Congress has power to govern war and the military and authority to control the nation's land mass.

Under the original Constitution, the people, through the House, and the states, through the Senate, must jointly agree to expend their human and economic resources in any given conflict. While wars are sometimes futile, usually wasteful, and rarely wanted, they are occasionally necessary. Prosperity invites aggressors, and we must preserve our inalienable rights.

Congress, and only Congress, can declare war—the president and the courts cannot. A president violates the Constitution if he declares war without the approval of Congress.

In the decades leading up to today, the United States has become embroiled in several undeclared wars—termed "armed conflicts"—in which the constitutional rules about engaging in war have been ignored. The Korean, Vietnam, and Gulf Wars are examples. We have paid for these unconstitutional wars in untold money and lives.

The Framers reluctantly saw the need for a modest standing army. They had seen monarchs use standing armies for unlawful conquest and wanted none of it. The original Constitution authorized military funding for two years only. At war's end, most soldiers returned to their homes. After World War II, however, the United States and its allies unwisely funded a strong Soviet military. When the Soviets later became the enemy, we were forced to build a large standing defensive military presence.[13] This has cost us dearly.

Also among the twenty powers of Congress is the authority to provide for and maintain a navy, punish crimes on the high seas, and establish rules for the armed forces. Congress can call up state militias, which are available to the federal government if needed. The states furnish officers and discipline, while the national government equips and trains them to maintain uniformity. Only three situations warrant federal use of state militias: executing the laws of the Union, suppressing insurrections, and repelling invasions.

Congress is authorized its own ten-square-mile land area known as the District of Columbia. Government needs its own exclusive territory for security purposes.

As needed, Congress can purchase and control areas within each state for "forts, magazines, arsenals, dockyards and other needful buildings." This land, the Founders assumed, would not include more than a very small percentage of any state—perhaps 1 or 2 percent. All states that enter the Union are to have control over the vast majority of their land areas.

The Constitution's rule for federal ownership of lands was broken when the Western states entered the Union. The federal government took permanent ownership of major portions of these incoming states without paying for them despite the states' objections and the unconstitutionality of the acts. Consequently, the federal government owns 45 percent of the land in Arizona and California, 64 percent of Idaho, 66 percent of Utah, 87 percent of Nevada, and 96 percent of Alaska, plus major parts of five other Western states.[14]

Nearly 30 percent of the United States land mass is currently held by the federal government without the consent of the states involved. This usurpation of land area denies revenue to the states and their citizens, which is unconstitutional.

As citizens, we have the right to fight only in declared wars and to have our state lands returned to us. It is time to insist on those rights.

9.13 | What Congress and the States Cannot Do

THE FOUNDING FATHERS identified not only what Congress could do, but what it could not do. In Article 1 Section 10, they placed restrictions on the states. Following are those not previously mentioned.

Congress was assigned to establish a postal system. Local postmasters originally operated from their homes and were paid per item. Benjamin Franklin organized a national postal system in 1753, which later became the United States Postal Service, with Franklin as the first postmaster general. Under Franklin's business genius, the postal system knew its greatest period of profitability. The first postage stamps were issued in 1847, and air mail service began in 1918.[15]

Congress sets citizenship rules to determine how immigrants can become United States citizens. Recent conflict over illegal immigration is the result of the federal government neglecting its duties in this matter.

Copyright laws and patents are established under the Constitution. They are set so that those in the creative process can protect their efforts for specified periods of time. Americans enjoy unprecedented scientific, industrial, and publication rights as a result of our superior laws in this regard.

Congress has established lower federal courts to bring justice close to the people where it meets their needs (and saves tax dollars).

What can Congress not do? First, it cannot suspend the writ of habeas corpus ("have the body"), meaning that those charged with a crime must be physically brought before the court. This prevents an individual from being jailed indefinitely without a trial to defend himself. We cannot be declared criminals and deprived of civil rights without a trial and conviction. After the terrorist attacks of September 11, 2001, the government drafted policies that jeopardize these rights. One example is the Military Commissions Act of 2006, which suspends the writ of habeas corpus in certain circumstances. This precedent should be a matter of concern for all Americans. These forms of injustice are favorites of repressive governments.

Congress cannot pass an ex post facto law to punish a person for a crime committed before the law was passed. It cannot confer titles of nobility, and no one in a position of authority for the United States can accept gifts, offices, or titles from any foreign country unless Congress agrees. Congress can only withdraw money from the Treasury when specifically authorized, and it cannot tax items exported from states.

As for actions forbidden to the states, they cannot make private war, create their own legal tender, or enter into agreements or compacts with another state or country. Both the North and South violated this last provision during the Civil War. The resulting conflict split the nation into a brother-against-brother conflict, costing more than a million American lives.

Some actions are specifically allowed to the states. They can impose duties, maintain troops in peacetime, and enter into agreements with other states, so long as Congress approves. States can engage in war without Congressional approval only if they are invaded or are in such danger that they must act before Congress can grant approval. In that case, they have the natural right of self-defense.

The Founders included every provision of the Constitution because they had seen repressive governments violate the rights of their citizens. They valued these rights because they had lived without them, so they built citizen protections into our freedom document.

Section Ten

——————— ⟡ ———————

THE CONSTITUTION: ENFORCING AND
INTERPRETING THE LAW

H ALF THE CONSTITUTION addresses the legislative branch of government because its duties are so varied. The duties of the president and Supreme Court were intended to be more limited and are therefore more easily defined.

Our Founders would be surprised to see how the office of president of the United States has become the most powerful political office in the world, for they did not intend it to be so. They advocated a policy of "friends with all and enemies of none" which would leave the United States independent of all other nations. It was not isolation they advocated, but freedom from the entanglements created by both allies and enemies in the international sphere. Easy relations with all nations would produce ease of government function, peace, and prosperity, both abroad and at home.

The Founders also anticipated a modest, limited federal government. We have discarded this ideal. The ratio of government workers to the populace is one hundred times greater in our day than it was in Washington's.[1]

Some say that the Founding Fathers held simplistic views. In our complicated world, they seem austere. Had we followed their governing prescriptions, however, we would be living in a world where simplicity was normal and enjoyable.

The Framers also gave the court system serious attention in the Constitution. Judges were expected to be "the most helpless and harmless members of the government."[2] The deliberate creation of a national court system was unparalleled, as no government in the past had set the pattern for what they did. Without a pattern, the court system they devised has shortcomings. These weaknesses have inadvertently created a court system with excessive power.

In addition to the executive and judicial branches, Articles II through VII of the Constitution deal with state unity, debts, supremacy of law, amendments, and ratification.

10.1 | What the President Does

T HE OFFICE of chief executive was originally intended to be one of limited responsibility, as the Constitution assigns only six duties to the president.

Over the last 225 years, the executive office has changed dramatically. Today, the president has duties connected to thousands of government departments. Innumerable current problems can be traced to this fact. The Founding Fathers feared that enlargement of this office would tend to transform the president into a king, and they tried to prevent it. By following their constitutional system, we could have avoided massive bureaucracy and regulation, as well as a monarchical president.

The chief executive's six constitutionally sanctioned duties, as found in the original Constitution, are listed below.

- Chief of state over all Americans, currently over 335 million.

- Commander-in-chief over the military, currently over 3 million.

- Chief executive officer over the executive branch of government. In this capacity, the president nominates Supreme Court justices, ambassadors, and consuls, who are confirmed by the Senate.

- Chief diplomat in handling foreign affairs, with power to enter into treaties with the consent of the Senate. If the treaty involves commercial transactions, the House must also ratify it.

- Chief instigator of needed legislation. The president may recommend but may not draft or lobby for legislation.

- Conscience of the nation in granting pardons or reprieves when justice requires them, but he cannot pardon for impeachment.

A partial list of just the major categories of presidential responsibilities today is almost incomprehensible. He is responsible to maintain full employment of the work force, ensure a high level of economic prosperity, and develop a national housing program. He supervises the underwriting of billions of dollars in private loans and insurance programs and administers Medicare, Medicaid, and Social Security. He oversees the education of our children, the environment, and major union-management disputes. He administers national health care and 30 percent of the nation's land area. He is responsible for our energy resources, our industries, our communications networks, and our food and drugs.

This gives us a clear definition of bloated government. Because it is impossible for one person to perform even minimal oversight in all the above-mentioned categories, the government has developed a massive bureaucracy to fulfill these responsibilities through a maze of regulations. This represents a far cry from limited government and shows what has gone seriously wrong.

This grand scale of government overreach is expensive and costs every tax-paying American thousands of dollars annually. It is also inefficient. Any voluminous organization tends to be sluggish, wasteful, and disorganized. Finally, it is susceptible to corruption. It places huge amounts of money in the hands of presidential appointees who use it to purchase programs, manipulate alliances, and influence the people. Bureaucrats and politicians alike benefit as Congress participates or looks the other way. Incoming presidents give political payoff for services rendered through bureauratic appointments, adding further expense.

The current system is expensive, inefficient, and fundamentally compromised. The original system worked very well for over one hundred years. We need it back.

10.2 | Serving as President

M OST SYSTEMS of government provide no way for removal of an unpopular head of state. Change often takes the form of political upheaval or assassination. Happily, the Founders crafted another way: we elect a president every four years. He must be at least thirty-five years of age, a native-born American citizen, and a United States resident for fourteen years. The vice-president, who succeeds him if he dies in office, must meet the same criteria.

Our president commits to faithfully execute his office and to defend the Constitution as it stands on his inaugural day—thus, the altered Constitution. Treason, bribery, or other high crimes and misdemeanors are the grounds on which a president can be impeached.

The presidential inaugural oath states: "I do solemnly swear [or affirm, as some religions prohibit swearing] that I will faithfully execute the Office of President of the United States, and will to the best of my ability, preserve, protect and defend the Constitution of the United States." On his first inauguration, President Washington added the words "so help me God," which became a tradition.

Washington served only two terms. This precedent was broken by Franklin D. Roosevelt, who died weeks into his fourth term in 1945. The Twenty-second Amendment, passed shortly after Roosevelt's death, limited the president's length of service to two terms.

The executive salary is modest to discourage greed. To prevent manipulation, it cannot be changed during a current term. Quoting Alexander Hamilton: "They (the Congress) might . . . either reduce him by famine, or tempt him by largess to surrender . . . his judgment to their inclinations."[3] Also to discourage manipulation, the Twenty-seventh Amendment set the same policy for Congress.

Benjamin Franklin commented on the vices that might accompany an excessive salary for our highest office: "Of what kind are the men that will strive for this profitable pre-eminence, through all the bustle of cabal, the heat of contention, the infinite abuse of parties, tearing to pieces the best of characters? It will not be the wise and moderate, the lovers of peace and good order, the men fittest for the trust. It will be the bold and the violent, [the] selfish." He said that there would "always be a party for giving more to the rulers, that the rulers may be able in return to give more to them."[4]

Several amendments pertain to the executive office. The Twelfth Amendment established separate ballots for president and vice-president, and the Twentieth Amendment reset the time for elected officials to take office.

The Twenty-fifth Amendment allows the vice-president to take over if the president is incapacitated. Under this amendment in 1973, Richard Nixon appointed Gerald R. Ford to fill the vacancy when Vice-President Spiro T. Agnew resigned. Later Nixon resigned, leaving Ford as president, and Ford appointed Nelson Rockefeller as vice-president. The United States then had both a president and vice-president who were not elected by the people—a worrisome precedent.

This amendment also allows the vice-president, with agreement from the president's cabinet, to declare the president incapable and take his place. This unwise provision carries the potential for serious abuse.

In order to have integrity in government, there must be integrity in the highest office in the land. The selection of the best man to serve as president was originally done by the Electoral College.

10.3 | Electing the President: The Electoral College

T HE ORIGINAL CONSTITUTION provided three unique ways to select three categories of officials. The House of Representatives used direct popular vote, the Senate was appointed by indirect vote through state legislatures, and the president was selected by the Electoral College as outlined in Article II. This was part of the genius of the original Constitution. Today, all are selected by popular vote, although an emasculated form of the Electoral College remains. Because of these changes, our form of government—a republic—comes dangerously close to a democracy, which can easily become a system of majority tyranny.

Because the public can easily be misled, the Framers considered it dangerous to leave the election of the president to popular vote. Founding Father Elbridge Gerry expressed this view: "The people are uninformed, and would be misled by a few designing men."[5]

The original Electoral College is far superior to the two-party system we currently use. The original process led to selection of the person most fit to govern. Our current system selects the most electable, most personable, and best financed candidate, rather than the best leader. The two-party system divides us, creates contention, is very expensive, and produces routine stalemate.

The original electoral system included four steps. First, the state legislatures selected wise men of sound reputation for a single term of service as electors. The number of electors for each state depended on its representation in Congress. Each was assigned to locate, research, and recommend two individuals as the best candidates for president. Only one could come from the elector's home state. Their sealed recommendations were sent to Congress. Second, the president of the Senate tallied the lists from each state while in legislative session. If a majority emerged for one individual, he became the president.

If this process did not produce a president, then, as the third step, the House of Representatives would vote immediately on the five names with the most votes, selecting the new president. The candidate with the next highest tally of votes became vice-president, with the Senate voting to break a tie, if necessary, as the fourth step. The Twelfth Amendment later provided for separate ballots for president and vice-president.

This original electoral selection process offered several substantial advantages. The electors had nothing to gain from the process. Their single term of service made corruption and outside influences unlikely. Because sealed recommendations were opened and all voting was done on the same day, little possibility existed for influence and intrigue to taint the process. Conspiracy and foreign influence were likewise eliminated. Because the electors were released after the election, elected officials had no group to which they owed favors.

The original electoral system was a rapid casualty in the process of constitutional decay. The two-party system, so prone to schemes and self-interest, soon emerged in its place. The electoral system now operating gives some minor benefit by balancing the votes of large and small states. The number of electors is determined by the total of Congressmen and Senators allotted to each state.

Today's Electoral College is ineffective compared to the original system. Periodic movements arise to eliminate it altogether. The wiser move, by far, would be to reinstate the Electoral College in its original form. Our presidential elections would select presidents of greater character and leadership with far less expense, harangue, and animosity.

10.4 | The Supreme Court of the Land

THE FOUNDING FATHERS aimed to create a government for the ages, free of oppression and power distortions. Jefferson spoke of "bind[ing men] down from mischief by the chains of the Constitution."[6]

These constitutional "chains" were for our protection. First, the Constitution gave only specific, limited powers assigned vertically at local, state, and federal levels and horizontally to the legislative, executive, and judicial branches. Second, self-correcting checks and balances chained the potential of a ravenous federal government. Third, the founding document's unyielding form made it difficult for power-hungry people to manipulate or control, providing that the system was followed. Another "chain" installed the Supreme Court as a guardian to strictly enforce the charter of freedom. It was to measure all legislation against our Constitution and the intent of the Founders.

No nation had used such a court system, so no pattern existed for the Founders to follow. Without that help, their structure had two fatal flaws. First, its judges were appointed for life and could not be removed. Second, their decisions were fixed and final, with no means of appeal. Judges later began to interpret the Constitution through political activism, and they continue to do so because no mechanism exists to counteract their improprieties or remove them from the bench.

Some of the Founders were unconcerned. Alexander Hamilton believed that without a means to force compliance, the courts were too weak to seize power. Thomas Jefferson, however, feared the court's potential for abuse. It was not that judges would be less honest, but that time and political parties would corrupt the process and turn judges into tyrants. Jefferson pleaded for a constitutional amendment to repair this omission. He believed that the seeds of destruction lay in the court system. His keen mind realized that the federal judiciary would ultimately draw all power to the federal government, with corruption as the inevitable result. His pleas went unheeded.

Jefferson's fears have come to pass. The Supreme Court now creates law with its judgments rather than studying and upholding constitutional law, as assigned. The court has overreached its bounds and changed the basic structure of government. Each decision of the court becomes law, similar to the force of a constitutional amendment, and is binding upon all Americans, present and future.

Two destructive decisions have already been noted. The 1936 *Butler* Supreme Court decision authorized the federal government to use public funds for anything it desired. The court's vastly expanded definition of commerce allows government control of all that affects commerce, including products consumed onsite at individual farms. Dozens of such decisions have changed the Constitution, defeated limited government, and curtailed personal freedom.

There are alternatives. All Supreme Court decisions require funding. Congress can refuse to fund these decisions and thus prevent their implementation, so that inappropriate "legislation from the bench" dies of malnutrition. This is a check of power built into the Constitution that would allow elected Representatives to curtail the high court's usurpation of power. We can insist that legislators not fund Supreme Court decisions that alter the Constitution. We can take the steps necessary to place constitutional limits on judicial terms and subject court decisions to some form of legislative review.

The Constitution was designed to remain firm against the attempts of unprincipled people so that its protections would endure. Keeping it firm keeps us safe.

10.5 | The Workings of the Courts: State and Federal

UNDER the Articles of Confederation, the United States had no judicial system with the authority to handle most federal issues. This left a serious blind spot in its governmental system.

Under the Constitution, the national government has a court system. Article III deals with federal courts. Each state also has its own court system structured according to its state constitution to deal with state matters. The two systems are to remain independent of each other.

State courts try most criminal matters and disputes in contracts, but some cases must be tried under federal jurisdiction. State and federal courts decide issues concerning both law and equity, or fairness. Originally, the Constitution allowed a citizen to sue a state. The Eleventh Amendment changed this when a citizen of South Carolina sued the state of Georgia and legislators deemed this action inappropriate.

Federal courts handle constitutional issues, matters with other countries (such as treaties and agreements, ambassadors, and foreign personnel), and maritime issues. The federal courts also try cases of treason, which can apply to any citizen or noncitizen receiving United States protection. They try any issue that involves multiple states—state to state, state to citizen of another state, or citizens disputing property in another state. Some cases must originate in the Supreme Court, while others may begin in lower federal courts.

Lower federal courts include district courts, courts of appeals, and specialized courts for matters such as bankruptcies and international trade. The highest federal court is the Supreme Court, which resolves conflicts with foreign countries and between states.

The Constitution provides for one Supreme Court of unspecified size, so the number of justices has changed through the years—we currently have nine. The Court meets from October through May. Federal judges are expected to maintain "good behavior" and can otherwise be impeached.

Their salaries cannot be altered while they are in office, which prevents their manipulation by those hungry for power. The Supreme Court is also the final appellate (review) court. Each year, it hears and reviews a small percentage of thousands of appeals and decisions of lower federal courts and some state courts. Most appealed decisions are not reviewed and remain final. The review process is expensive, clogs the system, and is usually unnecessary.

The original Constitution intended that federal courts not become involved in state matters. Each state must be independent in enforcing its own constitutional law. But, as with so many other issues, the state courts were invaded by federal court jurisdiction over time. Federal intervention now strips state courts of their power and often renders them ineffective, leaving state citizens subject to federal excess.

Jefferson spoke with concern generated by experience on this matter: "That body [the federal judiciary], like gravity, ever acting with noiseless foot and unalarming advance, gaining ground step by step and holding what it gains, is engulfing insidiously the [state] governments into the jaws of that which feeds them."[7] His fears have been realized as federal courts have increasingly inserted themselves into state matters.

Although the Founders did not adopt the full British system of courts, they retained one aspect of them designed to act as a check on rigid judicial interpretations of the law. The system of trial by a jury of one's peers made an ideal accompaniment to republican government, as will be seen.

10.6 | Trial by Jury

TRIAL BY JURY is a bulwark of modern personal liberty. The American system of justice is based on the right to trial by a jury of one's peers. This applies to all charges except that of treason, which is tried before the Senate. A great safeguard of a person's liberties, it is a pillar of free government. Those who know the accused, know the area in which he lives, and may know his character and situation hear his case and pass the fairest judgment.

Today's jury system embodies only part of the original protection of jury trials. Formerly, juries could pass judgment not only on the guilt or innocence of the individual, but on the validity of the law in that particular case. This is known as the common-law jury.

Until 1895, defendants were tried by common-law juries empowered to judge both the facts and the law itself. They could determine the meaning of the law in a particular situation and decide if that law was applicable and fair in the circumstances being considered. If the jury determined that the law was unjust in the matter at hand, the law could be set aside. While the jury could not use law to injure anyone and could not repeal a law, it could render it inoperative in a particular situation and return a "not guilty" verdict as a result.

John Jay, first chief justice of the Supreme Court in its first jury trial in 1794, explained: "You have a right to take upon yourselves the judge of both . . . law as well as the fact . . . both objects are lawfully within your power of decision."[8]

This right was designed to protect the accused from the ever-present possibility of government abuse. Alexander Hamilton declared that even those who disapproved of the Constitution believed that this practice would provide equal justice and fair government.[9] Because circumstances and individuals vary, it follows that conviction and consequences should vary as well. The inclusion of common-law juries was a mark of fairness and true justice for each individual citizen.

This startles Americans who are trained to believe that the law is universal and unyielding. It is difficult to believe that ordinary citizens had the right to set aside a particular law in a specific case. The right to trial by common-law jury was a British custom which dated from the time of the Magna Carta in 1215 and spread throughout the British Empire. The British gradually abandoned the practice of both juries and common-law juries in most cases, and the practice of trial by jury remains strong only in America.

Consider the difference it would have made to the character of Jean Valjean in *Les Misérables*, the classic novel by Victor Hugo, if a common-law jury had determined his case. He surely would not have spent nineteen years in prison for stealing a loaf of bread for his starving family.

Like so many principles of our original Constitution, this principle of legal flexibility has been erased by modern federal courts. Today, judges issue ironclad instructions to juries. The ability to spare one's neighbor an unjust penalty due to unusual circumstances is gone.

Law can be unfairly applied in some situations. The common-law jury sought to erase that unfairness.

10.7 | Unity of the States

IT WAS ESSENTIAL that citizens of the Union have freedom to travel and engage in commerce between states. Once the three horizontal branches of government were formed, the matter of unity among the states could be addressed. The Constitution would be little better than the Articles of Confederation if it did not provide working harmony among states. With their intact borders, individual states had freedom to create their own constitutions and programs.

Under Article IV of the Constitution, each state fully accepts as legal the acts, records, judicial proceedings, and privileges of all other states, with the federal government creating uniform paperwork. An issue illustrating the need for such unity among states is extradition—the agreement to return fugitives from justice who cross state lines to avoid prosecution.

The Constitution spelled out the rules for accepting states into the Union. These included the provision that new states could not be created out of existing ones without agreement from all concerned, including Congress. Congress received power to manage all its designated lands, including new territories. The Northwest Territory had just become part of the Union in 1787, so these rules were timely.

The United States expanded as new territories were added. The opportunity to include Canada in the Union had been written into the Articles of Confederation, but Canada refused the offer. The Louisiana Purchase of 1803 and the addition of Spanish Florida in 1819 greatly expanded the United States, as did the addition of Texas in 1845. Texas entered the Union with an agreement that allowed for its division into up to five states, if desired. This has not happened, of course, and Texas relishes its size.

After the war with Mexico ended in 1848, the United States purchased all the land between the Rocky Mountains and the Pacific coast. Congress bought Alaska from Russia in 1867 and voted it the forty-ninth state in 1959. Hawaii became a territory in 1900 and the fiftieth state in 1960. With the addition of the territories of Puerto Rico and Guam in 1898, the Virgin Islands in 1917, and American Samoa in 1929, the United States grew to what we recognize today as its full territory.

Article IV addresses other issues. When a state needs protection from domestic violence—meaning internal insurrection—it can ask for and receive federal assistance. This would quell any insurgence that threatens the whole.

Under republican principles, the federal government assures the right to vote. However, later amendments modified voting rights. The Twenty-third Amendment gave the vote to residents of the District of Columbia, the seat of government. The Twenty-fourth Amendment prevented charging a poll tax, and the Twenty-sixth Amendment inserted federal control when it required a national change of voting age from twenty-one to eighteen.

The United States guarantees the preservation of freely elected representative government in each state in the Union. No state can set up another form of government, such as a monarchy or oligarchy—states must maintain republican government. Under the original Constitution, the states had great latitude within their state governments. The altered Constitution has removed many matters, such as educational standards, from state jurisdiction.

Still, many variations on republican principles exist within the respective states, and rightfully so. This encourages states to become problem-solving laboratories for shared problems. Local needs and desires can thus be met.

10.8 | Amending the Constitution

James Madison, Father of the Constitution, said that the Founders "accomplished a revolution which has no parallel in the annals of human society . . . They formed the design of a great Confederacy, which it is incumbent on their successors to improve and perpetuate."[10] The "revolution" of which he spoke is the peaceful creation of a new government.

The Founders ensured that if the Constitution proved too severe, the means existed to tame it. If it was too weak, they provided the method to renew it to health and vigor. This means is the ability to amend and thus fine-tune the Constitution.

Two methods of amending the Constitution exist, only one of which has been used to produce the twenty-seven existing amendments. This method provides that two-thirds each of the House and Senate propose an amendment and send it to the states for ratification. No popular vote is taken. If three-fourths of the states—a substantial majority—ratify, the amendment becomes part of the Constitution.

The second, untried method available in Article V of the Constitution is designed for use when Congress ignores the needs of the people and the states, so that both lose confidence in the federal government. It allows the states to sidestep the federal process. Two-thirds of the state legislatures call for the amending convention and the proposed amendment(s) become law when three-fourths of the states ratify.

Some freedom-based groups are reluctant to use this second method. They fear the many enemies of the Constitution would seize control of the process and replace our Constitution with one of several freedom-destroying alternate constitutions known to exist. The movement to undermine our inspired Constitution is real and has been moving forward for well over one hundred years.

While no one knows whether a constitutional convention of the states would ultimately install a replacement document, the author's experience with President Carter's White House Conference on Families in 1980 is alarming. The declared intent of the conference was to provide everyday people an opportunity to tell government how to help families. The final results were skewed by a deliberate last minute rule change that effectively eliminated the conservative results of the conference and replaced them with an agenda that favored major government intervention in family affairs. In today's politically progressive climate, a constitutional convention of the states, sometimes called an Article V convention, could easily meet the same fate.

The amending process was intentionally made difficult in order to discourage reckless changes and tinkering with the document. Our Constitution is profoundly important to our freedom, protection, and prosperity—so much so that great caution must be used to alter it.

In his Farewell Address following his second term, George Washington offered insights invaluable to us today as he shared his perceptions over eight years as president. As our first president, he took the principles crafted by the fifty-five inspired, dedicated men who met in Philadelphia and made them into a real, working government. In his address, he carefully warned that changes to the Constitution must be made through the amendment process, saying: "Let there be no change by usurpation."[11]

His advice has been ignored. According to one former Supreme Court attorney and constitutional authority: "The . . . usurpation of authority by the executive and judicial branches [is] . . . responsible for the most serious problems presently assailing this country."[12]

10.9 | Debts, Law, and Religion

O NCE the major structure of the Constitution was complete, only the finishing details remained. Article VI deals with the important matters of debt, supremacy of law, and a state religion.

The Union had incurred seventy-nine million dollars of debt during the Revolutionary War. The Founders affirmed that those debts would be paid by the federal government, which accepted the war debts the states had incurred for national defense. Their actions increased American standing throughout the world. Commonly, European nations of the time reorganized, disclaimed previous debts, and left creditors unpaid.

French assistance during the war helped save America but had driven the extravagant French king further into debt. Refusing the advice of Jefferson, Franklin, and others, he levied more taxes on his already-impoverished people. This contributed to the bloodbath of the French Revolution, when four thousand members of France's leading families went to the guillotine.

Confidence in America increased among foreign bankers. The British underwrote a bank, chartered for twenty years, to help the nation pay its war debts. If this bank had continued past twenty years, it would have been harmful; but when controlled for this short term, its action helped. Twenty years later, Congress dissolved the bank as planned—over the protest of the British bankers, who wanted the profitable charter renewed. This led in part to the War of 1812 with England.

Article VI declared the Constitution itself, laws passed by Congress, and any treaties signed to be the supreme law of the land. One purpose of this "supremacy clause" was to prevent states from taking over federal responsibilities. It designated federal jurisdiction, committed states to abide by federal law, and made sure that the parts did not declare themselves above the whole.

Any government—local, state, or federal—can get out of control. In our day, the federal government has usurped state responsibilities. Citizens' vigilance is necessary at any and all levels of government to maintain proper balance.

The oath of office for government officials also appears in Article VI. No nation can survive without the fidelity of its officers. The major commitment made in the oath is to support, uphold, and defend the Constitution, so any federal officer who violates the Constitution is breaking his oath.

The final provision in Article VI states that no religious test shall be required as a qualification for any office in the federal government. Religion had been an engine of oppression in other governments, and persecution had historically been severe and prolonged. The Christian Crusades, the Spanish Inquisition, and the Jewish Holocaust are reminders of the sort of religious persecutions banned in the Constitution.

This clause acts as a guarantee of religious liberty. It forbids federal interference in any religious establishment, practice, or preference. Religious discrimination was not to be part of America's tradition. Still, religion and religious practices have become an issue. This is unconstitutional.

With these articles in place, the Constitution was very nearly complete. All that remained was to outline the ratification process.

10.10 | Ratification and Authorization

T HE FINAL PROVISION of the Constitution, Article VII, outlined the method to put it into action. While the rules required that nine states embrace it, the near-universal wish of the delegates was that all thirteen would ratify—which they did.

Delegates from the twelve states present at the Pennsylvania State House on September 17, 1787, to bring the Constitutional Convention to a close had invested heart and soul into the proposed new government. They believed that what they had created would stand as a testament to their wisdom and inspiration, but only time would make that sure.

Dr. Benjamin Franklin addressed this uncertainty as they prepared to affix their signatures. He related that he had learned through his long life that he was not always right: "The older I grow, the more apt I am to doubt my own judgment." Referring to the tendency of most people to think themselves in possession of all truth and those who doubt them to be in error, he related the story of "a certain French lady, who in a dispute with her sister, said, 'I don't know how it happens, Sister, but I meet with nobody but myself, that's always in the right.'"[13]

The delegates to the Constitutional Convention shared Franklin's apprehension. Personal courage mingled with serious trepidation within each man as he considered the reactions of the people back home. Each would face his state legislature as it dissected the document the Convention had written. They would have questions and would closely scrutinize the answers. Would the document pass muster?

One or more states might reject their previous covenant of perpetual union and go their own way. The South had already threatened secession over the issue of slavery. The creation of government, especially in a form that was new and untested, had been a volatile process. That the delegates proceeded to sign the new Constitution without flinching is a tribute to each of them and a blessing to us all.

The text of the Constitution closes thus, followed by the delegates' signatures, just as they signed:

Done in Convention by the Unanimous Consent of the States present the Seventeenth Day of September in the Year of our Lord one thousand seven hundred and Eighty seven and of the Independence of the United States of America the Twelfth. In Witness whereof We have hereunto subscribed our names,

G. Washington—presid. and deputy from Virginia

New Hampshire: John Langdon, Nicholas Gilman

Massachusetts: Nathaniel Gorham, Rufus King

Connecticut: Wm. Saml. Johnson, Roger Sherman

New York: Alexander Hamilton

New Jersey: Wil: Livingston. David Brearley, Wm Paterson, Jona: Dayton

Pennsylvania: B Franklin, Thomas Mifflin, Robt. Morris, Geo. Clymer, Thos. FitzSimons, Jared Ingersoll, James Wilson, Gouv Morris

Delaware: Geo: Read, Gunning Bedford Jun, John Dickinson, Richard Bassett, Jaco: Broom

Maryland: James McHenry, Dan. of St Thos. Jenifer, Danl Carroll

Virginia: John Blair—, James Madison Jr.

North Carolina: Wm. Blount, Richd. Dobbs Spaight, Hu Williamson

South Carolina: J. Rutledge, Charles Cotesworth Pinckney, Charles Pinckney, Pierce Butler

Georgia: William Few, Abr. Baldwin

Attest William Jackson Secretary

The Constitution was finished.

11

We the People

— ◌ —

THE BILL OF RIGHTS AND THE AMENDMENTS

THE FOUNDING FATHERS never intended that major changes be made to the Constitution—the government's birth certificate. It would, however, inevitably require adjustments, as few things are perfect at first.

Most delegates saw no need for a Bill of Rights; the entire document was a bill of rights. When some intended signers refused to support the finished product without specific guarantees of individual rights, the plan changed. The desired adjustments, passed in the first session of Congress under the Constitution, constitute the first ten amendments. The states made 189 suggestions. James Madison distilled them down to 17, Congress approved 12, and the states ratified 10.

The Bill of Rights would be better named the Bill of Federal Prohibitions, because it details what the federal government is not allowed to do. The Preamble makes this clear: "The Convention of a number of the States, having at the time of their adopting the Constitution, expressed a desire, in order to prevent misconstruction or abuse of its powers, that further declaratory and restrictive clauses should be added: And as extending the ground of public confidence in the Government will best ensure the beneficent ends of its institutions."

The Founders had expended time, energy, resources, and emotion to create this new republic. For some of them, it was not enough to know that personal liberty and chains to bind governmental abuse were written into the Constitution; they needed specific guarantees. They wanted freedom to ring from its pages, as the bells rang when the Declaration of Independence was read. Their document of freedom must declare boldly and unequivocally: "Government, these you cannot do!"

Only the first ten amendments constitute the Bill of Rights, although twenty-seven amendments have been proposed and accepted through the years. The first twelve amendments clarify the Constitution and are sound. Many of the remaining fifteen made questionable changes and are not prudent. The following pages discuss all the amendments.

Amendments are listed by topic in this section. See the Appendix for a chronological listing.

11.1 | First Amendment: The Right to Worship

No RIGHT is more important than freedom to worship as we choose. This liberty occupies first place in the freedoms mentioned in the Bill of Rights.

The Constitution states: "Congress shall make no law respecting an establishment of religion, or prohibiting the free exercise thereof." Without freedom of religion, political freedom is impossible. The people will not remain moral and respect the rights of others without a religious base. Christian principles formed the core of educational instruction and life in America. Universal religious fundamentals were central to America's schools. Some European philosophers believed that religion and liberty were antagonists; not so in America. The clergy, who preached moral strength and shunned partisan politics, helped to drive freedom.

The Constitution creates a wall between any specific church and the national government, but it does not place those limitations on the states. The Founders left the matter of a state religion exclusively to the state governments, which could make their own choices on this critical subject. Several states had state-sponsored religions. For example, New Jersey was Protestant, Massachusetts was Congregational, and Maryland designated Christianity.

At the state level, Jefferson had proposed religious instruction at the University of Virginia, which he established. He had encouraged religious professorships and attendance at religion classes on campus.[1] As governor of Virginia, he set religious holidays and fast days. These were all appropriate at the state level.

As national president, Jefferson took no actions that involved religion. He recognized that the federal government had no jurisdiction in religious matters. He understood that states could legislate and act in this critical area, but the federal government could not. However, during his second presidential term, Jefferson encouraged the states to discard their official churches and promote all religions to strengthen the national moral fiber.

Religious discrimination is again rearing its ugly head in America and worldwide.

Attorney Lance B. Wickman gave a speech entitled "The Threatened Demise of Religion in the Public Square" at the J. Reuben Clark Law Society Conference in February 2010. In it, he said: "The greatest challenge . . . [growing worldwide is] to religious liberty . . . A battle is looming over the effort to acquire civil *social* rights at the expense of civil *religious* rights. This battle represents the acceleration of a disturbing slide downward in the law regarding the place of religion in the public square." Speaking of the litigation surrounding Proposition 8 in California, he stated: "They [opponents of Proposition 8] essentially claim that the voters—from whom all authority in a democracy flows—may not consider religious views and values when deciding . . . social and cultural . . . rights . . . [This] threatens to eliminate any discussion of religion in the public square when social or cultural rights are at issue."[2] This would mean that religion, Christian values, and morality could not be a part of the decision-making process in any public or legal endeavor.

Thus, a nation founded by God, dedicated to God, and dependent on God could no longer mention God or make Him a part of public life.

This should not be the case. Our virtue and our belief in God are our safeguards of liberty. As a nation, we must ask daily for His assistance. If we pour out our hearts in prayer, He will hear and bless us. With His help, we can maintain our freedom of worship.

11.2 | First Amendment: The Right to Express Opinions

THE STATES based their recommendations for the Bill of Rights on their experiences with repressive British government. Their amendments reflect their determination to avoid the government coercions common in their past.

The First Amendment protects the right to voice opinions. Those aspects specifically mentioned are freedom of speech, freedom of the press, freedom to assemble in groups, and the right to petition the government.

The freedoms of speech and press are two arms of the same process—one spoken, one written. Both allow people freedom to express what they think. Freedom of the press defends the right to have access to truthful information on which to base decisions. This is absolutely necessary among a free people; without correct information, they cannot make wise choices. Those who want to control and manipulate the people always control the information they receive.

Some speech must be restricted, of course. One cannot slander another or falsely cry "Fire!" in a crowded theatre. If the act of free speech creates a hazard, such as obstructing traffic, some temporary limitations must be imposed. Sir William Blackstone, English judge and politician of the mid-1700s, said this of free speech: "Every freeman has an undoubted right to lay what sentiment he pleases before the public... But if he publishes what is improper, mischievous, or illegal, he must take the consequences of his own temerity."[3]

Control of the press today comes largely from ownership of the media by those who want to sway politics and public opinion. It takes hold when ideas and philosophies constantly present a particular slant to influence the public mindset. Control of information also includes ignoring what should be presented. Many watch the news without thought to what is *not* being reported and what philosophy underlies what is being reported.

We can peacefully assemble. British colonial governors repeatedly disbanded groups of colonial Americans who assembled to air their grievances. These acts of cancellation, or prorogue, fanned the flames for independence. The right to assemble to present our views, so long as this is done peacefully, is one of our inalienable rights from God. Of course, there are limitations. It is unlawful to assemble for purposes of fomenting violent government overthrow or conspiracy to commit a crime.

Americans cannot be prevented from expressing their grievances to the government. King George III ignored the colonial pleas for justice and relief from troops and taxation. Likewise, the French Revolution of 1789 resulted from oppressed people with no other action left to them but to seize the government. In both situations, the consequences of ignoring public opinion were harsh.

Despotic governments do not want to hear about their shortcomings. Free governments know that the people must be heard. This flow of information from citizens to government has many forms: petitions, letters, email messages, personal contact, paid lobbyists, and public demonstrations all send a message to officials. We have the responsibility to make our views known to our officials. Their primary task while in office is to respond to us. They cannot hear if we do not speak.

Communication between the governed and those who govern is essential to efficient administration. The First Amendment to the Bill of Rights guarantees this honest, uninhibited flow of information.

11.3 | Second Amendment: The Right to Protect Ourselves

IMAGINE trying to protect yourself without a weapon. You are faced with an armed intruder—those who want to hurt you will always have weapons—and you have nothing with which to protect yourself. This is not a pretty picture.

The Second Amendment gives us the right to bear arms—the right to protect ourselves with weapons.

Every successful, prosperous nation must defend itself against enemies, including those within the government. A major part of our protection comes from the Second Amendment, which reads: "Because a well-regulated state militia is necessary for the security of a free people, the right of the people to keep and bear arms shall not be infringed by the federal government."

During the colonial period of the United States, we largely protected ourselves through a resting citizens' militia. Free citizens were responsible to own and be able to use defensive weapons.

In the modern world, some argue that the Second Amendment does not guarantee the right of the people to bear arms, that only the state militia or the National Guard have that right. The Senate subcommittee on the Constitution, in its 1982 report entitled *The Right to Keep and Bear Arms,* investigated and reported the intent of the Founding Fathers on this topic, using direct quotations.

Patrick Henry said: "A well regulated militia, composed of gentlemen and freemen, is the natural strength and only security of a free government . . . The great object is that every man be armed."[4]

The 1787 pamphlet entitled *Letters from the Federal Farmer to the Republican,* attributed to Richard Henry Lee, reads: "To preserve liberty it is essential that the whole body of the people always possess arms and be taught alike, especially when young, how to use them."[5]

The subcommittee states: "The conclusion is thus inescapable that the . . . Second Amendment . . . indicates that . . . [the] individual right of a private citizen to own and carry firearms in a peaceful manner" is our constitutional right.[6]

The use of guns in modern terrorism and individual acts of violence has provoked cries to take our arms from us "for our own good." This makes no sense, since we can assume that only the law-abiding would comply.

Gun control does not curb crime. Senator Orrin Hatch (R-Utah), chairman of the Senate subcommittee on the Constitution, reasoned: "If gun laws . . . worked, the sponsors . . . should have no difficulty drawing upon long lists of examples of crime rates reduced by such legislation. That they cannot do so after a century and a half of trying . . . establishes the repeated, complete and inevitable failure of gun laws to control serious crime."[7]

Those who want to harm others or break the law will find ways to get weapons. If the government takes weapons from peaceable citizens, it leaves them at the mercy of criminals and despots. History demonstrates that a nation sliding into despotism typically forces gun registration, then provokes an incident that "requires" the confiscation of weapons. "George Mason, [a] drafter of the [Constitution and the] Virginia Bill of Rights, accused the British of having plotted 'to disarm the people— that was the best and most effective way to enslave them.'"[8]

Private citizens must not be left defenseless. We must retain the right to keep and bear arms.

11.4 | Third and Fourth Amendments:
The Right to Privacy

ALL OF US need privacy to restore and refresh ourselves. We gather family and friends in our homes and create moments of peace and contentment. The colonists' right to privacy was violated by an oppressive British government. Colonists chafed under these intrusions. When they accepted self-rule, they gave themselves the freedom of privacy.

During the enforcement of the Stamp Act, the colonists were forced to house British soldiers. This was repugnant to the colonists, and those in Massachusetts flatly refused. Their insistence eventually led to the Third Amendment: "No soldier shall, in time of peace, be quartered in any house without the consent of the owner, nor in time of war except in a manner prescribed by law."

When troops are quartered in a home, the residents are effectively placed under military law. In England, this dreaded practice was considered worse than a plague. It was expensive to provide for quartered soldiers. They often destroyed furniture and property. Much worse, residents in the home had no protection from ruthless soldiers who often abused the homeowners and defiled the women. Modern-day Americans have never had to submit to these atrocities precisely because we have the Third Amendment.

The Fourth Amendment states: "The right of the people to be secure in their persons, houses, papers and effects shall not be violated." Protection is given "against unreasonable searches and seizures." Search warrants are required, and "no warrant shall be issued by the courts unless based on probable cause, supported by an oath ... and describing the ... place to be searched and the person or things to be seized." These guarantees in the original Constitution have been seriously jeopardized by regulatory agencies put in place over the last several decades. These agencies are often the result of the Sixteenth Amendment, which imposes a graduated income tax on Americans. To verify that we pay our taxes, the government has increasingly invaded our personal lives, and our privacy has been sacrificed. This illustrates how one change in the Constitution can have far-reaching effects on our rights.

The Fourth Amendment's guarantees of privacy and protection are also jeopardized by government agencies such as the Occupational Safety and Health Administration (OSHA) and the more recent environmental agencies. These agencies are authorized to violate our privacy to assure that their policies are being carried out.

The government's actions allow administrative policies to take priority over personal rights. With emerging technologies—the Internet, data collection, electronic tracking and listening devices, and personal identification through biomarkers—our rights to privacy will diminish further. Acts of terrorism over the last several years have provided the government with reasons to erode our rights to privacy even more. When denied the right to privacy, we forfeit personal safety and freedom.

Some believe that we have no need for privacy if we are doing nothing wrong. This might be true with a moral, God-fearing government, all of whose agents act with full respect for our rights. However, a government staffed, even in part, by people who yield to the lust for power soon develops corrupt practices. Disrespect for individuals, their rights, and their property always follows.

No one is safe without privacy.

11.5 | Fifth through Eighth Amendments: The Rights of the Accused

ANY PERSON accused of a crime wants protection from mistreatment. Whether guilty or innocent, the accused has inalienable rights. The Fifth through Eighth Amendments provide this safety for the accused.

In ancient Rome and Britain, rulers routinely confiscated private property. The Fifth Amendment states that "life, liberty, and property can be taken only through fair operation of the law or with fair compensation." Unless caught in an act of wrongdoing, the accused appears before a grand jury to determine the facts. He cannot be forced to testify against himself or tried twice for the same crime. He receives a speedy public trial to prevent hidden injustice, unless publicity would injure him.

The Sixth Amendment states that the accused must be told what he is being tried for. During the Spanish Inquisition in the 1600s, those charged were not informed of the accusations against them, but they suffered severe penalties if they did not confess. This set up impossible jeopardy situations in which the accused convicted themselves.

The accused is entitled to legal help. He has the right to be confronted by his accusers; otherwise, the process against him becomes secretive. Witnesses can be compelled to testify in behalf of the accused. Without this right, a key witness might refuse to give testimony needed to prove guilt or innocence.

The Seventh Amendment guarantees the accused a fair trial by an impartial jury in any case that involves more than twenty dollars. (This amount has never been adjusted, and it would likely require an amendment to do so.) No appellate (review) court can ignore the findings of a previous court.

The Eighth Amendment provides that the court cannot assign excessive bail, excessive fines, or cruel and unusual punishment. This refers to bail set impossibly high or punishments out of proportion with the crime. The Magna Carta of 1215, which opened up rights to

Englishmen, defines excessive fines as those which deprive a man of his ability to earn a living or pursue his business. English law, under which the colonists had previously lived, allowed punishments out of proportion with the crimes committed, such as dismemberment, castration, branding on the cheek, and flogging.

The highest priority for early Americans was to ensure the freedom of the innocent. To them, the protection of the innocent was more important than the punishment of transgressors. While every attempt was made to bring the guilty to justice, early Americans believed that if the guilty escaped punishment in this life, God would deliver judgment in the hereafter. They preferred to err on the side of innocence.

If general rebellion arises, trial for the accused can be waived until order is restored. This is necessary during crisis but offers an opportunity for political mischief.

These four amendments constitute an impressive collection of legal protections for Americans. So long as these rights are respected, Americans are protected in the courts of law.

11.6 | Ninth and Tenth Amendments: Did We Forget Anything?

A NYONE who has ever tried to create a complete list knows how easy it is to omit something important.

This was the case with the Founders. The purpose of the Bill of Rights was to secure our liberties, and they feared that they would miss something critical. Any right omitted would be forfeited. Many of the Framers preferred not to draft a Bill of Rights for that reason.

The eventual solution was a pair of "catch-all" amendments. The Ninth Amendment reads: "The enumeration of certain rights in this Constitution shall not be interpreted to repudiate, deny or disparage other rights belonging to the people, but which have not been enumerated." In other words, "If we didn't mention it, that doesn't mean that it isn't important or that we don't get it."

The Tenth Amendment approaches this situation differently. It reads: "All powers not specifically delegated to the Congress of the United States by this Constitution, nor prohibited to the states by this Constitution, are reserved to the states, or to the people." Thus, any rights not assigned or restricted elsewhere, any future developments, or anything forgotten in the original plan becomes the right of the state to direct or the people to enforce. This cements the power of the states and strengthens their authority.

The Tenth Amendment is consistently ignored today, as the federal government works its way into emerging policies and regulations. The Seventeenth Amendment, which denies state governments a voice at the federal level, has effectively abolished the state authority granted in this amendment as well. This is another example of the havoc created by unwise amendments.

Because the people do not understand the imbalances such amendments have created, they blame everyone and everything else. The core problem is that our disabled Senate can no longer rein in government. Under the original Constitution, the Senate, made up of individuals who worked for the state governments, demanded its right to handle all matters not specifically assigned to the federal government. The states now stand defenseless, unable to demand their rights or exert their power. Senators, once occupied in protecting state interests, now spend their time currying favor with the people to win reelection.

With America's protectors—the states—gone, no one moves to stop the federal machine. Unchecked, it devours rights, programs, and benefits one after another. Tax money, made available by the passage of the Sixteenth Amendment, feeds its appetite. When tax dollars run dry, the Federal Reserve prints more money, and prices rise due to inflation. Boom-and-bust cycles impoverish the people as government spends our money to buy our votes.

Government bureaucracies have taken over education, business, safety, transportation, communications, and anything else they have encountered. Federal income taxes have gone up dramatically, from the 1 percent originally projected in 1913 to 28 percent and above. More and more Americans work for agencies and bureaucrats on the federal payroll. Regulations choke free enterprise as freedoms and privacy vanish.

Let this not be our epitaph. We can never have prosperity and freedom under the altered Constitution. To begin our national recovery, we must return the protective role of the states, as designated by the original Constitution. As we do so, we will regain the balance that gave us protection from a greedy federal government. Prosperity will be our reward.

11.7 | Amendments Eleven, Twelve, Twenty, Twenty-Two, Twenty-Five and Twenty-Seven: Polishing Procedures

THE CONSTITUTION is not a perfect document. Very few things are, initially. The fifty-five men who signed our founding charter knew their work would require refinements, and it did. They provided for peaceful adjustments through amendments, though not intending the core principles to change. Some of the amendments discussed below are also explained in Section 10.2.

The first change came just four years after the ten amendments of the Bill of Rights were added to the Constitution. Appropriately jealous of their sovereignty, the states ratified the Eleventh Amendment to declare they could not be sued without their consent. The states were heavily in debt from the inflation-ridden years under the Articles of Confederation. When it appeared citizens might sue the states over these debts, the states acted to protect themselves.

Several amendments pertain to the office of president. Time showed the need for corrections, some of which were "housekeeping" changes to polish the election process. Originally, the individual with the most votes became president, while the runner-up was named the vice-president; however, this plan was not working well. The Electoral College, to elect our chief executive, was already feeling the disruptions of the emerging two-party political system. Washington had warned about political parties in his farewell address eight years earlier. As a solution, the Twelfth Amendment established separate ballots for president and vice-president.

The Twentieth Amendment changed the dates for members of Congress, the president, and vice-president to take office. Too much time was elapsing between elections and installments of those elected. Those defeated for re-election remained in office, still making and passing laws in what came to be known as "lame duck" sessions.

The Twenty-second Amendment limits the president to two elected terms only. Washington had set the precedent of two terms, which was followed by all presidents until Franklin Delano Roosevelt. FDR's four terms in office challenged presidential tradition. When Roosevelt died just weeks into his fourth term, Congress and the states acted quickly to prevent an extended presidential term in the future. When a successor takes over after a president dies in office, he can only be elected once if he has served more than two years of the former president's term; that partial term equals a full term.

Amendment Twenty-five sets the vice-president as the official successor to the president, should he die or otherwise leave office. It also sets procedures for replacing the vice-president. The amendment addresses circumstances that have never arisen. It allows the president, if needed, to declare himself incompetent to serve and sets the procedure for him to later be reinstated. The vice-president and the president's cabinet can declare to Congress their belief that he should not resume his position. A vote of two/thirds of Congress prevails, however, and puts the president back in office.

The Twenty-seventh and final amendment declares that, if the House of Representatives votes itself a pay raise, the increase will not go into effect until after the next election cycle, to prevent mischief. This amendment was proposed along with the ten amendments of the Bill of Rights but was not ratified. It was proposed again and passed two hundred and one years after its initial proposal.

11.8 | Amendments Thirteen, Fourteen, Fifteen: The Right to Be Free

S LAVERY WAS A BLIGHT on America's soul; a stain on the collective conscience of a nation that claimed a divinely inspired Constitution. Cleansing this stain eventually cost the blood of a generation.

The Founders planned for the freedom of slaves. They wrote into the Constitution a twenty-year period to prepare for their manumission, or freedom. The first step to begin the freedom process was to end the importation of slaves. Writing an end to slavery into the Constitution was not possible in 1787, as three southern states had threatened to withdraw from the Union over the issue. Southern states had laws on emancipation and the Constitutional Convention had no authority to override them. In addition, the southern economy was based on slave labor and would have collapsed if slaves had been universally freed. This would have left the entire South destitute.

With the Civil War, the nation could no longer avoid the issue of slavery. Between 1865 and 1869, three amendments addressed the matter. The Thirteenth Amendment reads: "Neither slavery or involuntary servitude, except as a punishment for crime . . . shall exist within the United States or anyplace subject to their jurisdiction."

The Fourteenth Amendment grants automatic citizenship to children born in the US, unless born to foreign diplomats in residence. It requires due process of law—following standard legal procedures—where life, liberty and property are concerned, and establishes equal protection for all. It replaced the Constitution's three-fifths compromise that some mistakenly believe declared black people of lesser worth—discussed in Section 9.4.

The Fourteenth Amendment also imposed punishment on the South for the Civil War. It is a troublesome, vindictive amendment, passed by a Congress that wanted to punish the South for deserting the Union. Hurtful measures include reducing a state's representation in Congress if it interfered with black voters, denying public office to any who had taken the federal oath of office and then fought for the Confederacy, and denying payments of Southern war debts and losses to slave owners. While some clauses simply reiterate provisions of the Constitution, the Amendment's overall harsh effect on a country trying to heal itself further divided the nation.

Many of our current immigration problems stem from this amendment. Using the Fourteenth Amendment as justification, the 1965 Immigration Act declares that children of illegal immigrants born in the United States are citizens. These babies are known as "anchor babies"; they anchor illegal immigrant families to the United States, often drawing in extended family as well.

Amendment Fourteen's unforeseen consequences have caused many problems. This amendment has been repeatedly used by federal courts to tighten the federal chokehold on states. Through "substantive due process," the federal Bill of Rights, originally intended for the federal government only, is now applied to the states. Through court interpretations, nationally set standards prevent groups and states from adapting to unique circumstances, which is essential for personal liberty. For instance, the amendment's "equal treatment" clause wipes out necessary distinctions between genders. The courts are flooded with cases to determine equal treatment, and the judgments they render often ignore their negative effects.

The Fifteenth Amendment declares that the right to vote cannot be denied on the basis of race, color, or previous servitude. Section 11.9 discusses The Fifteenth Amendment.

11.9 | Amendments Fifteen, Nineteen, Twenty-Three, Twenty-Four, Twenty-Six: The Right to Vote

FEW ISSUES SPEAK of liberty more than the right to vote. By selecting leaders, we control outcomes, set standards, and protect property. This personal choice is essential; when voting rights disappear, tyranny quickly follows. A republic demands the unhampered voice of the people, and good government jealously protects the right to vote.

The original Constitution assigns the federal government to assure representative government—the right to vote—in the states (Article 4 Section 4). The states, however, determine who votes; the national government has no constitutional authority to determine voting eligibility.

At the time the Constitution was written, Southern states allowed only whites to vote, women left public matters and voting to their male heads-of-household, and young people voted at twenty-one. The culture changed and states changed with it, but some were slow to grant expanded voting rights. Congress inappropriately stepped in with amendments that brought the voting process under federal control. The states weakened themselves by ratifying these amendments, forfeiting substantial authority.

The objectives of these voting amendments were well-intended. The objections are to how the changes were made. In each, power was shifted from the states to the federal government. It is the state's duty to protect its citizens from a too-powerful federal government. This requires powerful states; weak states are poor protectors. With time, federal encouragement and social pressure from the other states would have led all the states to make the necessary changes in voting requirements. Patience would have been required, but important protections to our liberties would have remained in place. This could have forestalled the current problems with an abusive federal government.

The Fifteenth Amendment addressed slavery. It gives voting rights to persons of any nationality or skin color.

Ratified in 1870, shortly after the end of the Civil War, it states: "The right of citizens of the United States to vote shall not be denied or abridged (limited) by the United States or by any state on account of race, color, or previous condition of servitude."

Fifty years later, the Nineteenth Amendment gave women voting rights. It declares, "The right of citizens . . . to vote shall not be denied or abridged . . . on account of sex." The women's movement and World War I changed the culture and the vote for women was inevitable. Women had been voting in some states for decades: Wyoming for more than fifty years, Colorado, Utah, and Idaho for twenty-five years or so, and Washington State for ten.

The Twenty-third Amendment gave the vote to residents of the District of Columbia, the national seat of government. The District was intended to be neutral governing territory. Residents of the District could have voted in Maryland, the original owner of the District's territory, as an alternative. The District is not a state, and opponents feared this would set a precedent for cities to demand state privileges.

The Twenty-fourth Amendment prohibited a poll tax. Though the tax was only a few dollars to defray voting costs, some feared it could prevent the poor from voting.

The Twenty-sixth Amendment changed the voting age from twenty-one to eighteen. Eighteen year olds were being drafted and sent to war, so it seemed fair that they should vote on national matters. Opponents feared that eighteen year olds were not ready to make mature decisions on national matters.

11.10 | Amendments Sixteen, Seventeen, Eighteen and Twenty-One: Unwise Transfer of Power

THE FOUNDING FATHERS knew too well the lashing a powerful government could give its citizens. One of their core principles was that states would act as powerful buffers between citizens and federal aggression. Any move that diminished state authority disrupted the precise balance of power anchored in the Constitution.

Few amendments have done more to damage the delicate symmetry of the Constitution and strip citizen protection than the Sixteenth Amendment. This change to the Constitution gave Congress "the power to lay and collect taxes on incomes, from whatever source derived." The fairness of uniform taxation for all also perished.

Taxation would be applied ". . . without apportionment among the several states and without regard to any census or enumeration." This amendment is discussed in Section 9.7.

Equally damaging is the Seventeenth Amendment, which destroyed the balance between the people and the states in Congress. This amendment doubled input from the people and eliminated the states in policymaking. This brings us close to an unruly democracy, the most dangerous form of government. This amendment is explained in Section 9.6.

The Eighteenth and Twenty-first Amendments first invoked, then revoked, Prohibition, the federal government's attempt to control access to alcoholic beverages. The amendment to introduce Prohibition, effective in 1919, stated: "The manufacture, sale or transportation of intoxicating liquors for beverage purposes is hereby prohibited." Enforcement fell into both state and federal jurisdictions.

Going "dry" was a side-effect of World War I. Munitions manufactures required alcohol, so many states temporarily went dry to conserve the supply. Community life improved, and women across the country clamored for permanent national abstinence. After passage of the Eighteenth Amendment, opposition developed quickly. Along with hard liquor, beer and wine were prohibited. Soldiers returning from the war and ethnic groups who routinely consumed these lighter beverages protested.

Home breweries and secret bars, known as "speakeasies," sprang up in an era known as the Roaring Twenties and were backed by racketeers and an aggressive black market. Underground criminal activity and ruthless gangs absorbed the profitable, but forbidden, alcohol trade. Law enforcement and judges yielded to bribery and the great gangster era of America revved into high gear. When gang violence became rampant and the projected benefits of "failure to imbibe" did not materialize, the nation grew weary of temperance.

Fourteen years later, the Twenty-first Amendment repealed Prohibition. These amendments demonstrate the process of revoking one amendment by passing another. The Twenty-first Amendment did not make alcohol legal. It simply turned its control back to the states, where it was originally and should have remained.

Prohibition was not the answer to the alcohol problem. Taxation and penalties in the states, along with public education, could have made a difference. Americans have responded well to this method in curbing tobacco use. Government sometimes succumbs to the temptation to bring about a desired outcome "right now", rather than allowing states to act and natural events to produce change. Government interference often makes the matter worse.

There is folly in forcing people to do what is "right" in private decisions. Freedom and morality are intertwined, and laws must support the opportunity for moral behavior. However, it is not the purpose of the federal Constitution to codify, or put into law, specific moral actions. That behavior is a matter of personal choice.

Section Twelve

———————— ❧ ————————

WHO IS CHANGING THE CONSTITUTION?

B Y NOW it has become obvious that the Constitution has been changed dramatically. Through these changes, we have lost many of the freedoms and much of the prosperity that made America great.

This country was intended by God to be the incubator for religious freedom. Political freedom and religious freedom are inseparable—so much so that James Wilson of Pennsylvania referred to them as twin sisters.[1] Inspired, courageous leaders have been brought forward by divine intervention to guide us. Our Founding Fathers were wise and moral men. Their courage and commitment to principles of liberty have few parallels in history. They were both tenacious in pursuing independence and patient as they sifted out the components of workable government. Our system of government has roots in England and in the Middle East of the ancient Israelites. When we keep the commandments and make and keep covenants, we receive the blessings of a watchful God.

America is a constitutional republic. We rule ourselves. We loan part of our rights to those we elect to create our laws. This makes us a republic—the most stable government ever known in the world.

Those to whom we loaned our authority have failed us. They have violated their oaths to protect our freedoms. We have also failed ourselves because we have not watched our representatives carefully, nor removed them from office when they betrayed our trust. These failures have endangered our freedoms.

There are several reasons why our liberties are in jeopardy. In the following pages, we will look at four of these reasons: godless philosophies, misuse of constitutional amendments, unconstitutional changes by the Supreme Court, and the decline in public virtue.

We can correct our course. When we do, we will regain the priceless heritage of freedom, protection, prosperity, and peace that we have lost.

12.1 | Godless Philosophies: God versus Lucifer

GOD INSPIRED the United States Constitution, as the Framers frequently affirmed. George Washington repeatedly acknowledged God's hand in America. "When I contemplate the interposition of Providence . . . in guiding us through the revolution, in preparing us for the reception of a general government, and in conciliating the good will of the people of America . . . after its adoption, I feel myself . . . almost overwhelmed with a sense of the divine munificence [generosity]."[2]

The Constitution was given to the American colonists by God because their morality and virtue entitled them to the blessings of liberty. Only virtuous people respect the rights and freedoms of others as they respect their own. Such people need few laws and limited government. Their motivation comes from within, not from an external source such as law. They can be trusted with self-government. Alexis de Tocqueville, the Frenchman who studied America in detail and wrote *Democracy in America,* stated: "Morality [is] the best security of law, and the surest pledge of . . . freedom."[3]

Lucifer, or Satan, wants to destroy our morality. He is determined to bring bondage and unhappiness to all God's children. He is an enemy to liberty and all that it entails: freedom, or individual choice; the safety that comes with protection; prosperity, which is the ability to preserve one's individual interests; and ownership of property, which secures all other rights. He is assuredly an enemy of peace. As an enemy of God, Lucifer is in direct opposition to the Constitution of the United States of America. His corroding hand is at work to overthrow God's document of freedom.

The adversary has conquered the hearts of some and blinded the eyes of others to his influence. He has enlisted both groups to do his bidding. He wants to control—to destroy God's work. We can see the results of his influence in the Bible. He interrupted the peace of the Garden of Eden with his temptations. He convinced Cain to take the life of his brother Abel, thus introducing the sin of murder—the ultimate destruction of individual freedom.

Anything that takes away our right of personal choice or that leaves us without the ability to protect ourselves violates our God-given rights. Any force or organization that impairs our economy, takes our property from us without our consent, or destroys our peace of mind also operates under the influence of our eternal adversary.

Satan wants to be worshipped. His temptation of Jesus after His forty-day fast in the wilderness demonstrates this. Satan offered Christ all the kingdoms of the world if He would only fall at his feet and worship him (Matthew 4:1–10).

In his lust for glory, Satan has created his own religion. It is a counterfeit which substitutes worship of God with worship of self and things. Cunningly, he caters to the ego and self-interest of those he entices. Satan's religion suppresses the individuality of men, which forces their conformity and denies them individual choices. This religion is secular humanism.

When we use our knowledge of God's liberty and Satan's bondage as tools of measurement, we can identify those who undermine our Constitution. They remove our choices and our means of protection. They destroy our economy, shackle our prosperity, and pervert our peace.

12.2 | Godless Philosophies: Secular Humanism

A NEW "religion" under the direction of Lucifer has emerged worldwide. Rather than worship of deity, this officially recognized religion, called secular humanism, worships man.

Three versions of the Humanist Manifesto, the official statement of belief, appeared between 1933 and 2002. Humanist beliefs have gained wide acceptance. Many Christians unwittingly embrace some of these beliefs, which stand in stark contrast to traditional Christian values.

Humanism makes man the center of its religion. Belief in a supreme God who hears and answers prayers, according to humanists, is irrelevant, for God is powerless and faith is outmoded. Humanism says that deity cannot save us—we must save ourselves. There is no heaven and no life after death. Humanists view traditional religion as an obstacle to human progress.

Humanist dogma states that the purpose and meaning of life come from man's supreme importance. Answers come through technology, science, and the intelligent mind, not from God. The goal, however, is not scientific advancement for its own sake. Through science, humanists believe that mankind can alter human progress, unlock new powers, reduce disease, modify behavior, and conquer poverty. Humanists could then restructure the world according to their own plan. They encourage these developments in many ways, one of which is by influencing educational curricula.

The goal of humanism is the good life, here and now. Traditional morality, it claims, inhibits humans from experiencing their full humanity. All sexual conduct between consenting adults is an acceptable means of personal expression. Abortion, divorce, suicide, and euthanasia are all approved.

Secular humanism ignores basic facts of human nature. For instance, though humanists join Christians in encouraging all to work for their necessities, they assert that those unable—or even unwilling—to do so are entitled to a guaranteed income and goods given by the state.[4] This philosophy has resulted in our current American welfare system. We, along with many other countries, prove every day that this approach does not work. Many abuse the system, earning resentment from those whose taxes support it. An ever-expanding welfare class, permanent dependency, and destructive idleness are the universal effects.

Secular humanism is riddled with contradictions. Differences in social values are permitted, but all moral values are expected to be uniform. Political preferences are allowed, but all are pressured to embrace the same political system. Freedom of religion is given, yet God-centered religions are vilified. Tolerance is encouraged, yet only humanism's standards are deemed acceptable. The philosophy permits individual choices but dictates the outcome. This is not possible.

Choice does not exist when individuals are required to arrive at a conclusion that has been dictated to them. Uniformity rarely results from freedom; only coercion produces uniformity. Freedom produces diversity precisely because it allows individual choice.

Humanism professes freedom but discourages property ownership in favor of government ownership. When individuals do not own property, they are dependent for their needs on those who do, which violates the core concept of freedom. Humanism allows a variety of economic systems, yet the liberty of free enterprise, with its attendant prosperity, is unacceptable. Humanism espouses a world economy with no anticipated rewards for individual efforts. Under worldwide humanism, the United States would no longer have a separate economy and inviolate borders. Her resources and labors would belong to the world. Her national character would vanish, and her standard of living would plummet.

Secular humanism cannot offer freedom, protection, prosperity, or peace.

12.3 | Godless Philosophies: Creating Dependence

SECULAR HUMANISM has now made its way into our educational system.[5] Its pervasive presence in educational materials is thoroughly documented, and its influence encourages a culture of dependence.

Education has been highly prized in America for centuries. The earliest settlers in America took personal responsibility for teaching their children. Most colonial children could read before they entered school. Their textbooks were the Bible and the McGuffey Readers, which taught a wide variety of subjects incorporating religion and Christian values.

In *Democracy in America,* de Tocqueville said: "The instruction of the people powerfully contributes to the support of the democratic republic; and . . . is not separated from the moral education."[6] Under widespread moral instruction, America rose to heights previously unknown, which other countries tried to imitate.

The vocabulary of colonial Americans, which far exceeds ours today in its variety and sophistication, offers insight about their educational levels. As an example, it is wise to have a dictionary on hand when reading de Tocqueville, *The Federalist Papers,* or the Founders' letters.

In the mid-1800s, Horace Mann and his disciple John Dewey, influenced by the secularism of the widely admired Prussian school system of their day, began a crusade in America against moral education from Columbia Teachers College. They advocated government educational control to replace traditional instruction from parents. Their standard was the beliefs of men, not the words of God. They sought "a new religion, with the state as its true church, and education as its messiah."[7] Their approach increasingly discouraged parents from participating in their children's education.

As secular humanism infiltrated Europe and the Americas, John Dewey—an original signer of the first Humanist Manifesto and first president of the American Humanist Association—expressed his beliefs: "There is no god, and there is no soul . . . Truth is also dead and buried. There is no room for . . . moral absolutes."[8] Called educational progressivism, this movement preached self-actualization rather than proficiency in the traditional basics of reading, writing, and arithmetic. The shift of goals has been so subtle that many teachers today do not realize what they are teaching. Nevertheless, Mann's and Dewey's aims have been realized. The teaching of right and wrong is largely absent from school curricula today.

The gradual encroachment of humanist philosophies in our schools has placed emphasis on the self, diminished focus on core academics, and encouraged an entitlement mentality and general moral decay. The attitude of getting as many benefits as possible for as little effort as possible has proliferated in our society. These attitudes, encouraged by inflated self-importance, have fostered a diminished work ethic and resulted in a nation dependent on government.

Most Americans believe that today's classrooms are free of religious instruction. They are not. They are free of Christian moral instruction, but the secular humanism incorporated into many widely used educational materials has been declared a religion by the Supreme Court.

The field of education has moved far from its original goal of moral instruction in basic topics. Parents are now only marginally involved in decisions about their children's education. Concern surrounding this topic has fueled the move to private schools, Christian schools, and home schooling. As an initial step to counteract the problem of secular humanism in public education, we can increase parental involvement in curriculum selection and development.

12.4 | Godless Philosophies: Setting the Stage

BEGINNING shortly after the turn of the nineteenth century, the great bankers and financiers of Europe sought to harness the bounty of America. Their organization worked under the Rothschild banner to establish two successive central banks in the United States.[9]

These men put in motion a plan to control the American economy and eliminate competition—which, by default, would introduce the principles of secular humanism into America. This course of action, which works against the inalienable right of man's freedom, must have originated with the great adversary of liberty—Lucifer. Implementing it involved several major steps.

First, our free-market economy had to be disrupted. In a free economy, people trade: "I give you money; you give me goods." Both buyer and seller are satisfied. Under the socialism arising from secular humanism, which advocates government control of all property, the federal government controls transactions through regulations, if not outright ownership.[10]

Second, our moral values as a nation had to be degraded. Moral people reverence God, not themselves, as humanism advocates. Prayer and instruction about God were removed from schools.[11] The entertainment industry sullied our language, perverted our sexual standards, and immersed us in violence. Our music became dissonant and tuneless, its lyrics obscene.[12] We work less and play more. Materialism and vanity distract us.

Third, Americans had to be misled. Destructive policies are commonly enacted in secret. The news media is responsible to keep Americans informed on these matters of public interest. It has failed to do so. News has become entertainment, frequently devoid of necessary information. Trivial events occupy people's attention, while critical matters go unheralded. It is hard to discover and discuss information necessary to make wise choices.

Fourth, political correctness had to introduce national embarrassment into American politics and society. Political correctness teaches that defending what is right or true is unacceptable because individuals or groups might be offended. However, while some favored groups and people must never be criticized, others can be disparaged at will. Often, those who offend long-held social values are not expected to change or apologize, while those who adhere to these values, if they take offense, are blamed for being offended. They are expected to conform to accepted opinions and to compromise their principles.

Godless philosophies flourish in a climate of fear that obscures the good in our world. The media, largely controlled by those who hold humanist beliefs, endlessly air events and circumstances that generate fear. People feel unsafe and cling to a paternalistic government for reassurance.

On the other hand, humanism has difficulty taking root among people who feel safe and content. Faith—the opposite of fear—is the mark of a people who respect God. Faith in people and events leads us to expect what is good—to hope. Charity, or love for others expressed in action, follows. The scriptures group faith, hope, and charity to demonstrate a pleasant progression from belief to expectation to action. God reassures us that life is good and that well-being is our natural gift. "For God hath not given us the spirit of fear; but of power, and of love, and of a sound mind" (2 Timothy 1:7).

We reject godless humanist philosophies. We must live Christian values and teach them to our children. Our homes can be places of peace. Each of us can choose faith over fear.

12.5 | Godless Philosophies:
      | Our Government Today

OUR FLIRTATION with secular humanism and socialism, the political
system which advocates its beliefs, has changed America's
perception of what government is responsible to do. The distinctions
between liberty and policies that violate liberty have become blurred.

When socialism is aided by misguided elected representatives, it is
known as democratic socialism. W. Cleon Skousen, noted constitutional
authority, discussed this fact, using a quotation from de Tocqueville.

*The fascinating aspect of democratic socialism is that while the people
lose their inherent freedoms in exchange for . . . security, they think
they still have their freedom because they get to choose their leaders
at the polls . . .*

*Very gradually the economic and political choices of the people are
circumscribed by a network of regulations, rituals and rules which
the people begin to accept as the normal pattern of life. Thus, the
people lose their freedom without ever realizing exactly when it
happened.*

*"It [democratic socialism] covers the surface of society with a network
of small, complicated rules, minute and uniform, through which
the most original minds and the most energetic characters cannot
penetrate . . . The will of man . . . [is] seldom forced by it to act,
but . . . [is] constantly restrained from acting. Such a power does
not destroy, but it prevents existence; it does not tyrannize, but it
compresses . . . extinguishes and stupefies a people, till [the] nation
is reduced to be nothing better than a flock of timid and industrious
animals, of which the government is the shepherd."*

Of course this does not go on forever, because eventually the bribery, cheating, conniving and internal conspiratorial forces operating in such a system initiate a cancerous rot of social self-destruction. That is when a nation either disintegrates or generates sufficient fire in its soul to reach up once more for the glory of the past.[13]

This sobering description hits uncomfortably close to home. America teeters on the brink of democratic socialism.

The federal welfare system has been a major pathway to bring socialist, or secular humanist, philosophy into our national life.[14] Socialism's redistribution of wealth has created federal dependence, and it can also infuse the lust for power into those who direct such programs. Power is a seductive master, and the ability to compel others to action can go to the heads of ordinary people.

The federal welfare program is a compulsory charity—one to which we are forced to give. The federal government takes from the middle class (and from the rich who neglect to shelter their wealth from federal taxation). It bestows goods alike on the needy and those who masquerade as needy. Fraud frequently spoils the integrity of the programs, among both recipients and administrators. Once entrenched, the system is difficult to dislodge.

Assistance to the truly needy is important, but it must not create dependence on government. Our founding document forbids government from plundering some in order to bestow goods upon others. With serious, committed effort and strength of will, we can find the means to restructure our welfare system. If we benefit the truly needy and assist those capable of supporting themselves to do so, we will elevate our national character. That increased moral stature will enlarge our freedoms. Americans can do difficult things. Delay will only prolong our discomfort.

	Misuse of Constitutional
12.6	Amendments: A Wise
	Amendment

A SECOND destructive force against the Constitution is the misuse of constitutional amendments, as discussed.[15] The Framers wisely provided a previously unknown means to adjust our political system. Their process operates cautiously to prevent capricious changes, since each amendment modifies the entire system. While the first ten amendments were essential, many of the remaining seventeen are troublesome and might wisely be overturned.

Honorable individuals have proposed the Liberty Amendment as a possible approach to restore some of the freedoms of the original Constitution.

It originated with Willis E. Stone, a journalist concerned by encroaching federal powers. He researched and succeeded in getting the amendment introduced in the House of Representatives in 1959. It is nonpartisan and nonpolitical, driven by ordinary people to wrestle their state and local governments from federal usurpation.

The Liberty Amendment reads:

Section 1
The Government of the United States shall not engage in any business, professional, commercial, financial or industrial enterprise except as specified in the Constitution.

Section 2
The constitution or laws of any State, or the laws of the United States, shall not be subject to the terms of any foreign or domestic agreement which would abrogate [abolish] this amendment.

Section 3
The activities of the United States government which violate the intent and purposes of this amendment shall, within a period of three years from the date of ratification of this amendment, be liquidated and the properties and facilities shall be sold.

Section 4
Three years after the ratification of this amendment the Sixteenth...
Amendment to the Constitution of the United States shall stand
repealed and thereafter Congress shall not levy taxes on personal
incomes, estates and/or gifts.

This drafted amendment addresses taxation, international interference, and competing government businesses that siphon commerce from private businesses into bureaucracies. With few exceptions, federal projects are more expensive, less efficient, and of inferior quality to those of the private sector.

Additionally, this amendment would shrink government and dramatically decrease taxes. Bureaucratic jobs lost could be absorbed by revitalized private enterprise. Funds from the sale of government businesses could reduce the national debt. Needs addressed by Social Security, Medicare, federal finance programs, and federal departments such as transportation would be met better and more economically in the private sector.

With the repeal of the graduated income tax, every citizen would receive, in effect, an equivalent pay raise. Additional income, smaller federal government, and reduced regulation would create plentiful jobs in a thriving economy and revitalize our free enterprise system. This happened under the original Constitution.

Because many political, business, and financial entities benefit from the current system, the Liberty Amendment has lain idle in Congress, but it is viable and sound. Nine states have passed resolutions in favor of it. Reintroduced in Congress in 2003, 2007, and 2009, this amendment is just one example of legislation to eliminate bureaucratic and economic bondage. In addition, the actions of Willis Stone prove that one individual can make a difference. It would be wise to encourage your elected representatives to support this or a similar amendment.

12.7 | Supreme Court Decisions: Judicial Review

THE THIRD destructive change to the Constitution involves decisions of the Supreme Court. Unconstitutional decisions have come about through the process of judicial review. Under judicial review, the courts evaluate acts of the president and Congress to be sure that they adhere to the Constitution.

The Supreme Court established judicial review in 1803. Chief Justice John Marshall set the precedent in a case judged between outgoing president John Adams and incoming president Thomas Jefferson.

Because the Framers had no pattern for the court system they created, their system was not fully formed with appropriate checks and balances. President Jefferson requested an amendment to correct the omissions. His request was ignored, to our detriment.

Under the original Constitution, judicial review worked well. Supreme Court justices struck down any law or act that did not comply strictly with the Constitution. Personal opinions did not influence their decisions. Under this watchful oversight, the Constitution was safe from distortions and changes and remained firm, protecting the integrity of our political system.

Time and individuals with questionable ethics have compromised judicial review and the integrity of the high court. Rulings gradually began to follow the opinions of the justices or society at large. Like ceaseless storms beating against stone, these unwise decisions have eroded the Constitution. The document Americans ratified in 1787 is no longer our legal standard. Court judgments have made basic changes to government without the consent of elected representatives or the people. This is unconstitutional. This body, formed to guarantee constitutional law, has done much to demolish it.

Various excuses attempt to justify the irresponsibility of the Supreme Court. Some declare that the Constitution is deliberately vague to permit modern adaptations. It is not vague. Our national charter is clear and simple. It is a document of unchanging human nature. The principles behind the Constitution must remain unchanged as well.

Some claim that the Founders intended these adaptations to be made over time. The Framers did allow for minor adjustments in the Constitution, but only through the amendment process. Only the states or Congress can amend the Constitution. Only the Legislature has authority to make new laws. The Supreme Court is not authorized to do so.

Some claim the changes have not really altered the Constitution. This is obviously untrue. The media has failed in its responsibility to create public awareness of Supreme Court actions that alter our government.

Two hundred years of faulty judicial review have injured our Constitution. Today's professors of law are often unaware that judicial review was not included in the original Constitution. New attorneys frequently emerge from law universities untrained to revere our founding document.

Changes made to the Constitution to gratify the wishes of society or to showcase the justices' opinions violate their oaths to the people. To capriciously change our national contract of freedom is tantamount to changing the scriptures so as to alter God's commandments. In the book of Proverbs, we read: "The just man walketh in his integrity" (Proverbs 20:7). This is what we ask of our Supreme Court justices: that they abide by their constitutionally assigned responsibilities to interpret law rather than create it. We ask that they act with integrity.

We can restore our Constitution and restructure our Supreme Court to demand integrity in judicial review. We need the necessary legislation to do so.

12.8 | Supreme Court Decisions: A Fixed Standard

MANY BELIEVE that the Constitution should adapt to a changed world. Our modern Supreme Court embraces this attitude. Making changes from the judicial bench, however, is fundamentally unethical.

The Constitution is a contract between government and the people. When two parties have signed a contract, its terms cannot be changed by anyone without the knowledge and consent of the parties involved.

Consider these examples of the damage done when a contract changes terms. An individual who has contracted to buy a home is notified that the bank has changed the terms of the contract, and he now owes three hundred dollars more each month on his mortgage payment. A mother signs a contract with her son's orthodontist, who then alters it to read that he is responsible only for installation of the braces and not for their maintenance or removal. A printer is purchased with a three-year warranty, but when the warranty is needed, the buyer is informed that the company no longer honors the warranty.

A contract must maintain its terms in order to protect the rights of the signers. The contract between government and the governed—the people of the United States—is no different. Changes made must be carefully considered and agreed to by all parties. Allowing the Supreme Court to alter our national contract without our approval through its interpretations is like allowing a third party to alter a contract we have already signed. The Constitution is a fixed standard against which all of our rights are measured. Fixed standards govern our world. A standard that changes is useless and even dangerous.

The entire world operates on Coordinated Universal Time, maintained on a carefully guarded clock in Greenwich, England. Every business, transportation schedule, and human endeavor on our planet ultimately measures itself against the clock at Greenwich. Consider the consequences if that clock was changed, especially without public notification. Gradual shifts in individual timepieces would leave the entire world without the knowledge of what time it was. Confusion would rule, schedules would be useless, planes and trains would collide, missed deliveries would be routine, and medical errors would increase as the effects compounded. A standard is essential to keep accurate time.

One pound is exactly sixteen ounces. This measurement is kept and protected by the federal government, as assigned in the Constitution. If the government changed that measure to fifteen ounces this year and seventeen ounces a decade later, we would have widespread confusion. Every business that uses ounce measurements would flounder. A set standard for weights and measures is vital.

Our world depends on set standards to maintain accuracy. They protect us from those who might change the measures and cheat us. Set standards give dependability to our transactions. We can establish schedules for the present and accurately plan for the future because we have set standards.

The Constitution is our set standard for government. It is not a temporary document contrived from shallow theories. God gave it to us through the wisdom of inspired and prepared men. The Constitution brings together solid political principles that have been yearned for, spoken of, and written about by the great men of past centuries. We have the good fortune to live under its freedoms.

We must not allow anyone to change it without our express consent.

<table>
<tr><td>12.9</td><td>Supreme Court Decisions:
Unconstitutional Changes</td></tr>
</table>

S UPREME COURT decisions create law through the interpretations they render. Their decisions are given the power to amend the Constitution, violating our political charter. Only Congress and the states are authorized to amend our Constitution.

Some Americans welcome a powerful national government. They want the benefits it awards to some individuals. The social programs of big government do award "goodies" as gifts to the people. Their supporters fail to realize that the money for these giveaways comes from their own pockets. They fail to see that they have traded freedom for meager benefits. The damage done is far greater than any benefit gained.

We have discussed usurpations of power through Supreme Court decisions. Each decision has led to additional court decisions and hundreds of abuses of power. Some of these court decisions are summarized here.

As part of President Franklin D. Roosevelt's New Deal, the Supreme Court ruled on the 1936 *Butler* case. Though the case concerned an agricultural issue, the Court's ruling created a new federal power. Its interpretation of the general welfare clause empowered the federal government to introduce social programs and giveaways for all or some of its citizens. Under the original Constitution, government protected its citizens from foreign interference and put a basic structure of services in place—that was all. Today's bloated federal welfare bureaucracy, funded by our tax dollars, began with this interpretation by the Supreme Court of the *Butler* case. The judgment of the justices amended the Constitution without authority.

The commerce clause in the Constitution gave the federal government jurisdiction over trade between the states. Through a series of Supreme Court decisions, the commerce clause has expanded to include almost any physical activity in the nation. Rather than just goods that cross state boundaries, all goods—even what is grown and consumed on a family farm—fall under federal control. Any method of transportation for goods, which also includes communication, falls under federal control. Almost every object produced in the United States or that enters the country now falls under federal jurisdiction. The Founders did not intend these developments, but Supreme Court decisions made them law.

The Supreme Court's interpretation of the Fourteenth Amendment now allows the federal government to control state and local matters. They have extended the federal Bill of Rights to the states. In an earlier decision, the Supreme Court had ruled that the Bill of Rights did not pertain to state and local governments. It was a restriction on the federal government only. This followed the intent of the Founders.

Through a series of later decisions, the court reversed this position and gave national government power to supervise, and thus control, the policies of states and communities. The federal government now makes local government decisions from Washington, D.C. This has changed the balance of power in government, degrading the authority of the states.

Natural laws underlie the Constitution. Men cannot simply create any law they want, because good laws rest on a foundation of natural, or inalienable, rights. Laws that do otherwise can neither endure nor create freedom. The renowned Roman statesman Cicero called true law "right reason." He was correct.

<table>
<tr><td>12.10</td><td>Decline in Public Virtue: American Morality</td></tr>
</table>

AMERICANS have lost their liberty because so many have abandoned noble moral standards. Only moral people can be trusted with freedom in government. Benjamin Franklin said: "Only a virtuous people are capable of freedom. As nations become corrupt . . . they have more need of masters."[16] To understand our loss of freedoms, we must examine our virtues as a people.

Troublesome statistics confront us. The information that follows, gleaned from various websites in February 2012 in order to be as current as possible, serves as a moral report card for America.

There are 1.37 million abortions performed in the United States each year, with 64 percent performed on never-married women and 20 percent performed on teenagers.[17]

Pornography has become a huge business, with 12 percent of total Internet websites dedicated to it. Twenty-five percent of all search engine requests on an average day are for pornography sites. Almost 43 percent of Internet users view pornography, and 80 percent of fifteen- to seventeen-year-olds have had multiple exposures to hard-core pornography. Pornography produces over thirteen billion dollars in revenue yearly in the United States.[18]

Dishonesty in taking tests is rampant among students. Fifty percent say that they think it is "no big deal." Two in three students copy the homework of friends, and 80 percent of top students cheat on tests. By comparison, in the 1940s, only 20 percent admitted to cheating on high school tests.[19]

Family debt skyrockets as more families live beyond their means. The average debt approaches five thousand dollars each for every man, woman, and child in the country. One in three families describe their debt situation as hopeless or precarious. Less than one in four are free of debt. Fifty-two percent of families attribute their precarious financial standing to poor management. The typical family has thirteen credit cards. Minimum payments made at the current rate of interest will require twenty-five years for a family to pay off its credit card debt if no new debt is added.[20]

We have embraced greater materialism. Our homes grow larger, despite a decrease in family size. We now own almost one television set per person in the country. The number of shopping malls has increased nationwide by two-thirds since 1985. The average person now adds forty-eight new items of apparel each year to his or her wardrobe.

These sobering statistics indicate that, collectively, Americans have lost their moral base as they have embraced materialism, promiscuity, dishonesty, and irresponsible behavior toward others.

These are not the statistics of a virtuous people prepared to handle freedom. They paint the picture of a people without an inner moral compass who are in need of masters. The federal government is anxious to comply.

The ancient prophet Job described virtue to us. "As God liveth ... while my breath is in me ... my lips shall not speak wickedness, nor my tongue utter deceit . . . Till I die I will not remove mine integrity from me" (Job 27:5). Job could have been trusted with freedom in government. When we individually embrace Job's integrity, we can also be trusted with freedom.

12.11 | Decline in Public Virtue: Religious Worship

THE AMERICAN CONSTITUTION was written, ratified, and implemented during a time of strong moral virtue. That period continued for well over one hundred years. Exceptional prosperity came from the combination of moral citizens and a political document of personal liberty through limited government.

Early colonists regularly attended services to worship Christianity's God. Integrity, virtuous relationships, and clean language were the common expectation. Children naturally learned moral values. They heard Bible stories from infancy at home.

The Bible was the colonial textbook—often the only book in colonial homes. Children learned to read and write from its pages. Families gathered regularly to read together, and individuals searched its pages daily. The version read by early Americans was the Geneva Bible, with its marginal commentaries on a wide variety of practical matters. The Bible provided answers to the daily events of life.

Many of our Founders were deeply Christian and formed Bible study groups. These men included Benjamin Rush, a signer of the Declaration of Independence who began America's first Sunday School organization, and orator and statesman Rufus King, who signed the Constitution. John Jay, the first Supreme Court chief justice, also formed a Bible study group.[21]

The Bible shaped political views on topics that ranged from welfare and abolition of slavery to land management and separation of powers. Early presidents talked about God, religion, and morality in personal and official writings. President Washington said in his Farewell Address: "Of all the dispositions and habits which lead to political prosperity, religion and morality are indispensable supports. In vain would that man claim . . . patriotism who should . . . subvert these great pillars of human happiness."[22]

We have drifted far from those religious standards, and we have lost our political freedoms in proportion to our moral drift.

Religious worship in America has declined substantially. A respected Christian research organization recently found that 40 percent of Americans today go more than a month without attendance at a religious service, and 23 percent of American adults attend church less than once a year.[23] Some churches have embraced secular humanism and its agenda of social activism. In these churches, the worship of man has replaced the worship of God. The Sabbath, no longer holy, is a day for national athletic contests. Businesses and recreation facilities are often busiest on Sundays. Apparently, God is unimportant or unknown to many people.

Citizens and churches ignore God's commandments to care for the poor, the widows, and the fatherless. The needy rely on the federal government, whose unwise charity leaves them idle and dependent.

God is outlawed from schools and public places. Filthy words and ideas are the common language in school hallways and entertainment venues. Revealing clothing is commonplace. Tables and benches in public places are chained to nearby trees to prevent theft. Graffiti defaces public monuments and buildings. Too many public officials are no longer honest, exemplary men, and half of all American babies born to mothers under age thirty enter fatherless homes.[24]

We can change society and government by changing ourselves. The transformation begins with each person who makes a commitment to increase personal virtue and encourages others to follow. We will restore America's freedom as we restore our moral foundation.

12.12 | Decline in Public Virtue:
      | Morality in Government

A VIRTUOUS GOVERNMENT is a free and prosperous government. The original Constitution remained sound and unchanged while the American people remained morally strong.

Samuel Adams, who began American independence in 1764 from the rostrum in Boston's Faneuil Hall, connected virtue and liberty. "While the people are virtuous, they cannot be subdued; but . . . once they lose their virtue, they will be ready to surrender their liberties to the first external or internal invader . . . [Yet] if virtue and knowledge are diffused among the people, they will never be enslaved. This will be their great security."[25]

His cousin John Adams agreed: "Statesmen . . . may plan and speculate for liberty, but it is religion and morality alone, which can establish the principles upon which freedom can securely stand . . . Religion and virtue are the only foundation . . . of all free governments."[26]

A government without virtue or integrity cannot govern fairly and preserve the inalienable rights of its citizens. When government and its people follow the same wise standards, freedom and prosperity abound. Virtuous people tell the truth, keep their word, and honor their commitments. Moral people who are honest and live the Golden Rule produce prosperity. Our concepts of right and wrong come from our virtue, and without virtue there is little use for truth.

Moral government must also tell the truth. A government that deceives its people and breaks its promises will inevitably fall. Government, as well as people, must know right from wrong and live those principles.

Systems of totalitarian government disrespect morals, integrity, and individuals. As an example, Soviet leaders created worldwide havoc in the last century. Lenin, their early leader, urged his followers: "Be prepared to resort to every possible . . . subterfuge, trick, illegal device calculated to conceal the truth."[27] The actions of Stalin, his successor, demonstrated this philosophy well. Life under a political system that ignores morality is ugly.

Other governments sometimes operate with force. They pass laws that make people do or not do what government wants, without regard to the inalienable rights of citizens. Many otherwise rational people tolerate compulsion from government that they would not accept in their personal lives.

We sometimes sanction governmental control (usually over others, rarely over ourselves) in the belief that we must make people do what is right. God does not force us to do what is right. He gives us correct principles and allows us to govern ourselves. This is Cicero's "right reason." The Golden Rule is the basis of government. We do to others only what we want others to do to us, politically and personally. Government should not do what the people themselves cannot do.

Politics and morality often seem at odds with each other, but they are not natural enemies. Government can maintain virtue, and leaders can act with integrity. The same rules that apply to government also apply in all areas of human involvement.

Mark Levin, author of *Ameritopia,* said it well: "When virtue is gone, the republic is gone."[28] So did Solomon: "When the wicked . . . rule, the people mourn" (Proverbs 29:2).

We can require integrity from elected representatives. We can hold them accountable, remove them from office when necessary, and replace them with those who will uphold moral principles. When we do, our prosperity under the Constitution will increase.

12.13 | Decline in Public Virtue: Entitlement Mentality

AN ENTITLEMENT mentality has swept America and the world. An ever-expanding number of people believe that they are entitled to goods and services that they need not work to earn. This attitude has unsettled our society. Since before civilization began, people have understood that they are responsible to earn the goods that feed, clothe, and house them. God explained this to Adam and Eve before they left the Garden of Eden: "In the sweat of thy face shalt thou eat bread, till thou return unto the ground" (Genesis 3:19).

Some will always have more of the world's goods, and some will have less. Individuals vary, the marketplace shifts, and public needs and fancies come and go. These change the success and profitability of livelihoods. The Declaration of Independence does not promise equality of goods and lifestyles. It promises the equal opportunity of freedom.

Some believe that they deserve a certain standard of living regardless of what they do, or do not do, to earn it. This is the entitlement mentality, fostered by secular humanism.[29] It comes from experimentation with a caretaker government that makes our decisions, solves our problems, and tries to make us equal in "stuff."

President Grover Cleveland, our twenty-second president,[30] was outspoken about the role of government: "I can find no warrant for such an appropriation [fixing all our problems] in the Constitution, and I do not believe that the power and duty of the General Government ought to be extended to the relief of individual suffering . . . Though the people support the government, the government should not support the people."[31]

This dependence is fostered by Godless philosophies that rob us of the guidance of morality and integrity. Combined, these forces have led us into entitlement. Whole segments of society believe that they cannot take care of themselves and rely on the labors of others to feed and clothe them.

It is now impossible to live in normal society without feeling the impact of the welfare state. Even the employed accept government handouts in the form of tax breaks, benefits, and "freebies" for which they have paid with their own tax money. It seems logical to take advantage of them. The tentacles of federal dependence reach everywhere.

While the concept of modern welfare professes compassion, its outcome is not compassionate. Federal funds support some who choose not to work. Mistakes and fraud are rampant as those who work pay to support those who will not. Usurping the rights of the employed, these individuals live according to false precepts. They do not learn the law of cause and effect. Those who labor learn the lesson of the Little Red Hen: "He who does not work does not eat." Those who receive welfare unfairly learn this principle differently: "He who does not work eats the bread of him who does."

Not all of the massive amounts of federal funding given to help the needy reach them. A paid bureaucracy administers these federal programs from Washington, D.C. Many of these funds finance an industry devoted to poverty, with social networks and businesses that cater exclusively to welfare programs.

As a society, we are responsible for the defective lessons we have taught to generations of federal welfare recipients. It is time to change. There are just and honest ways to care for the deserving poor.

12.14 | Decline in Public Virtue: Moral Welfare

GOD has better help for the poor than federal welfare. The Founders of early America practiced wise public assistance through their churches. Their system illuminates our way back to healthy charity. Colonists understood charity as a charge from God and preached it regularly from Christian pulpits. It began with the family. Husbands, wives, and children pooled their resources to assist each other, along with the extended family when needed. When the family had exhausted its resources, the community stepped in.

Sound principles—firm, but kindly—guided colonial compassion. Charity was locally administered and addressed basic human nature. It was a personal process—not the impersonal giving of money, but a commitment of action and immediately usable goods. Both givers and receivers were neighbors and friends, which encouraged accountability. The givers supervised as the recipients used the assistance wisely.

Moral behavior was a prerequisite for assistance. Early Americans did not share our modern reluctance to dictate standards to recipients of charity. The morality of one affected the liberty of all, so charity was part of the moral principle of right and wrong. Those who drank to excess, broke the law, or gambled were taught moral principles to reform them. Nor did the colonials accept our modern belief that all people want to work—that unemployment comes from lack of opportunity to rise from adverse circumstances and that society is to blame for neediness. Those who refused to work were compelled to do so.

Early Americans were "hard-headed but warm-hearted."[32] They offered opportunities, not blind charity. They believed that most people, if given the choice, would choose idleness. Those who received assistance did not have that choice—they worked for what they received. Colonists viewed those who gave assistance unwisely as transgressors of divine principles. Compassion was temporary, and it aimed at teaching future independence through mastery of a skill. Personal responsibility was mandatory.

To those unable to work, early Americans freely and kindly extended care for the time needed. They took orphans, the impaired, the bedridden, and the elderly into their private homes. The entire church congregation contributed a modest stipend for their care.

Benjamin Franklin explained England's public assistance in the mid-1700s: "I am for doing good for the poor, but I differ in . . . the means . . . The best way of doing good to the poor, is not making them easy in poverty, but leading or driving them out of it . . . The more public provisions were made for the poor, the less they provided for themselves, and of course became poorer . . . The less was done for them, the more they did for themselves, and became richer . . . You offered a premium for the encouragement of idleness, and you should not now wonder that it has had its effect in the increase of poverty."[33]

Thomas Jefferson described charitable assistance in the colonies. Trustworthy men in the congregation evaluated and oversaw funds given for assistance. "Vagabonds" were put into poorhouses, where they were cared for and required to work. He explained that throughout the Americas, "you will seldom meet a beggar."[34]

The colonists practiced wise compassion. The United States government does not. Our first step to improve the system is to bring welfare back to the local level, where we can supervise and refine it. There we can make it personal.

12.15 | Decline in Public Virtue: Distraction

Prosperity is the natural result of a solid work ethic and moral strength. With prosperity comes the opportunity for leisure and entertainment. In moderation, these refresh us; in excess, they damage our freedom by diverting our attention from things that matter.

Entertainment, when used unwisely, creates idleness, which reverses the prosperity from which it rose. America is trapped in this cycle. We ride on the coattails of prosperity from a century ago. Many have discarded the work ethic that brought us success and instead embrace lethargy and continual entertainment. Such is the perpetual cycle that so often defeats success—we struggle to maintain that which has brought us greatness.

Early Americans had little entertainment. They worked long and hard for food and shelter, and the entertainment they created often revolved around more work—barn raisings, crop harvests, and feast days were their recreation. Their hardships spared them the distractions of idleness.

To fill our idle hours, we have turned increasingly to social media, online gaming, music, reality shows and sports. Little of long-term worth comes from idle online chitchat, beating the odds on a computer screen, discordant music or watching grown men crash into each other on a grassy field. As these activities take center stage, our liberties quietly dissipate.

Substantial entertainment profits have muddled the values of the media and invited corruption and perversion. Power and profits accumulate as the media glamorize violence, incivility, and immorality. Vices are presented so attractively and subtly that we brush them aside with no sense of disgust. Children and youth are programmed to accept self-interest, promiscuity, and crime as reasonable and even desirable lifestyles. The entertainment industry has become a tool to distract and pollute our values. As our values slide, so does our liberty. Freedom and morality are branches on the same tree, and anything that disparages our values leads us into political bondage.

Our common moral standards have been influenced by ongoing Supreme Court decisions concerning the First Amendment right of free speech. Our Founding Fathers drafted this freedom to protect us from government oppression. Today, amid declining morals, we labor to define obscenity and to determine what should and should not be allowed under the banner of free speech. Supreme Court decisions have imposed broad leeway in moral standards, licensing the entertainment industry to peddle rubbish.[35] This reinforces our national need for a means to subject the Court's decisions to some form of review.

These problems ultimately result from our declining integrity. Our entertainment media would stop producing objectionable materials if no one bought them. The fact that the media continue to present these dubious offerings proves that public sales make them profitable. We will continue to struggle with base and offensive entertainment until we reinstate strong principles of right and wrong in our individual and family lives.

In the meantime, we can elevate our entertainment standards and refuse to participate in activities with little redeeming value. We can register our dislike of value-devoid entertainment at the ticket booth and checkout register. We can invest our time in the better things in life, rather than the mediocre and wasteful. We can request that states exercise their options to encourage quality entertainment within their borders, as allowed by the Tenth Amendment. Surprising innovations could emerge from state efforts.

12.16 | Decline in Public Virtue: Apathy—and Hope

A MAJOR REASON for the destructive changes to our freedom document is apathy. Americans are often indifferent and do not want to get involved. Their apathy takes many forms.

Some are voluntarily blind. Their world of personal events and interests forms a secluded bubble separating them from freedom's decline. They laugh at those who try to open their eyes and say that they "cry wolf" unnecessarily. To them, the problems are not real.

Some are asleep. No conflicts between freedom and oppression exist in their dreamlike world. They are impervious to events and the efforts of others to awaken them. They have always felt free; of course it will continue. They wish to be left alone on the topic.

Many are distracted. They are immersed in important or trivial things that press heavily on their time and attention. Yes, there are problems. Yes, they are important. Yes, something must be done. But someone else will have to fix it. They have too much to do; their time is too valuable.

Some do not care. The entire concept of freedom in jeopardy is an illusion. If it were true, the media or the military or *somebody* would tell us so. Those people who worry about freedom are just a bunch of "crazies." Ignore them, and the problem will go away.

Some see the problems and are concerned. They want them fixed, but it is just too upsetting to think about. The topic makes them depressed, so they ignore it for their own well-being. They would prefer that you not bring the topic to their attention.

Finally, some do not really want the problems fixed. They want the government "goodies." Give the federal government all the power it wants, and bring those benefits on! Who cares about the freedoms lost? What difference does it make, anyway? It's not going to affect them. They just want to watch the ballgames and reality shows on TV and hang out with friends.

***

More and more Americans have awakened to the seriousness of our national situation. They talk to each other about their concerns. They discuss solutions and question sources of information. They watch current events intently and look for the real stories behind the scenes.

These Americans now scrutinize elected officials carefully. More good people run for office. They get involved in local and regional politics and contact their elected representatives with opinions. Concerned Americans form groups across the country to study, work, and share to restore freedom and welcome back prosperity.

Public prayers more often mention freedom and liberty as we pray for leaders and country. Parents teach their children about freedom and question schoolteachers about their curricula.

Americans are waking up. Hope has begun to sing its beautiful song throughout the country. A renewed spirit wafts in the breezes that float our Stars and Stripes.

Patriots gave their lives, their fortunes, and their sacred honor for American liberty. We should do no less. We began as a free country, and we will, with effort, stay a free country. America may be shackled at present, but those chains will soon be broken. Apathy is not our national spirit—action is. Freedom is not free. We have to work for it. We are ready.

Section Thirteen

─────────────── ❧ ───────────────

FOUR ACTIONS TO REGAIN OUR ORIGINAL FREEDOMS

THE UNITED STATES OF AMERICA has lost much of its liberty. We have reached the danger point in the erosion of our inalienable rights. Our losses escalate daily. Some fear that it is too late. It is not, but we must act now.

God is an economical being. He works in eternal ways. He has invested centuries of individual effort and commitment in our nation, and he will not abandon it. He will help us restore our freedoms if we show Him that we care and if we earn His intervention. We can save our beloved nation and our freedom document, but we must begin now. Our circumstances have progressed too far to do this difficult work of restoration alone. We must prove by our actions that freedom is important to us.

Americans have become aware of the seriousness of our situation. Many have begun to ask what can be done to right the ship of state. Organizations and causes have sprung up across the country.

Our focus must be on the basics of restoration: personal virtue, a knowledge of and love for the Constitution, and involvement in government. We have to supervise our elected officials. We must put our country ahead of ourselves—not in occasional, agitated outbursts of emotion, but in the sustained, steady dedication of a lifetime.

Our conversations with others about politics and government must be civil and persuasive. When we argue, we foster contention. God's Spirit departs when contention prevails.

The four actions we can take to restore the blessings of the Constitution are to align with God, to build strong families, to learn the principles that made America the greatest nation on earth, and to get involved in the governing process by casting informed ballots and continuously overseeing our elected officials. These actions will improve our cities, states, and nation. We will now study these in greater detail.

To restore our liberty under our original Constitution, we must have God's help. We must begin the work to earn His help. The longer we wait, the more freedoms we lose and the harder the task becomes.

13.1 | Simple Truths in the Constitution

"THE THINGS of God are always simple."

That statement from an otherwise unremembered church sermon of years ago rings true of our United States Constitution. It is a simple document, free of political monologues and extravagant flourishes—a few pages of print in normal type. Its abbreviated length hides the decades of thoughtful study, the years of political experience, and the months of intense discussion required to bring it to life.

It is the small and simple things that bring grand results. The United States Constitution has kept the ship of state afloat and viable for over two centuries. Our country is a vast conglomerate of peoples accumulated from many nations of the world. The Constitution is our instruction manual for the peaceful coexistence of this hubbub of humanity.

Hidden in the brevity of the Constitution are profound truths layered in a political organization of moral standards. Those who read the Constitution in the dialect of the Holy Spirit will learn that God testifies of its truth.

The uninformed could miss the handiwork of the fifty-five political masterminds who poured heart and soul into its principles. The uninitiated will marvel at the reverence bestowed upon the Constitution. Hundreds of millions of people throughout its 225-year history have pledged allegiance to the country it created.

While the principles themselves are simple, our ability to keep them alive is not always easy. Without firm guidance, our ship of state will break against the reefs. The unprincipled and the ignorant have begun to dismantle the Constitution. They do not see its worth or value its restraint. They chafe at its restrictions and reject the inspiration and studied investment of the Founders, whose divine stewardship led to a bold government for a bold new nation. They pick at its parts and disturb its balance. They rail at its deliberate structure and rue the wear and tear on the original. They want to replace it with a new, chic model. Those hungry for power anticipate that eventual outcome for our country.

Those who dismantle our powerful Constitution do so contrary to the will of God. He is not dissatisfied with the Constitution; man is. God has not asked that we replace or streamline it; man has. God designed, sanctioned, and verified it, and He has sustained it. There is no need for another.

Our generation has the privilege to defend the Constitution. The law of reciprocal effort is in force. The Constitution gave us freedom, and it is our duty and honor to restore it.

The work required of us is not extreme. There are no physical battles, no parades or marches in the streets. What we need to do remains well within the laws of the land, because any who take the law into their own hands break the law by their actions.

We are asked to do the simple things that bring about peace. These things are to be done within our homes and communities.

Our Founding Fathers dedicated their lives, their fortunes, and their sacred honor to the creation of America. We can do the work to return America to the glorious days she knew under the protection of the United States Constitution.

We will now discuss four ways to restore integrity and honor in government.

13.2 | Look to God for Freedom

THE FIRST of the four things we must do to qualify for God's help in the restoration of our Constitution is to look to God as the source of our freedoms.

God's efforts formed our nation and its Constitution. He has a great interest in our affairs and efforts. The United States has been chosen to be the flagship of freedom in the modern world. In America, we fought for freedom, made it real, and made a government to keep it. Our early citizens lived with freedom until our nation began to lose its way. Now we are at work to find the path of freedom again.

We need God's help to find that path. He is the author of liberty. He gives us the inalienable right of individual choice. He revealed the principles of free government thousands of years ago and kept them alive in the minds of great men until America was ready to employ them. He preserved the American continent and protected it until people were ready to endow its shores with liberty.

He is an all-knowing God of power and glory. John tells us in the book of Revelation that He is "king of kings and lord of lords" (Revelation 19:16). Those words have rung true through the centuries, and they are true now. This glorious God knows what must be done to restore freedom to the United States.

He is all-powerful, capable of all He sets His hand to. The prophet John praises Him: "Alleluja: for the Lord God omnipotent reigneth" (Revelations 19:6). Godless philosophies and destructive government policies will fall before His powerful hand.

He is all-loving and is no respecter of persons. He has no favorites. His only criteria to assist us are individual and national virtue. He tells us that He will protect us: "How often would I have gathered thy children together, even as a hen gathereth her chickens under her wings, and ye would not!" (Matthew 23:37). In this plea, we hear His longing to shield us from danger.

He is a God of government. Isaiah tells us: "The government shall rest upon His shoulders . . . Of the increase of His government and peace there shall be no end" (Isaiah 9:6–7). He offers His continually outstretched hand.

Surely this powerful, gracious, and loving God is able to restore America's government. What He gave originally, He can bring back.

Why has He not done so? He has not done so because we have not sufficiently asked, because we have not wanted it enough, because we have not yet earned it. When we pray, God listens. When we obey, God acts.

All that has gone wrong can change—in an instant for the individual, and in a short time for our nation. Many Americans watch our totalitarian drift with anguish. Their desire for our original freedoms can sweep this land with great speed when each of us commits to carry the message of liberty forward. We will reach those who are worried and concerned for America. We will invest ourselves to bring back our base of liberty.

It is to God that we can look for our peace under liberty. He invites us all to do so. Patriots will heed His call.

13.3 | Quality Family Life: Prayer

THE SECOND recommendation to preserve freedom is to create strong individuals and strong families.

The family is the most important element of society—the most basic unit of government. What happens in families determines what happens in the state and nation. When families are happy, secure, and gainfully employed, the nation is peaceful and prosperous.

Our national liberty depends on families that teach strong moral beliefs and healthy citizen behaviors. Only a virtuous people can maintain freedom. Those who destroy our freedoms undermine the family. Those who improve a nation work to build vibrant families.

Strength comes to a family that prays together. Parents can do nothing better than to pray together with their families morning and night. Family prayer is a bond that ties family members to each other and to God. The time spent each day in prayer together anchors the day and brings greater peace into the family. Love and cooperation grow between siblings. Prayer in the morning wraps God's protection around family members as they go out into the world. Prayer at night sends family members to bed with a sense of security.

Family prayer is a great teaching tool for children. As parents and grandparents pray, they convey the principles that really matter. As children hear their parents pray for important things, their values are strengthened, and lifelong lessons are ingrained. A mother who tells God in family prayer how much she loves her child leaves impressions on the child's heart that last a lifetime. A father who shares family goals with God in family prayer imprints those goals on his children's hearts. A child who learns to talk with God openly in the security of the family circle will be more secure and will honor God throughout life. All members of the family are uplifted as they communicate to God the successes and sorrows of the day. Family prayer is a time to recommit to family goals.

Prayer is a powerful tool for teaching children and grandchildren moral values such as patriotism. Children who hear parents pray for national leaders to be wise and moral will expect leaders to be wise and moral. When they reach voting age, they will use their ballots to select such leaders. Parents who pray for freedom encourage their children to value freedom. Children who hear parents thank God for His inspired Constitution will believe the Constitution is worthy of their study and protection.

Parents can also pray together as a couple. This practice unites parents in their goals and strengthens their partnership. They become a team of three that includes God. Cooperation increases, and each understands more fully his or her role in the parental unit.

Personal prayer is one of the most powerful forces in the universe. God loves us. He listens, He answers, and He respects the desires we carry in our hearts.

When we commit to pray in private, as couples, and as families, we can make a real difference in our country. We can pray for our prosperity and peace. We can pray for the restoration of our freedoms under the Constitution and for the return of limited government. We can pray for those who lead us, who make our laws, and who set our national standards.

Power comes into our lives and families when we pray together.

13.4 | Quality Family Life: Family Time Together

STRONG FAMILIES spend time together. Families can enjoy each other, even though every family has occasional bumps on the road to family harmony. Few things in life bring more satisfaction than the laughter and conversations of people who share family ties, commitments, and past memories.

Wise parents and grandparents look for opportunities to strengthen family ties through constructive activities. Families can build shared memories and have fun while participating in valuable lessons. We can combine time, instruction, and common values to create family time as a tradition in our homes.

Our families deserve quality time. Wise parents plan for and prioritize time together. Many families set a specific time during the week when the family takes priority over all else. This family time is dedicated to activities that draw the family closer and reinforce important values.

Family time can take many forms. It can be a time for games and fun foods. It can be attendance at one child's ball game or dance recital. A family work project, with teams that race to get the job done and root beer floats afterward, makes for fun family time. A picnic dinner and a drive to see the fall leaves draw the family closer. Family time can include helping an elderly neighbor, or taking turns weekly to share individual talents and interests with family members.

Family time is for parents to teach their children the things that matter. The world teaches many things of questionable value. It creates distractions for parents, who want more time with their families but always have other demands. When a family commits to spend a few hours together each week, free of distractions, family unity and family bonds improve. Love grows, and contentment improves. Parents feel peace as they focus on the most important things in life. Children know that their parents care about them.

Important concepts to teach during family time are lessons on faith in God, the benefits of prayer, and commitment to keep God's commandments. Lessons can center on the importance of good grades in school, love for extended family members, and the joy of service to others. A lesson could even deal with the need for everyone to get their chores done on time.

Family time provides the perfect opportunity for families to study principles of virtue in government. Parents and children can learn the history, divine guidance, and freedom principles behind and within the Constitution. Family time creates the opportunity to read and discuss together God's hand in the creation of the United States and its founding document. Current events provide important opportunities to examine values and discuss personal responsibility. Events of the day can be used to teach wise citizen involvement. The lives of our Founders offer beneficial moral instruction.

Prayer to open and close the occasion adds an extra dimension to the learning process, as does a treat at the end.

Strong families are the bedrock of society. Any political system that guarantees inalienable rights depends on families who are committed to personal and national virtue.

Anything that strengthens the family strengthens the nation and each of us as well. Family time held in individual families will help our nation remain free.

13.5 | Quality Family Life: Study God's Word

THE BIBLE is a persuasive collection of human virtues. These virtues are explained in the lives of the great figures revealed on its pages.

Our colonial forefathers had only the Bible from which to learn and to instruct their children. No other text was needed. Its stories included all the lessons of virtuous manhood and dedicated womanhood. We can wisely follow their lead and teach ourselves and our families the traits and beliefs of a moral, free society from the pages of the Bible.

These stories of greatness and staunch leadership are available to all of us. Job compels us to cultivate unfailing diligence and patience in the face of adversity. The lives of Abraham and Sarah show a committed marriage, strong family bonds that carry through generations, and the responsibilities of grandparents to their extended families. The story of Joseph sold into Egypt offers many lessons. It shows the hand of God as it operates through human foibles. It sets a pattern for forgiveness. Joseph's experience in Potiphar's house teaches us to flee from evil. We also learn that rewards for virtue come on God's timetable.

The story of Jonah teaches us what happens to those who evade responsibility. That of Daniel in the lion's den shows us faith and courage. Ruth's story teaches us kindness, as well as putting honorable priorities into action. Relations between Jacob and Esau show us the opposite perspectives of those who do and do not honor and value priorities. Rehoboam's reign helps us see the wisdom of age and the folly of those who ignore wisdom. From Esther, we learn of courage and sacrifice for the good of others.

These scriptural figures give us role models. In a world where virtuous role models are hard to find, these individuals illuminate a darkened road. Each of us who commit to live lives of goodness and integrity—adults and children alike—will face times in our lives when we have to stand alone against a crowd. When those times come, it helps to know that others have done the same. The notable characters of the Bible show us the way to deal with these problems.

Wise parents provide their children with armor against the adversary. Wise individuals strengthen themselves against assaults to their standards. As we read their stories, these Bible heroes become part of our lives and benefit us in important ways. Like friends in the flesh, their support gives us courage to do the hard things as we study their lives and emulate their virtues.

Make Bible stories the backbone of your family time. Any one of these stories could make an evening's lesson. The family can read together the scriptural account and discuss the story afterward. Young children can read the simple words. The scripture hero will come to life and will surface as a guide when needed in the future.

Individuals who pray to develop the qualities of their scripture heroes receive moral strength. As each person studies the scriptures and emulates the lives of great scriptural figures, our nation's freedoms increase. Ours is a collective effort. Only people of integrity and virtue can sustain freedom. Holy writ strengthens the moral code in all of us.

13.6 | Quality Family Life: Faith, Hope, and Charity

W<small>E CAN STRENGTHEN</small> our nation and receive divine help as we exercise our faith, activate our hope, and practice charity.

We must believe that it is possible to restore our Constitution and regain its original peace and prosperity. This requires faith. Then we must expect divine help. That expectation is hope. As we believe and expect change, we will step forward and do our part to make it happen. When we do so with kindness and love for others in the name of moral principles, we practice charity.

The great prosperity epoch of the United States would have been a wonderful time in which to live. The nation was vibrant and alive with industry. Creative ideas flowed from the minds of great inventors. Citizens were involved in their communities, jobs were plentiful, and families were stable and happy.

Our prosperity era began its sad decline in 1913 with the presidency of Woodrow Wilson. In one year, the state legislatures lost their representation in federal government, the federal government began to levy taxation on income, and control of our national economy was given to a group of private individuals. This was a national disaster of the first order.

Our faith, hope, and charity, as demonstrated by action, can repair the damage.

The Old Testament story of Esther shows faith, hope, and charity in action. Queen Esther faced a challenge that resembles our situation today. Her story reads like a modern movie script. It would make a stimulating and instructive family time lesson.

Raised by her cousin Mordecai, Esther won the heart of Ahasuerus, king of Persia and Media, and became his queen. Political intrigue brought Mordecai into conflict with Haman, the king's arrogant and ambitious underling. Haman used his position of influence to defame the Jews. He obtained approval to have all the Jews put to death—men, women, and children.

Esther became the hope of salvation for her people. Mordecai asked her to go before the king to plead for the Jews. He entreated her with these words: "Who knoweth whether thou art come to the kingdom for such a time as this?" (Esther 4:14).

Esther understood the seriousness of the threat to her people. She also knew that any individual who went before the king unbidden could be sentenced to death. She accepted the challenge but asked her people to help her. Esther instructed the Jews to fast with her and her maidens for three days prior to her approach to the king. Then she presented herself before Ahasuerus unbidden. His favorable response resulted in the salvation of the Jewish people. The evil Haman was hanged on the gallows constructed for Mordecai, and the Jewish people were saved from death.

Esther believed and expected to make a difference in behalf of her people. She then acted on her belief by using the spiritual tool of fasting—voluntary abstinence from food to gain spiritual strength—as her action step.

Faith, hope, and charity in action give us tools to make needed changes. The spiritual tool of fasting is available to us as well.

The United States stands at a crossroads. With these spiritual tools, we can correct our national course through decisive action.

13.7 | Study the Constitution, Teach It to Our Families

THE THIRD PRINCIPLE to earn God's help is to study and teach the Constitution and the sacrifices of the Founders to our families.

Few people study the Constitution. This is not because it is hard to study. It is a simple document, easily read in a pleasant hour. It is not difficult to understand, although the educational level of its writers is far above the levels of modern instruction.

We do not read the Constitution because we have forgotten that it matters. We take it for granted, just as we have taken our freedoms for granted. We can no longer afford the luxury of indifference. We must instill in the next generation a love for this founding document to keep it alive, viable, and active. Adults need to revive their love and understanding of the Constitution. If we do not defend it, we may lose it.

Sometimes we ignore the Constitution because we have accepted the philosophies of its enemies. Many voices influence our opinions on national policies. Each of us must carefully evaluate those who lead and who dispense information on government. The responsibilities of limited government are few. Government is to protect our lives, liberty, and property. It is to require that we do our duty but is not authorized to create new duties for us. It is responsible to punish us when, and only when, we violate our duties. That is all government should be responsible for. Once we understand, we can accurately evaluate the actions of government.

The original Constitution is taught in schools today more as a lesson in history than as a practical, workable system of government, and certainly not as a product of inspiration. The growing influence of secular humanism encourages our children to see the Constitution as flawed and outdated. The family may be the best source of accurate information on the Constitution.

We can set goals to review the Constitution frequently. Early Americans studied it regularly and deeply so that they could supervise their elected officials. We must do the same. We cannot supervise them properly without knowledge of the Constitution's principles and intent.

Wonderful family times await parents who teach their children about the Founding Fathers. Young people love hearing about the miracles of the Revolutionary War: the story of Henry Knox and the cannon from Ticonderoga, the fighting tale of old Sam Whittemore, the barricades that appeared overnight on Boston's Dorchester Hill, and many, many more.

Young people can learn compassion as they read of George Washington's sacrifice. He gave up sixteen years at his beloved Mount Vernon to fight the Revolutionary War and serve as our first president. Our children can read John Adams's powerful words in defense of freedom and independence. They can laugh at the description of Patrick Henry lifting and twirling his tattered wig when he got excited.

We can teach them about checks and balances, the separation and limitations of power, and the need for effective legislation to limit the Supreme Court. Youth can develop critical thinking skills through family discussions and prepare to become involved. Families can visit city council meetings, museums, and national history sites for family time activities.

Study of the Constitution will develop generations of patriots in America. Our country will thrive under their influence.

13.8 | **Get Involved: Local Efforts, National Effects**

THE FINAL VIRTUE necessary to restore freedom is to become involved in the process of government. Our wise votes are needed at every election. We must acquaint ourselves with candidates and platforms and select those best qualified to make the laws that rule us. We cannot leave their selection to chance or indifference.

The logical place to begin is at the local level. We must actively improve our communities, counties, and states. These efforts will have a national effect. As we receive training in the governing process, we can accept responsibilities at higher government levels if we choose.

Our personal virtue affects the nation. All movements begin with one person, and that one can make a difference if he or she is moral, diligent, and prayerful.

States can affect national policy as they test new ideas and programs. As provided by the Tenth Amendment, states are free to adapt, improvise, legislate, and conduct business that benefits their citizens. Fifty creative experimental laboratories operating cooperatively would find solutions for difficult local and national problems. Our world embraces new technologies, wider communication, worldwide travel, and the social challenges that accompany each. Our resourcefulness as a nation would multiply if we first addressed these challenges at the state level with imagination and ingenuity. All humanity would benefit.

The Seventeenth Amendment, which hobbled the states, denied us the discoveries of these experimental state laboratories. We will never know what creative solutions we might have had if strong states had operated to our collective advantage.

If we citizens become involved, we can energize local and state political affairs and influence representatives to restore balance in our political system. The change must begin with elected statesmen who uphold moral values rather than "the party line," the money trails, and the "good old boy" network. They must be individuals of good character who understand the purposes and principles of the Constitution and the intent of the Founders and who work to preserve them. They must be committed to God, not to men.

Many worthwhile organizations attract the efforts and attention of patriots. They should be properly screened for their true intent. Sometimes, well-intentioned individuals apply their efforts to the wrong things. Sincere individuals often propose alternatives that are as constitutionally inept as the problems they attempt to correct. When improperly structured, the cure can be worse than the disease. The Seventeenth Amendment is the classic example of just such a toxic solution.

Join with an organization whose mission is to restore our original Constitution. The first place to start is with the passage of necessary legislation to replace the Seventeenth Amendment. This will restore our checks and balances. Until they are restored, no other effort will have a permanent effect. Other unwise amendments can then be replaced, accompanied by action to prevent the Supreme Court from creating legislation through judicial decisions.

God will help restore our prosperity and freedoms as we become involved. He brought great individuals forward in the crises of 1776 and 1787. He is doing so again.

We are those people. We are being trained for the work He will bring about. We must ask for His help and follow His instructions. We cannot waste any more time.

14

We the People

insure domestic Tranquility, provide for the common and our Posterity, do ordain and establish this Con

Section Fourteen

------------------------------ ℃ℛ ------------------------------

THE VISION FOR AMERICA

WE HAVE DISCUSSED the Constitution from its ancestry to its future. We know that lives, fortunes, and sacred honor have been invested to create and preserve America's charter of freedom. Great dangers confront our country as the Constitution faces multiple assaults. We have pledged to help restore our past prosperity and virtue.

None who read this book have lived and done business in the robust free-enterprise system that was the hallmark of our original Constitution. Our downfall began in 1913—more than one hundred years ago. Our sorrowful retreat from freedom and virtue has been erratic. Some government administrations have inched in that direction, while others have rushed headlong to embrace socialism and secular humanism.

The political expediency of compromise has increased the speed of our descent. While compromise between two good forces is wise, compromise between good and evil, or between freedom and bondage, plunges us unfailingly toward serfdom. Our unfortunate choice has been between the latter options of freedom and bondage.

As we close our study, it is essential that we see the United States of America dressed again in the robes of freedom, protection, prosperity, and peace. To fully understand the present and the past, we must see the future—our lives as they will be when we again have our freedoms under the original Constitution. We must see the hope that waits for us.

The images that close this book are deliberately simple, perhaps even idyllic. Some people will find them too simplistic and therefore impossible. Liberty is possible. We can regain our freedoms and have the peace and plenty that are portrayed in the next few pages.

The task will not be easy. Powerful adversaries will move to stop us.

The strength of three great forces will be needed in this effort. First, we must be a virtuous people. Second, we must elect officials to Congress with the moral courage to restore our heritage. Finally, we must embrace God as our ally. His power surpasses all else. With Him on our side, we cannot fail.

14.1 | Economics

The economy of a nation and the liberty of its citizens are bound together. A sound economy will strengthen every family and make prosperity possible in each home.

When we return to our original Constitution, we will put our economy back under the control of our elected officials, as the Constitution intended. We will no longer be controlled by the demands of a private bank. As the means are found, we can retire the national debt and free ourselves of the interest payments that bleed our prosperity and our people.

With our money system back under Congress, we can eliminate inflation. We can balance available dollars with the goods and services available for purchase. When the dollar maintains its value for years to come, we will be free of the constant creep and occasional crescendo of inflation. Everyone will benefit.

Interest rates will stabilize. People will want to save and invest because the economy is predictable in the long term. Individuals, families, and businesses can become self-sufficient with stable, long term investments.

We can return to a banking system backed by precious metals. This will give us real money rather than the fabricated money that comes from fractional banking and a privately run money system

These policies, taken together, will stabilize our economy. We can plan wisely for the future and minimize the financial crises that knock families and businesses into bankruptcy.

We will pay few taxes. Government will shrink, and we will pay for our smaller government mostly with duties on imports and exports, The money paid in taxes, which currently comprises about half the average breadwinner's salary, will double useable family income. What can you envision your family doing with that new, discretionary income? Rather than spending it all, the prudent will save for future expenses and emergencies. This will greatly reduce the need for assistance when inevitable bumps occur in the economy.

Our economy will benefit all equally, rather than practicing favoritism. The free market economy, with ample jobs, will substantially reduce the poor among us. We can teach and encourage those who will not work, or who squander the help given, and we can refuse to offer unwise assistance. Individuals, families, churches, and local government can identify the honestly needy, rendering temporary help and teaching skills to encourage independence. Americans have proven to be generous if their contributions are used wisely.

Honesty in government will increase and attract people of integrity who will give moral leadership. Our watchful eye will reward virtue and punish corruption. Our greater morality will translate into greater peace with other countries. Responsible citizens will again become part of the resting citizen militia that will provide national strength and discourage foreign encroachment.

America will demonstrate its stable government and prosperous economy to the world. As we provide a pattern, we will encourage other nations to follow our lead. However, we will leave them free to solve their own problems, fund their own economies, and develop their own political systems.

There will still be problems under a restored constitution. Economic dips, temporary market fluctuations, and conflicts of opinion will still exist. We will need to use creativity and proper principles to find solutions. The problems will be short-lived, and we will preserve our freedoms and national integrity.

14.2 | Education

When we restore our original Constitution, we will have freedom of choice in education. Everyone will benefit—parents, students, teachers, communities, and the nation.

Parents will resume their God-given responsibility to direct their children's education. Concerned parents, working for the good of their children, can dramatically improve the quality of education, offering greater freedom in educational choices. These new options will make learning more enjoyable, and happier children will make life easier for parents.

An inevitable advance in children's education will be an increase in parent-directed home schooling. This movement is currently sweeping the nation, carrying its traditionally high standards and self-directed independent study into education. Homeschooling is renowned for its ability to tailor learning to the individual student while fostering a love for learning—goals of all quality education.

Parents who prefer public education will directly influence standards and goals for schools and customize curricula. Their initiatives, rather than those of bureaucrats, will direct local, district and state educational decisions. Parent-led programs traditionally produce creative excellence, as no one cares more for the well-being of children than their parents.

The federal government will not be involved in education. Its involvement is unconstitutional. Federal money, and national standards set to accomodate the lowest students, will no longer directly or indirectly control education. States will set policies and provide funding, but only as directed by their citizens. Our mobile society will need smooth transitions between state educational systems for students who move to new locations. Cooperative systems that facilitate this will be developed—again, unfettered by direct or indirect federal money and control.

We can reinstate the teaching of right and wrong, faith in God, and morality in the classroom. Objectionable philosophies and political correctness, with its fear that truth will offend, can be eliminated. Parents can constructively address school dropout rates and encourage respect for a broad range of occupational endeavors, encouraging youth to judge careers by their integrity and service rather than their projected salaries.

Public school teachers can teach what students want and need to learn, rather than "teaching to the tests". Working as a team with parents and students, they can explore and ignite a love of learning and regain their lost positions as guides to true education.

Schools will be healthier, safer, more pleasant places for students and teachers. Christian morals and ethics can again be taught in public classrooms to counteract negative ideas in the culture. Students will behave better, show more respect and exercise greater self-discipline. Crime and vandalism will be greatly reduced as self-esteem, dress, and language improve. As teachers insist that students treat each other with kindness, they will spend less time trying to make students work and behave.

Patriotism can fill our homes and schools as we teach a renewed love of country, filling textbooks, math story problems, and written assignments with true stories of patriots, prophets and everyday heroes. We can again pledge our "allegiance to the flag of the United States of America and to the republic for which it stands" in our classrooms.

Our invigorated educational systems will stimulate our society, reinstituting critical thinking skills in youth who can think for themselves. American prosperity will thrive on creative new ideas. Under the educational freedom of our restored original Constitution, morals-based instruction can be our top educational priority.

14.3 | Business

BUSINESSES will flourish and jobs will be plentiful when honor, virtue, and constitutional freedoms are restored to the marketplace.

In early America, a man with woodworking skills could open a carpentry shop at home. A woman could sell baked goods from her kitchen. Young people apprenticed themselves to learn trades. This was free enterprise at work. Ingenuity and a solid work ethic produced a comfortable income for a family.

In today's regulated world, these freedoms have been hobbled. They can be restored, with corresponding benefits to employers, employees, and consumers.

Businesses will return to the United States when the free-market system restores America's robust workplace. Well-managed companies will succeed; poorly managed companies will be replaced by successful businesses that understand customer needs. Profits will depend on real success rather than government favoritism, subsidies, tax breaks, and bailouts.

Government businesses, with their unfair advantages, will no longer compete with private industry. Government favoritism that encourages giant corporations will no longer drive smaller companies out of business. Companies can expect success when they no longer fear shutdowns or fines if they violate obscure agency rules that carry the force of law.

With a sound economy, taxes and business debt will be reduced. Increased profits will bring higher wages to employees. With greater integrity in the marketplace, people will honor their word and practice the Golden Rule. New cooperative programs will emerge to assist in deciding wages and working conditions for owners and employees. Those formerly employed in the diminished government sector will move to the rapid growth of the private sector.

Some supervision is necessary in the commercial world. Without federal control, we will meet those needs at the state level and through trade groups, citizen groups, and private industry, just as we did in more prosperous times. Industries police themselves to protect their profits when government does not usurp that responsibility. This principle was proven in the profitable free-enterprise economy of the past.

We will still require protection from force, fraud, monopoly, and debauchery. Government will still require us to obey laws and punish transgressors. Beyond this, we can police ourselves better than the federal government. Much of this responsibility will fall within the renewed powers of the states. Supervision will still be required. Excessive zoning and licensing laws, which stifle the growth of new and home-based businesses under the guise of protecting us, often originate at the state or local level. Citizens in the community must insist on wise local laws that allow freedom to businesses.

It will take creativity to bring freedom to the marketplace. Americans today have never lived without bureaucratic control. We are conditioned to believe that we will be cheated without government to protect us and that ordinary people cannot supervise themselves. When government controls us, some people believe that they do not need to control themselves. We are capable of thinking for ourselves, setting rules, and putting protections in place. With virtue restored, we will be free to create a common attitude of respect and integrity.

Things will still go wrong. There will be fraud, inferior products, and dishonest contracts. We are people, and people make intentional and unintentional mistakes. Will our response be to take freedom away, or will we find honest solutions and continue to trust the Constitution?

American ingenuity will triumph in the marketplace if we honor and keep the principles that founded this nation.

14.4 | Agriculture

MOST OF US rarely consider government control in agriculture. We assume that the industry's goods will always fill our stores. Few areas of commerce need liberty more than agriculture, yet few are more heavily regulated.

The universal need for food should make agriculture solidly profitable. It has been in the past and will be again under a renewed free-market system.

At present, government control regulates the ability of farmers and ranchers to use existing land and water for their animals and crops. This has hobbled their efforts to produce the food we consume and has raised our food prices. Under a restored free-enterprise system, grazing rights, water rights, and roads and waterways that access public lands will be available as needed. Decisions about crops and herds will be made by those who produce and manage them, rather than by distant bureaucrats ignorant of needs and regional variables. Layers of regulations that piggyback on each other will be removed. Farms and ranches will regain privacy when government agents no longer invade their property to look for violations of government regulations.

Agriculture will shed the web of outside control from environmental agencies, land management agencies, and animal-rights groups. A free-market economy will eliminate subsidies, trade barriers, and price supports that distort market prices and disrupt competition. Farmers will be free to select crops, grow what sells, and sell at competitive but fair prices.

The advantages of large agribusinesses over small farmers will be reduced when bureaucratic red tape is eliminated. The costs of environmental and land agency rules drive small operations out of business, but large businesses with greater profits can survive. Hence, government regulations discriminate against small farmers. Fair, accessible, competitive markets will result when mammoth growers can no longer manipulate the markets.

With economic freedom, small farmers can sell their produce to any buyers available. Ranchers, who must currently limit the size of their herds according to standards set by distant bureaucrats, will be free to increase herd size. Competing energy markets, upon which agriculture is so dependent and which are currently highly regulated by government, will drive down energy prices for food producers. The healthy market that develops will reduce food prices and improve business for large and small operations.

Excessive taxes that eat profits and drive prices up will be eliminated. Agriculture can adopt sound economics rather than the current debt-based system, with interest that threatens disaster during difficult years. Those who manage their operations profitably will succeed. The demise of unsuccessful operations will create space for new businesses and make it profitable and satisfying for young people to remain on the family farm.

Proper application of the commerce clause in the Constitution will lift government controls on transportation and equipment and allow products to move throughout the market without disruption. Because the Constitution gives the federal government the responsibility to manage exports and imports, it will do so for the benefit of our economy and agriculture.

Farmers and ranchers are dedicated to their land and lifestyle. They are protective of the natural resources they require to survive. Their work has many challenges, including long hours and unpredictable weather and natural elements. They need free-market forces in their favor and freedom from government control to give every possible edge for profitability.

American agriculture can produce ample goods to feed us well. We can profitably export substantial quantities to foreign countries with a free-market economy that allows agriculture to flourish.

14.5 | The Family

ALL THAT HAPPENS in America, whether good or bad, ultimately affects the core unit of our nation—the family. When families are strong, free, and healthy, the nation prospers.

How will a return to the original Constitution affect our families?

Families will be happier and more stable. We will be a nation of moral people who live the Golden Rule. Religious worship can be a core family activity. Family time, family prayer, and family religious study will increase our strength.

The virtue generated in our families will flow to schools, the workplace, churches, and government. As some families set the example, others will find this desired moral power. The movement to build strong, moral families will lift neighborhoods and communities. It will spread upward to the state and influence the nation with the blessings of integrity.

In a free-market economy, breadwinners will have secure jobs. Family finances will improve. With more money in the family bank account, parents will have fewer worries and stress. Shorter work hours will be needed to provide an adequate income. More mothers can stay at home to care for their children when they choose to.

Parents and children can plan a family budget together, or save for future purchases or to strengthen their future security. In these family councils, children will learn to avoid debt, manage their money to meet expenses, and save for the future. Activities such as selling cold water at a hot parade can teach them the free-enterprise system. Skills learned in the family will promote a strong economy for the next generation.

Parents can give children and grandchildren the gift to love work, take it seriously, and give an honest day's labor for an honest wage. They can focus their children's attention on service rather than the "stuff" in their lives. Families can work together on worthwhile projects, from yard work to community service. They can help the widows, the fatherless, and the truly needy, as Jesus Christ taught us to do. They can pool their strengths to help other families with common needs.

A strong sense of community will grow from shared kindness. Generosity of funds, time, and service will bring blessings into our homes. Towns and neighborhoods will unify to work for the good of all in the community.

School and family will be extensions of each other. As parents volunteer in the classroom, participate on committees to select and approve materials, and carry out special projects, they will lighten the load for teachers and save valuable school funds. Teachers and parents will team up to work for the progress of all children in the school. Parents can offer creative solutions in the classroom and the school.

Parents have the great opportunity to instill a love for the Constitution and our Founders in their children. Our youth rely on moral parents to prepare them for their future leadership roles. Guiding them as they ready themselves is a privilege and an honor.

We hold the future of our families, our nation, and our liberty in our own hands. With the strength of our youth, we will replace moral decay and political erosion with virtue and honor. The next generation will someday direct society and operate our government. Now is the time to prepare them to do so with integrity.

Love of God and love of country, planted in the hearts of children in the family circle, will create unimaginable power. Virtue and morality, our national legacy, will rise to bless all families with freedom, protection, prosperity—and through these, peace. This is our privilege; this is our heritage; we claim this birthright.

.

Epilogue

α

THE AUTHOR'S PERSPECTIVE

DECADES AGO, I read a book whose title I can no longer remember. The main character in this volume of historical fiction died as the story closed. I was mesmerized by the epilogue to this story. I read it many times as I engraved it on my heart.

The author wished to demonstrate that the main character, Elizabeth, lived on after death. He portrayed this continuation to a place beyond life with the main character stepping from a lighted circle into the mysterious darkness of another realm.

The main character had been preceded in death by the man she loved, and he waited for her, unseen in the darkness. His kind, loving voice coaxed her onward through her fears of the unknown. "Come, Elizabeth, just step into the darkness. I am here, waiting for you. You need only step in faith into the dark. You must trust me. Once you have taken the first step, you will feel my hand, and I will draw you to me, but you must take the first step alone. Just one step—that is all." The story drew to an end as Elizabeth took her step of faith past the lighted circle to embrace her future.

This tender epilogue has much to teach us. Our own circumstance comes late in the story of the Constitution of the United States. We have pondered the course to restore our treasured liberties and Constitution. While we know some steps necessary to accomplish that goal, we do not know them all, nor do we know how the unknown will come about.

Like Elizabeth, we are asked to step into the unknown with faith and to trust in God, who will help us reinstate our Constitution. Once we trust in Him, He will reach out His hand to pull us to safety. We do not yet know the full means to restore our precious rights, but He does. We have only to ask His help and take the step of faith, through our actions, into the darkness beyond sight and human understanding. In this, we show our trust and willingness to follow His instructions.

Isaiah describes the process: "For precept must be upon precept . . . line upon line . . . here a little, and there a little" (Isaiah 28:10). We must take one step at a time, one step after another. There will be a new idea here and there, and new understanding will come as we proceed. Once we prove our willingness to follow, He will teach us more. "Come now, and let us reason together, saith the Lord" (Isaiah 1:18). As we are ready, He will explain additional steps to reestablish full freedom in America.

It is uncomfortable to begin a journey with a step into the unknown. Fear causes us to hesitate. It is, however, the only way to begin any journey. Faith must come before we receive the miracle.

We must know for ourselves that this crusade to restore our freedom, our protections, our prosperity, and thus our peace under the original Constitution is possible and wise. We must study the issues and decide where and how we will use our time, talents, and resources in the current campaign. Prayer will help us make those decisions wisely.

Each of us can assist in the work to restore our inalienable rights. We must, if we are to be free. It is time to begin!

APPENDIX
❧

The Declaration of Independence

IN CONGRESS, July 4, 1776.

The unanimous Declaration of the thirteen united States of America,

When in the Course of human events, it becomes necessary for one people to dissolve the political bands which have connected them with another, and to assume among the powers of the earth, the separate and equal station to which the Laws of Nature and of Nature's God entitle them, a decent respect to the opinions of mankind requires that they should declare the causes which impel them to the separation.

We hold these truths to be self-evident, that all men are created equal, that they are endowed by their Creator with certain unalienable Rights, that among these are Life, Liberty and the pursuit of Happiness.—That to secure these rights, Governments are instituted among Men, deriving their just powers from the consent of the governed, —That whenever any Form of Government becomes destructive of these ends, it is the Right of the People to alter or to abolish it, and to institute new Government, laying its foundation on such principles and organizing its powers in such form, as to them shall seem most likely to effect their Safety and Happiness. Prudence, indeed, will dictate that Governments long established should not be changed for light and transient causes; and accordingly all experience hath shewn, that mankind are more disposed to suffer, while evils are sufferable, than to right themselves by abolishing the forms to which they are accustomed. But when a long train of abuses and usurpations, pursuing invariably the same Object evinces a design to reduce them under absolute Despotism, it is their right, it is their duty, to throw off such Government, and to provide new Guards for their future security.—Such has been the patient sufferance of these Colonies; and such is now the necessity which constrains them to alter their former Systems of Government. The history of the present King of Great Britain is a history of repeated injuries and usurpations, all having in direct object the establishment of an absolute Tyranny over these States. To prove this, let Facts be submitted to a candid world.

He has refused his Assent to Laws, the most wholesome and necessary for the public good.

He has forbidden his Governors to pass Laws of immediate and pressing importance, unless suspended in their operation till his Assent should be obtained; and when so suspended, he has utterly neglected to attend to them.

He has refused to pass other Laws for the accommodation of large districts of people, unless those people would relinquish the right of Representation in the Legislature, a right inestimable to them and formidable to tyrants only.

He has called together legislative bodies at places unusual, uncomfortable, and distant from the depository of their public Records, for the sole purpose of fatiguing them into compliance with his measures.

He has dissolved Representative Houses repeatedly, for opposing with manly firmness his invasions on the rights of the people.

He has refused for a long time, after such dissolutions, to cause others to be elected; whereby the Legislative powers, incapable of Annihilation, have returned to the People at large for their exercise; the State remaining in the mean time exposed to all the dangers of invasion from without, and convulsions within.

He has endeavoured to prevent the population of these States; for that purpose obstructing the Laws for Naturalization of Foreigners; refusing to pass others to encourage their migrations hither, and raising the conditions of new Appropriations of Lands.

He has obstructed the Administration of Justice, by refusing his Assent to Laws for establishing Judiciary powers.

He has made Judges dependent on his Will alone, for the tenure of their offices, and the amount and payment of their salaries.

He has erected a multitude of New Offices, and sent hither swarms of Officers to harrass our people, and eat out their substance.

He has kept among us, in times of peace, Standing Armies without the Consent of our legislatures.

He has affected to render the Military independent of and superior to the Civil power.

He has combined with others to subject us to a jurisdiction foreign to our constitution, and unacknowledged by our laws; giving his Assent to their Acts of pretended Legislation:

For Quartering large bodies of armed troops among us:

For protecting them, by a mock Trial, from punishment for any Murders which they should commit on the Inhabitants of these States:

For cutting off our Trade with all parts of the world:

For imposing Taxes on us without our Consent:

For depriving us in many cases, of the benefits of Trial by Jury:

For transporting us beyond Seas to be tried for pretended offences

For abolishing the free System of English Laws in a neighbouring Province, establishing therein an Arbitrary government, and enlarging its Boundaries so as to render it at once an example and fit instrument for introducing the same absolute rule into these Colonies:

For taking away our Charters, abolishing our most valuable Laws, and altering fundamentally the Forms of our Governments:

For suspending our own Legislatures, and declaring themselves invested with power to legislate for us in all cases whatsoever.

He has abdicated Government here, by declaring us out of his Protection and waging War against us.

He has plundered our seas, ravaged our Coasts, burnt our towns, and destroyed the lives of our people.

He is at this time transporting large Armies of foreign Mercenaries to compleat the works of death, desolation and tyranny, already begun with circumstances of Cruelty & perfidy scarcely paralleled in the most barbarous ages, and totally unworthy the Head of a civilized nation.

He has constrained our fellow Citizens taken Captive on the high Seas to bear Arms against their Country, to become the executioners of their friends and Brethren, or to fall themselves by their Hands.

He has excited domestic insurrections amongst us, and has endeavoured to bring on the inhabitants of our frontiers, the merciless Indian Savages, whose known rule of warfare, is an undistinguished destruction of all ages, sexes and conditions.

In every stage of these Oppressions We have Petitioned for Redress in the most humble terms: Our repeated Petitions have been answered only by repeated injury. A Prince whose character is thus marked by every act which may define a Tyrant, is unfit to be the ruler of a free people.

Nor have We been wanting in attentions to our Brittish brethren. We have warned them from time to time of attempts by their legislature to extend an unwarrantable jurisdiction over us. We have reminded them of the circumstances of our emigration and settlement here. We have appealed to their native justice and magnanimity, and we have conjured them by the ties of our common kindred to disavow these usurpations, which, would inevitably interrupt our connections and correspondence. They too have been deaf to the voice of justice and of consanguinity. We must, therefore, acquiesce in the necessity, which denounces our Separation, and hold them, as we hold the rest of mankind, Enemies in War, in Peace Friends.

We, therefore, the Representatives of the united States of America, in General Congress, Assembled, appealing to the Supreme Judge of the world for the rectitude of our intentions, do, in the Name, and by Authority of the good People of these Colonies, solemnly publish and declare, That these United Colonies are, and of Right ought to be Free and Independent States; that they are Absolved from all Allegiance to the British Crown, and that all political connection between them and the State of Great Britain, is and ought to be totally dissolved; and that as Free and Independent States, they have full Power to levy War, conclude Peace, contract Alliances, establish Commerce, and to do all other Acts and Things which Independent States may of right do. And for the support of this Declaration, with a firm reliance on the protection of divine Providence, we mutually pledge to each other our Lives, our Fortunes and our sacred Honor.

The 56 signatures on the Declaration appear in the positions indicated:

Georgia:
  Button Gwinnett
  Lyman Hall
  George Walton

North Carolina:
  William Hooper
  Joseph Hewes
  John Penn

South Carolina:
  Edward Rutledge
  Thomas Heyward, Jr.
  Thomas Lynch, Jr.
  Arthur Middleton

Massachusetts:
  John Hancock
Maryland:
  Samuel Chase
  William Paca
  Thomas Stone
  Charles Carroll of
  Carrollton
Virginia:
  George Wythe
  Richard Henry Lee
  Thomas Jefferson
  Benjamin Harrison
  Thomas Nelson, Jr.
  Francis Lightfoot Lee
  Carter Braxton

Pennsylvania:
  Robert Morris
  Benjamin Rush
  Benjamin Franklin
  John Morton
  George Clymer
  James Smith
  George Taylor
  James Wilson
  George Ross

Delaware:
  Caesar Rodney
  George Read
  Thomas McKean

New York:
  William Floyd
  Philip Livingston
  Francis Lewis
  Lewis Morris

New Jersey:
  Richard Stockton
  John Witherspoon
  Francis Hopkinson
  John Hart
  Abraham Clark

New Hampshire:
  Josiah Bartlett
  William Whipple

Massachusetts:
  Samuel Adams
  John Adams
  Robert Treat Paine
  Elbridge Gerry

Rhode Island:
  Stephen Hopkins
  William Ellery

Connecticut:
  Roger Sherman
  Samuel Huntington
  William Williams
  Oliver Wolcott

New Hampshire:
  Matthew Thornton

Constitution of the United States

WE THE PEOPLE of the United States, in order to form a more perfect union, establish justice, insure domestic tranquility, provide for the common defense, promote the general welfare, and secure the blessings of liberty to ourselves and our posterity, do ordain and establish this Constitution for the United States of America.

ARTICLE I

Section 1. All legislative powers herein granted shall be vested in a Congress of the United States, which shall consist of a Senate and House of Representatives.

Section 2. The House of Representatives shall be composed of members chosen every second year by the people of the several states, and the electors in each state shall have the qualifications requisite for electors of the most numerous branch of the state legislature.

No person shall be a Representative who shall not have attained to the age of twenty-five years, and been seven years a citizen of the United States, and who shall not, when elected, be an inhabitant of that state in which he shall be chosen.

Representatives [and direct taxes][1] shall be apportioned among the several states which may be included within this Union, according to their respective numbers, [which shall be determined by adding to the whole number of free persons, including those bound to service for a term of years, and excluding Indians not taxed, three- fifths of all other persons][2]. The actual enumeration shall be made within three years after the first meeting of the Congress of the United States, and within every subsequent term of ten years, in such manner as they shall by law direct. The number of Representatives shall not exceed one for every thirty thousand, but each state shall have at least one Representative; [and until such enumeration shall be made, the state of New Hampshire shall be entitled to choose three, Massachusetts eight, Rhode Island and Providence Plantations one, Connecticut five, New York six, New Jersey four, Pennsylvania eight, Delaware one, Maryland six, Virginia ten, North Carolina five, South Carolina five, and Georgia three][3].

When vacancies happen in the representation from any state, the executive authority thereof shall issue writs of election to fill such vacancies.

The House of Representatives shall choose their speaker and other officers, and shall have the sole power of impeachment.

Section 3. The Senate of the United States shall be composed of two Senators from each state, [chosen by the legislature thereof,][4] for six years; and each Senator shall have one vote.

---

1 The words in brackets have been modified by Amendment 16.
2 The words in brackets have been modified by Section 2 of Amendment 14.
3 he words in brackets have been obsolete since 1793.
4 The words in brackets have been modified by Amendment 17.

Immediately after they shall be assembled in consequence of the first election, they shall be divided as equally as may be into three classes. The seats of the Senators of the first class shall be vacated at the expiration of the second year, of the second class at the expiration of the fourth year, and of the third class at the expiration of the sixth year, so that one-third may be chosen every second year; [and if vacancies happen by resignation, or otherwise, during the recess of the legislature of any state, the executive thereof may make temporary appointments until the next meeting of the legislature, which shall then fill such vacancies][5].

No person shall be a Senator who shall not have attained to the age of thirty years, and been nine years a citizen of the United States, and who shall not, when elected, be an inhabitant of that state for which he shall be chosen.

The Vice President of the United States shall be president of the Senate, but shall have no vote unless they be equally divided.

The Senate shall choose their other officers, and also a president pro tempore in the absence of the Vice President, or when he shall exercise the office of President of the United States.

The Senate shall have the sole power to try all impeachments. When sitting for that purpose, they shall be on oath or affirmation. When the President of the United States is tried, the Chief Justice shall preside; and no person shall be convicted without the concurrence of two-thirds of the members present.

Judgment in cases of impeachment shall not extend further than to removal from office, and disqualification to hold and enjoy any office of honor, trust, or profit under the United States; but the party convicted shall nevertheless be liable and subject to indictment, trial, judgment, and punishment, according to law.

Section 4. The times, places, and manner of holding elections for Senators and Representatives shall be prescribed in each state by the legislature thereof; but the Congress may at any time by law make or alter such regulations, [except as to the places of choosing Senators][6].

The Congress shall assemble at least once in every year, [and such meeting shall be on the first Monday in December,][7] unless they shall by law appoint a different day.

Section 5. Each house shall be the judge of the elections, returns, and qualifications of its own members, and a majority of each shall constitute a quorum to do business; but a smaller number may adjourn from day to day, and may be authorized to compel the attendance of absent members, in such manner and under such penalties as each house may provide.

Each house may determine the rules of its proceedings, punish its members for disorderly behavior, and, with the concurrence of two-thirds, expel a member.

Each house shall keep a journal of its proceedings, and from time to time publish the

---

5 The words in brackets have been modified by Amendment 17.
6 The words in brackets have been superseded by Amendment 17.
7 The words in brackets have been modified by Section 2 of Amendment 20.

same, excepting such parts as may in their judgment require secrecy; and the yeas and nays of the members of either house on any question shall, at the desire of one-fifth of those present, be entered on the journal.

Neither house, during the session of Congress, shall, without the consent of the other, adjourn for more than three days, nor to any other place than that in which the two houses shall be sitting.

Section 6. The Senators and Representatives shall receive a compensation for their services, to be ascertained by law and paid out of the treasury of the United States. They shall in all cases, except treason, felony, and breach of the peace, be privileged from arrest during their attendance at the session of their respective houses, and in going to and returning from the same; and for any speech or debate in either house, they shall not be questioned in any other place.

No Senator or Representative shall, during the time for which he was elected, be appointed to any civil office under the authority of the United States which shall have been created, or the emoluments whereof shall have been increased, during such time; and no person holding any office under the United States shall be a member of either house during his continuance in office.

Section 7. All bills for raising revenue shall originate in the House of Representatives; but the Senate may propose or concur with amendments as on other bills.

Every bill which shall have passed the House of Representatives and the Senate shall, before it become a law, be presented to the President of the United States. If he approve he shall sign it, but if not he shall return it, with his objections, to that house in which it shall have originated, who shall enter the objections at large on their journal and proceed to reconsider it. If after such reconsideration two-thirds of that house shall agree to pass the bill, it shall be sent, together with the objections, to the other house, by which it shall likewise be reconsidered, and if approved by two-thirds of that house, it shall become a law. But in all such cases the votes of both houses shall be determined by yeas and nays, and the names of the persons voting for and against the bill shall be entered on the journal of each house respectively. If any bill shall not be returned by the President within ten days (Sundays excepted) after it shall have been presented to him, the same shall be a law, in like manner as if he had signed it, unless the Congress by their adjournment prevent its return, in which case it shall not be a law.

Every order, resolution, or vote to which the concurrence of the Senate and House of Representatives may be necessary (except on a question of adjournment) shall be presented to the President of the United States; and, before the same shall take effect, shall be approved by him, or, being disapproved by him, shall be repassed by two- thirds of the Senate and House of Representatives, according to the rules and limitations prescribed in the case of a bill.

Section 8. The Congress shall have power to lay and collect taxes, duties, imposts, and excises, to pay the debts and provide for the common defense and general welfare of the United States; but all duties, imposts, and excises shall be uniform throughout the United States;

To borrow money on the credit of the United States;

To regulate commerce with foreign nations, and among the several states, and with the Indian tribes;

To establish an uniform rule of naturalization, and uniform laws on the subject of bankruptcies throughout the United States;

To coin money, regulate the value thereof, and of foreign coin, and fix the standard of weights and measures;

To provide for the punishment of counterfeiting the securities and current coin of the United States;

To establish post offices and post roads;

To promote the progress of science and useful arts by securing for limited times to authors and inventors the exclusive right to their respective writings and discoveries;

To constitute tribunals inferior to the Supreme Court;

To define and punish piracies and felonies committed on the high seas, and offenses against the law of nations;

To declare war, grant letters of marque and reprisal, and make rules concerning captures on land and water;

To raise and support armies, but no appropriation of money to that use shall be for a longer term than two years;

To provide and maintain a navy;

To make rules for the government and regulation of the land and naval forces;

To provide for calling forth the militia to execute the laws of the Union, suppress insurrections, and repel invasions;

To provide for organizing, arming , and disciplining the militia, and for governing such part of them as may be employed in the service of the United States, reserving to the states respectively the appointment of the officers and the authority of training the militia according to the discipline prescribed by Congress;

To exercise exclusive legislation, in all cases whatsoever, over such district (not exceeding ten miles square) as may, by cession of particular states and the acceptance of Congress, become the seat of the government of the United States, and to exercise like authority over all places purchased by the consent of the legislature of the state in which the same shall be, for the erection of forts, magazines, arsenals, dockyards, and other needful buildings;-And

To make all laws which shall be necessary and proper for carrying into execution the foregoing powers, and all other powers vested by this Constitution in the government of the United States, or in any department or officer thereof.

Section 9. [The migration or importation of such persons as any of the states now existing shall think proper to admit shall not be prohibited by the Congress prior to the year one thousand eight hundred and eight, but a tax or duty may be imposed on such importation, not exceeding ten dollars for each person.][8]

The privilege of the writ of habeas corpus shall not be suspended, unless when in cases of rebellion or invasion the public safety may require it.

No bill of attainder or ex post facto law shall be passed.

No capitation [or other direct tax][9] shall be laid, unless in proportion to the census or enumeration herein before directed to be taken.

No tax or duty shall be laid on articles exported from any state.

No preference shall be given by any regulation of commerce or revenue to the ports of one state over those of another; nor shall vessels bound to or from one state be obliged to enter, clear, or pay duties in another.

No money shall be drawn from the treasury but in consequence of appropriations made by law; and a regular statement and account of the receipts and expenditures of all public money shall be published from time to time.

No title of nobility shall be granted by the United States; and no person holding any office of profit or trust under them shall, without the consent of the Congress, accept of any present, emolument, office, or title, of any kind whatever, from any king, prince, or foreign state.

Section 10. No state shall enter into any treaty, alliance, or confederation; grant letters of marque and reprisal; coin money; emit bills of credit; make anything but gold and silver coin a tender in payment of debts; pass any bill of attainder, ex post facto law, or law impairing the obligation of contracts; or grant any title of nobility.

No state shall, without the consent of the Congress, lay any imposts or duties on imports or exports, except what may be absolutely necessary for executing its inspection laws; and the net produce of all duties and imposts, laid by any state on imports or exports, shall be for the use of the treasury of the United States; and all such laws shall be subject to the revision and control of the Congress.

No state shall, without the consent of Congress, lay any duty of tonnage; keep troops or ships of war in time of peace; enter into any agreement or compact with another state, or with a foreign power; or engage in war, unless actually invaded or in such imminent danger as will not admit of delay.

ARTICLE II

Section 1. The executive power shall be vested in a President of the United States of America. He shall hold his office during the term of four years and, together with the Vice President, chosen for the same term, be elected as follows.

Each state shall appoint, in such manner as the legislature thereof may direct, a number

---

8 This paragraph has been obsolete since 1808, when Congress outlawed the further importation of slaves into the United States.
9 The words in brackets have been modified by Amendment 16.

of electors equal to the whole number of Senators and Representatives to which the state may be entitled in the Congress; but no Senator or Representative, or person holding an office of trust or profit under the United States, shall be appointed an elector.

[The electors shall meet in their respective states and vote by ballot for two persons, of whom one at least shall not be an inhabitant of the same state with themselves. And they shall make a list of all the persons voted for, and of the number of votes for each; which list they shall sign and certify, and transmit sealed to the seat of the government of the United States, directed to the president of the Senate. The president of the Senate shall, in the presence of the Senate and House of Representatives, open all the certificates, and the votes shall then be counted. The person having the greatest number of votes shall be the President, if such number be a majority of the whole number of electors appointed; and if there be more than one who have such majority, and have an equal number of votes, then the House of Representatives shall immediately choose by ballot one of them for President; and if no person have a majority, then from the five highest on the list the said house shall in like manner choose the President. But in choosing the President, the votes shall be taken by states, the representation from each state having one vote; a quorum for this purpose shall consist of a member or members from two-thirds of the states, and a majority of all the states shall be necessary to a choice. In every case, after the choice of the President, the person having the greatest number of votes of the electors shall be the Vice President. But if there should remain two or more who have equal votes, the Senate shall choose from them by ballot the Vice President.][10]

The Congress may determine the time of choosing the electors and the day on which they shall give their votes, which day shall be the same throughout the United States.

No person except a natural-born citizen, [or a citizen of the United States at the time of the adoption of this Constitution,][11] shall be eligible to the office of President; neither shall any person be eligible to that office who shall not have attained to the age of thirty-five years and been fourteen years a resident within the United States.

[In case of the removal of the President from office, or of his death, resignation, or inability to discharge the powers and duties of the said office, the same shall devolve on the Vice President, and the Congress may by law provide for the case of removal, death, resignation, or inability, both of the President and Vice President, declaring what officer shall then act as President; and such officer shall act accordingly until the disability be removed or a President shall be elected.][12]

The President shall, at stated times, receive for his services a compensation, which shall neither be increased nor diminished during the period for which he shall have been elected; and he shall not receive within that period any other emolument from the United States, or any of them.

---

10 This paragraph has been superseded by Amendment 12.
11 The words in brackets are no longer applicable.
12 The words in brackets have been modified by Amendment 25.

Before he enter on the execution of his office, he shall take the following oath or affirmation: "I do solemnly swear (or affirm) that I will faithfully execute the office of President of the United States, and will, to the best of my ability, preserve, protect, and defend the Constitution of the United States."

Section 2. The President shall be commander-in-chief of the army and navy of the United States, and of the militia of the several states when called into the actual service of the United States; he may require the opinion, in writing, of the principal officer in each of the executive departments upon any subject relating to the duties of their respective offices; and he shall have power to grant reprieves and pardons for offenses against the United States, except in cases of impeachment.

He shall have power, by and with the advice and consent of the Senate, to make treaties, provided two-thirds of the Senators present concur; and he shall nominate, and by and with the advice and consent of the Senate shall appoint, ambassadors, other public ministers and consuls, judges of the Supreme Court, and all other officers of the United States whose appointments are not herein otherwise provided for, and which shall be established by law; but the Congress may by law vest the appointment of such inferior officers as they think proper in the President alone, in the courts of law, or in the heads of departments.

The President shall have power to fill up all vacancies that may happen during the recess of the Senate, by granting commissions which shall expire at the end of their next session.

Section 3. He shall from time to time give to the Congress information of the state of the Union, and recommend to their consideration such measures as he shall judge necessary and expedient; he may, on extraordinary occasions, convene both houses, or either of them, and in case of disagreement between them with respect to the time of adjournment, he may adjourn them to such time as he shall think proper; he shall receive ambassadors and other public ministers; he shall take care that the laws be faithfully executed; and shall commission all the officers of the United States.

Section 4. The President, Vice President, and all civil officers of the United States shall be removed from office on impeachment for, and conviction of, treason, bribery, or other high crimes and misdemeanors.

ARTICLE III

Section 1. The judicial power of the United States shall be vested in one Supreme Court, and in such inferior courts as the Congress may from time to time ordain and establish. The judges, both of the Supreme and inferior courts, shall hold their offices during good behavior, and shall, at stated times, receive for their services a compensation, which shall not be diminished during their continuance in office.

Section 2. The judicial power shall extend to all cases, in law and equity, arising under this Constitution, the laws of the United States, and treaties made, or which shall be made, under their authority; to all cases affecting ambassadors, other public ministers, and consuls; to all cases of admiralty and maritime jurisdiction; to controversies to which the United States shall be a party; to controversies between two or more states;

[between a state and citizens of another state;][13] between citizens of different states; between citizens of the same state claiming lands under grants of different states; and between a state, or the citizens thereof, and foreign states, [citizens, or subjects][14].

In all cases affecting ambassadors, other public ministers, and consuls, and those in which a state shall be party, the Supreme Court shall have original jurisdiction. In all the other cases before mentioned, the Supreme Court shall have appellate jurisdiction, [both as to law and fact,][15] with such exceptions and under such regulations as the Congress shall make.

The trial of all crimes, except in cases of impeachment, shall be by jury; and such trial shall be held in the state where the said crimes shall have been committed; but when not committed within any state, the trial shall be at such place or places as the Congress may by law have directed.

Section 3. Treason against the United States shall consist only in levying war against them or in adhering to their enemies, giving them aid and comfort. No person shall be convicted of treason unless on the testimony of two witnesses to the same overt act, or on confession in open court.

The Congress shall have power to declare the punishment of treason, but no attainder of treason shall work corruption of blood or forfeiture except during the life of the person attainted.

ARTICLE IV

Section 1. Full faith and credit shall be given in each state to the public acts, records, and judicial proceedings of every other state. And the Congress may by general laws prescribe the manner in which such acts, records, and proceedings shall be proved, and the effect thereof.

Section 2. The citizens of each state shall be entitled to all privileges and immunities of citizens in the several states.

A person charged in any state with treason, felony, or other crime, who shall flee from justice and be found in another state, shall, on demand of the executive authority of the state from which he fled, be delivered up to be removed to the state having jurisdiction of the crime.

[No person held to service or labor in one state, under the laws thereof, escaping into another, shall, in consequence of any law or regulation therein, be discharged from such service or labor, but shall be delivered up on claim of the party to whom such service or labor may be due.][16]

Section 3. New states may be admitted by the Congress into this Union; but no new state shall be formed or erected within the jurisdiction of any other state; nor

---

13 The words in brackets have been superseded by Amendment 11.
14 The words in brackets have been superseded by Amendment 11.
15 The words in brackets have been modified by Amendment 7.
16 The words in brackets have been superseded by Amendment 13.

any state be formed by the junction of two or more states, or parts of states, without the consent of the legislatures of the states concerned as well as of the Congress.

The Congress shall have power to dispose of and make all needful rules and regulations respecting the territory or other property belonging to the United States; and nothing in this Constitution shall be so construed as to prejudice any claims of the United States, or of any particular state.

Section 4. The United States shall guarantee to every state in this Union a republican form of government, and shall protect each of them against invasion, and on application of the legislature, or of the executive (when the legislature cannot be convened), against domestic violence.

ARTICLE V

The Congress, whenever two-thirds of both houses shall deem it necessary, shall propose amendments to this Constitution, or, on the application of the legislatures of two-thirds of the several states, shall call a convention for proposing amendments, which, in either case, shall be valid to all intents, and purposes as part of this Constitution when ratified by the legislatures of three-fourths of the several states, or by conventions in three-fourths thereof, as the one or the other mode of ratification may be proposed by the Congress; provided [that no amendment which may be made prior to the year one thousand eight hundred and eight shall in any manner affect the first and fourth clauses in the ninth section of the first article; and][17] that no state, without its consent, shall be deprived of its equal suffrage in the Senate.

ARTICLE VI

All debts contracted and engagements entered into before the adoption of this Constitution shall be as valid against the United States under this Constitution as under the Confederation.

This Constitution, and the laws of the United States which shall be made in pursuance thereof, and all treaties made, or which shall be made, under the authority of the United States, shall be the supreme law of the land; and the judges in every state shall be bound thereby, anything in the constitution or laws of any state to the contrary notwithstanding.

The Senators and Representatives before mentioned, and the members of the several state legislatures, and all executive and judicial officers, both of the United States and of the several states, shall be bound by oath or affirmation to support this Constitution; but no religious test shall ever be required as a qualification to any office or public trust under the United States.

ARTICLE VII

The ratification of the conventions of nine states shall be sufficient for the establishment of this Constitution between the states so ratifying the same.

Done in convention by the unanimous consent of the states present, the seventeenth day of September in the year of our Lord one thousand seven hundred and eighty-

---

17 The words in brackets have been obsolete since 1808.

seven, and of the independence of the United States of America the twelfth. In witness whereof we have hereunto subscribed our names.

Signers of the Constitution

Go. Washington--Presidt: and deputy from Virginia

NEW HAMPSHIRE
John Langdon
Nicholas Gilman

MASSACHUSETTS
Nathaniel Gorham
Rufus King

CONNECTICUT
Wm. Saml. Johnson
Roger Sherman

NEW YORK
Alexander Hamilton

NEW JERSEY
Wil: Livingston
David Brearley
Wm. Paterson
Jona: Dayton

PENNSYLVANIA
B Franklin
Thomas Mifflin
Robt Morris
Geo. Clymer
Thos. FitzSimons
Jared Ingersoll
James Wilson
Gouv Morris

DELAWARE
Geo: Read
Gunning Bedford jun
John Dickinson
Richard Bassett
Jaco: Broom

MARYLAND
James McHenry
Dan of St. Thos. Jenifer
Danl Carroll

VIRGINIA
John Blair
James Madison Jr.

NORTH CAROLINA
Wm. Blount
Richd. Dobbs Spaight
Hu Williamson

SOUTH CAROLINA
J. Rutledge
Charles Cotesworth Pinckney
Charles Pinckney
Pierce Butler

GEORGIA
William Few
Abr Baldwin

Attest William Jackson
Secretary

Amendments to the Constitution of the United States of America

The first Ten Amendments to the Constitution constitute the Bill of Rights, which was ratified by the states and became effective December 15, 1791.

PREAMBLE TO THE BILL OF RIGHTS

THE Conventions of a number of the States, having at the time of their adopting the Constitution, expressed a desire, in order to prevent misconstruction or abuse of its powers, that further declaratory and restrictive clauses should be added: And as extending the ground of public confidence in the Government, will best ensure the beneficent ends of its institution.

Amendment I

Congress shall make no law respecting an establishment of religion or prohibiting the free exercise thereof, or abridging the freedom of speech or of the press, or the right of the people peaceably to assemble and to petition the government for a redress of grievances.

See 7.8, 11.1, 11.2, 12.15 for information on this amendment.

Amendment II

A well-regulated militia being necessary to the security of a free state, the right of the people to keep and bear arms shall not be infringed.

See 11.3 for information on this amendment.

Amendment III

No soldier shall, in time of peace, be quartered in any house without the consent of the owner, nor in time of war but in a manner to be prescribed by law.

See 11.4 for information on this amendment.

Amendment IV

The right of the people to be secure in their persons, houses, papers, and effects against unreasonable searches and seizures shall not be violated, and no warrants shall issue but upon probable cause, supported by oath or affirmation, and particularly describing the place to be searched and the persons or things to be seized.

See 11.4 for information on this amendment.

Amendment V

No person shall be held to answer for a capital or otherwise infamous crime unless on a presentment or indictment of a grand jury, except in cases arising in the land or naval forces, or in the militia, when in actual service in time of war or public danger;

nor shall any person be subject for the same offense to be twice put in jeopardy of life or limb; nor shall be compelled in any criminal case to be a witness against himself, nor be deprived of life, liberty, or property without due process of law; nor shall private property be taken for public use without just compensation.

See 11.5 for information on this amendment.

Amendment VI

In all criminal prosecutions, the accused shall enjoy the right to a speedy and public trial by an impartial jury of the state and district wherein the crime shall have been committed, which district shall have been previously ascertained by law, and to be informed of the nature and cause of the accusation; to be confronted with the witnesses against him; to have compulsory process for obtaining witnesses in his favor; and to have the assistance of counsel for his defense.

See 11.5 for information on this amendment.

Amendment VII

In suits at common law, where the value in controversy shall exceed twenty dollars, the right of trial by jury shall be preserved, and no fact tried by a jury shall be otherwise reexamined in any court of the United States than according to the rules of the common law.

See 11.5 for information on this amendment.

Amendment VIII

Excessive bail shall not be required, nor excessive fines imposed, nor cruel and unusual punishments inflicted.

See 11.5 for information on this amendment.

Amendment IX

The enumeration in the Constitution of certain rights shall not be construed to deny or disparage others retained by the people.

See 11.6 for information on this amendment.

Amendment X

The powers not delegated to the United States by the Constitution, nor prohibited by it to the states, are reserved to the states respectively, or to the people.

See 11.6, 11.7, 12.15, 13.8 for information on this amendment.

Amendment XI (Ratified February 7, 1795)

The judicial power of the United States shall not be construed to extend to any suit, in law or equity, commenced or prosecuted against one of the United States by citizens of another state, or by citizens or subjects of any foreign state.

Note: Article III, section 2, of the Constitution was modified by amendment 11.

See 10.5, 11.7 for information on this amendment.

Amendment XII (Ratified June 15, 1804)

The electors shall meet in their respective states and vote by ballot for President and Vice President, one of whom, at least, shall not be an inhabitant of the same state with themselves; they shall name in their ballots the person voted for as President, and indistinct ballots the person voted for as Vice President, and they shall make distinct lists of all persons voted for as President and of all persons voted for as Vice President, and of the number of votes for each, which lists they shall sign and certify, and transmit sealed to the seat of the government of the United States, directed to the president of the Senate. The president of the Senate shall, in the presence of the Senate and House of Representatives, open all the certificates, and the votes shall then be counted. The person having the greatest number of votes for President shall be the President, if such number be a majority of the whole number of electors appointed; and if no person have such majority, then from the persons having the highest numbers, not exceeding three, on the list of those voted for as President, the House of Representatives shall choose immediately, by ballot, the President. But in choosing the President, the votes shall be taken by states, the representation from each state having one vote; a quorum for this purpose shall consist of a member or members from two-thirds of the states, and a majority of all the states shall be necessary to a choice. [And if the House of Representatives shall not choose a President whenever the right of choice shall devolve upon them, before the fourth day of March next following, then the Vice President shall act as President, as in the case of the death or other constitutional disability of the President.]*

The person having the greatest number of votes as Vice President shall be the Vice President, if such number be a majority of the whole number of electors appointed; and if no person have a majority, then from the two highest numbers on the list, the Senate shall choose the Vice President; a quorum for the purpose shall consist of two-thirds of the whole number of Senators, and a majority of the whole number shall be necessary to a choice. But no person constitutionally ineligible to the office of President shall be eligible to that of Vice President of the United States.

Superseded by section 3 of the 20th amendment.

Note: A portion of Article II, section 1 of the Constitution was superseded by the 12th amendment.

See 10.2, 10.3, 11.7 for information on this amendment.

Amendment XIII (Ratified December 6, 1865)

Neither slavery nor involuntary servitude, except as a punishment for crime whereof the party shall have been duly convicted, shall exist within the United States, or any place subject to their jurisdiction.

Congress shall have power to enforce this article by appropriate legislation.

Note: A portion of Article IV, section 2, of the Constitution was superseded by the 13th amendment.

See 11.8 for information on this amendment.

Amendment XIV (Ratified July 9, 1868)

All persons born or naturalized in the United States, and subject to the jurisdiction thereof, are citizens of the United States and of the state wherein they reside. No state shall make or enforce any law which shall abridge the privileges or immunities of citizens of the United States; nor shall any state deprive any person of life, liberty, or property without due process of law, nor deny to any person within its jurisdiction the equal protection of the laws.

Representatives shall be apportioned among the several states according to their respective numbers, counting the whole number of persons in each state, [excluding Indians not taxed]*. But when the right to vote at any election for the choice of electors for President and Vice President of the United States, Representatives in Congress, the executive and judicial officers of a state, or the members of the legislature thereof is denied to any of the male inhabitants of such state, being twenty-one years of age and citizens of the United States, or in any way abridged except for participation in rebellion or other crime, the basis of representation therein shall be reduced in the proportion which the number of such male citizens shall bear to the whole number of male citizens twenty-one years of age in such state.

No person shall be a Senator or Representative in Congress, or elector of President and Vice President, or hold any office, civil or military, under the United States, or under any state, who, having previously taken an oath, as a member of Congress, or as an officer of the United States, or as a member of any state legislature, or as an executive or judicial officer of any state, to support the Constitution of the United States, shall have engaged in insurrection or rebellion against the same, or given aid or comfort to the enemies thereof. But Congress may, by a vote of two-thirds of each house, remove such disability.

The validity of the public debt of the United States, authorized by law, including debts incurred for payment of pensions and bounties for services in suppressing insurrection or rebellion, shall not be questioned. But neither the United States nor any state shall assume or pay any debt or obligation incurred in aid of insurrection or rebellion against the United States, or any claim for the loss or emancipation of any slave; but all such debts, obligations, and claims shall be held illegal and void.

The Congress shall have power to enforce, by appropriate legislation, the provisions of this article.

Changed by section 1 of the 26th amendment.

Note: Article I, section 2, of the Constitution was modified by section 2 of the 14th amendment.

See 11.8, 12.9 for information on this amendment.

Amendment XV (Ratified February 3, 1870)

The right of citizens of the United States to vote shall not be denied or abridged by the United States or by any state on account of race, color, or previous condition of servitude.

The Congress shall have power to enforce this article by appropriate legislation.

See 11.8, 11.9 for information on this amendment.

Amendment XVI (Ratified February 3, 1913)

The Congress shall have power to lay and collect taxes on incomes, from whatever source derived, without apportionment among the several states and without regard to any census or enumeration.

Note: Article I, section 9, of the Constitution was modified by amendment 16.

See Prologue, 9.6, 9.7, 11.4, 11,6, 11.10 for information on this amendment.

Amendment XVII (Ratified April 8, 1913)

The Senate of the United States shall be composed of two Senators from each state, elected by the people thereof, for six years; and each Senator shall have one vote. The electors in each state shall have the qualifications requisite for electors of the most numerous branch of the state legislatures.

When vacancies happen in the representation of any state in the Senate, the executive authority of such state shall issue writs of election to fill such vacancies, provided that the legislature of any state may empower the executive thereof to make temporary appointments until the people fill the vacancies by election as the legislature may direct.

This amendment shall not be so construed as to affect the election or term of any Senator chosen before it becomes valid as part of the Constitution.

Note: Article I, section 3, of the Constitution was modified by the 17th amendment.

See Prologue, 9.5, 9.6, 9.7, 11.6, 11.10, 13.8 for information on this amendment.

Amendment XVIII (Ratified January 16, 1919)

[After one year from the ratification of this article, the manufacture, sale, or transportation of intoxicating liquors within, the importation thereof into, or the exportation thereof from the United States and all territory subject to the jurisdiction thereof for beverage purposes is hereby prohibited.

The Congress and the several states shall have concurrent power to enforce this article by appropriate legislation.

This article shall be inoperative unless it shall have been ratified as an amendment to the Constitution by the legislatures of the several states, as provided in the Constitution, within seven years from the date of the submission hereof to the states by the Congress.]*

*This amendment was repealed by Amendment 21.

See 11.10 for information on this amendment.

Amendment XIX (Ratified August 18, 1920)

The right of citizens of the United States to vote shall not be denied or abridged by the United States or by any state on account of sex.

Congress shall have power to enforce this article by appropriate legislation.

See 11.9 for information on this amendment.

Amendment XX (Ratified January 23, 1933)

The terms of the President and Vice President shall end at noon on the twentieth day of January, and the terms of Senators and Representatives at noon on the third day of January, of the years in which such terms would have ended if this article had not been ratified; and the terms of their successors shall then begin.

The Congress shall assemble at least once in every year, and such meeting shall begin at noon on the third day of January, unless they shall by law appoint a different day.

If, at the time fixed for the beginning of the term of the President, the President-elect shall have died, the Vice President-elect shall become President. If a President shall not have been chosen before the time fixed for the beginning of his term, or if the President-elect shall have failed to qualify, then the Vice President-elect shall act as President until a President shall have qualified; and the Congress may by law provide for the case wherein neither a President-elect nor a Vice President-elect shall have qualified, declaring who shall then act as President, or the manner in which one who is to act shall be selected, and such person shall act accordingly until a President or Vice President shall have qualified.

The Congress may by law provide for the case of the death of any of the persons from whom the House of Representatives may choose a President whenever the right of choice shall have devolved upon them, and for the case of the death of any of the persons from whom the Senate may choose a Vice President whenever the right of choice shall have devolved upon them.

Sections 1 and 2 shall take effect on the fifteenth day of October following the ratification of this article.

This article shall be inoperative unless it shall have been ratified as an amendment to the Constitution by the legislatures of three- fourths of the several states within seven years from the date of its submission.

Note: Article I, section 4, of the Constitution was modified by section 2 of this amendment. In addition, a portion of the 12th amendment was superseded by section 3.

See 10.2, 11.7 for information on this amendment.

Amendment XXI (Ratified December 5, 1933)

The eighteenth article of amendment to the Constitution of the United States is hereby repealed.

The transportation or importation into any state, territory, or possession of the United States for delivery or use therein of intoxicating liquors, in violation of the laws thereof, is hereby prohibited.

This article shall be inoperative unless it shall have been ratified as an amendment to the Constitution by conventions in the several states, as provided in the Constitution, within seven years from the date of the submission hereof to the states by the Congress.

See 11.10 for information on this amendment.

Amendment XXII (Ratified February 27, 1951)

No person shall be elected to the office of the President more than twice, and no person who has held the office of President, or acted as President, for more than two years of a term to which some other person was elected President shall be elected to the office of the President more than once. But this article shall not apply to any person holding the office of President when this article was proposed by the Congress, and shall not prevent any person who may be holding the office of President, or acting as President, during the term within which this article becomes operative from holding the office of President or acting as President during the remainder of such term.

This article shall be inoperative unless it shall have been ratified as an amendment to the Constitution by the legislatures of three- fourths of the several states within seven years from the date of its submission to the states by the Congress.

See 10.2, 11.7 for information on this amendment.

Amendment XXIII (Ratified March 29, 1961)

The district constituting the seat of government of the United States shall appoint, in such manner as the Congress may direct, a number of electors of President and Vice President equal to the whole number of Senators and Representatives in Congress to which the district would be entitled if it were a state, but in no event more than the least populous state; they shall be in addition to those appointed by the states, but they shall be considered, for the purposes of the election of President and Vice President, to be electors appointed by a state; and they shall meet in the district and perform such duties as provided by the twelfth article of amendment.

The Congress shall have power to enforce this article by appropriate legislation.

See 10.7, 11.9 for information on this amendment.

Amendment XXIV (Ratified January 23, 1964)

The right of citizens of the United States to vote in any primary or other election for President or Vice President, for electors for President or Vice President, or for Senator or Representative in Congress, shall not be denied or abridged by the United States or any state by reason of failure to pay any poll tax or other tax.

The Congress shall have power to enforce this article by appropriate legislation.

See 9.3, 10.7, 11.9 for information on this amendment.

Amendment XXV (Ratified February 10, 1967)

In case of the removal of the President from office or of his death or resignation, the Vice President shall become President.

Whenever there is a vacancy in the office of the Vice President, the President shall nominate a Vice President, who shall take office upon confirmation by a majority vote of both houses of Congress.

Whenever the President transmits to the president pro tempore of the Senate and the speaker of the House of Representatives his written declaration that he is unable to discharge the powers and duties of his office, and until he transmits to them a written declaration to the contrary, such powers and duties shall be discharged by the Vice President as acting President.

Whenever the Vice President and a majority of either the principal officers of the executive departments, or of such other body as Congress may by law provide, transmit to the president pro tempore of the Senate and the speaker of the House of Representatives their written declaration that the President is unable to discharge the powers and duties of his office, the Vice President shall immediately assume the powers and duties of the office as acting President. Thereafter, when the President transmits to the president pro tempore of the Senate and the speaker of the House of Representatives his written declaration that no inability exists, he shall resume the powers and duties of his office unless the Vice President and a majority of either the principal officers of the executive department, or of such other body as Congress may by law provide, transmit within four days to the president pro tempore of the Senate and the speaker of the House of Representatives their written declaration that the President is unable to discharge the powers and duties of his office. Thereupon Congress shall decide the issue, assembling within forty-eight hours for that purpose if not in session. If the Congress, within twenty-one days after receipt of the latter written declaration, or, if Congress is not in session, within twenty-one days after Congress is required to assemble, determines by two-thirds vote of both houses that the President is unable to discharge the powers and duties of his office, the Vice President shall continue to discharge the same as acting President; otherwise, the President shall resume the powers and duties of his office.

Note: Article II, section 1, of the Constitution was affected by the 25th amendment.

See 10.2,11.7 for information on this amendment.

Amendment XXVI (Ratified July 1, 1971)

The right of citizens of the United States, who are eighteen years of age or older, to vote shall not be denied or abridged by the United States or by any state on account of age.

The Congress shall have power to enforce this article by appropriate legislation.

Note: Amendment 14, section 2, of the Constitution was modified by section 1 of the 26th amendment.

See 10.7, 11.9 for information on this amendment.

Amendment XXVII (Ratified May 7, 1992)

No law varying the compensation for the services of the Senators and Representatives shall take effect until an election of Representatives shall have intervened.

See 10.2, 11.7 for information on this amendment.

NOTES
ᆸ

Section One: Waiting

[1] Moreau de Saint-Méry, *Voyage aux États-Unis de l'Amérique, 1793–1798*, 302–3, cited in Sherrill, *French Memories of Eighteenth-Century America*, 124.

[2] Barbé-Marbois, *Our Revolutionary Forefathers*, 78, cited in Bowen, *Miracle at Philadelphia*, 167.

[3] Address to the South Carolina constitutional convention, May 14, 1788, cited in Elliot, *The Debates in the Several State Conventions on the Adoption of the Federal Constitution*, 4:331.

[4] This and the subsequent quotations in this subsection come from Farrand, *The Records of the Federal Convention of 1787*, 2:666–67, cited in Bowen, *Miracle at Philadelphia*, 238–39.

[5] See Jefferson to Edmund Pendleton, August 13, 1776, cited in Skousen, *The Making of America*, 1:31.

[6] Skousen, *The 5000 Year Leap*, 132.

[7] Militia Act of 1903, 32 Stat. 775 (1903).

[8] "The Nature of Peace," sermon presented October 1943, cited in Newquist, *Prophets, Principles and National Survival*, 482.

Section Two: Preparing for Freedom

[1] Benson, *An Enemy Hath Done This*, xi.

[2] Bradford, *Of Plymouth Plantation*, 120–21.

[3] Goodman, "Squanto," 25–31.

[4] Bradford, *Of Plymouth Plantation*, 114.

[5] Marshall and Manuel, *The Light and the Glory*, 175.

[6] Sanford H. Cobb, *The Rise of Religious Liberty in America*, 162, cited in Marshall and Manuel, *The Light and the Glory*, 227–28.

[7] Winthrop to Mary Winthrop, October 20, 1629, cited in Bremer, *John Winthrop*, 161.

[8] Sanford H. Cobb, *The Rise of Religious Liberty in America*, 162, cited in Marshall and Manuel, *The Light and the Glory*, 228.

[9] Mather, *Magnalia Christi Americana*, 2:300.

[10] Winthrop, *The History of New England*, 2:277.

[11] Cited in Marshall and Manuel, *The Light and the Glory*, 277–80.

[12] Rowlandson, *The Sovereignty and Goodness of God*, second remove, cited in Marshall and Manuel, *The Light and the Glory*, 228–33.

[13] Marshall and Manuel, *The Light and the Glory*, 294.

[14] Force, *American Archives*, 1:77, cited in Niles, *Principles and Acts of the Revolution in America*, 198.

[15] Speech to the Lords and Commons of Parliament, March 21, 1609, cited in Thornton, *The Pulpit of the American Revolution*, 74.

Section Three: Conflict and Independence

[1] All anecdotes in this section are cited in Pratt, *American History Stories You Never Read in School but Should Have,* 1:8–21, 50–51, 85–88.

[2] Cited in Marshall and Manuel, *The Light and the Glory,* 345–46.

[3] Washington to Martha Washington, June 18, 1775, cited in Ballard, *The American Covenant,* 1:171.

[4] Speech delivered June 16, 1775, cited in McCullough, *1776,* 49.

[5] Parry et al., *The Real George Washington,* 125.

[6] Jefferson to William Johnson, October 27, 1822, cited in Parry et al., *The Real George Washington,* 615–17.

[7] Unknown Native American chieftain, speech given near Kanawha River, Ohio, fall of 1770, reported by eyewitness James Craik to George Washington Parke Custis, cited in Parry et al., *The Real George Washington,* 48–49.

[8] Adams to Timothy Pickering, August 6, 1822, cited in Allison, *The Real Thomas Jefferson,* 63.

[9] This story appears as cited in Ballard, *The American Covenant,* 1:372. Other accounts record an entire address given by an elderly man whom none of the delegates recognized. Claims that the speaker was either Patrick Henry or John Hanson are unfounded, as neither one attended the Second Continental Congress.

[10] Cited in Benson, *This Nation Shall Endure,* 27. This quotation, widely attributed to Morton as early as 1888, may be a traditional family story among his descendants.

[11] Cited in Allison, *The Real Thomas Jefferson,* 358–59. This undocumented story appears in numerous histories as early as 1901. The anonymous speaker is described only as a well-educated Northerner.

[12] Allison, *The Real Thomas Jefferson,* ix.

[13] Knox to Lucy Knox, July 6, 1776, cited in McCullough, *1776,* 136.

[14] Adams to Abigail Adams, July 3, 1776, cited in Marshall and Manuel, *The Light and the Glory,* 391.

[15] Diary of John Adams, June 25, 1774, cited in McCullough, *John Adams,* 23.

[16] Attributed to John Adams by Daniel Webster in a speech given August 2, 1826, cited in *American Oratory,* 491–93.

[17] Speech to the First Continental Congress, July 1–2, 1776, cited in Marshall and Manuel, *The Light and the Glory,* 388–89.

[18] Benjamin Rush to John Adams, August 2, 1811, cited in Barton, *Faith, Character, and the Constitution.*

[19] Pratt, *American History Stories You Never Read in School but Should Have,* 1:75–77. Slight changes have been made in formatting.

[20] Cited in Ballard, *The American Covenant,* 1:394. Numerous other sources cite the same words.

Section Four: War and Victory

[1] Marshall and Manuel, *The Light and the Glory,* 367–68.

[2] Greene to Marquis de Lafayette, May 1, 1781, cited in ibid., 418.

[3] Diary of Henry Knox, January 10, 1776, cited in McCullough, *1776,* 84.

[4] Diary of Archibald Robertson, March 4, 1776, cited in McCullough, *1776*, 93.

[5] Howe's statement, repeated in many sources with slight variations, appears as cited in McCullough, *1776*, 93.

[6] James Grant to Richard Rigby, September 2, 1776, cited in McCullough, *1776*, 192.

[7] Sermon, May 17, 1776, in Witherspoon, "The Dominion of Providence over the Passions of Men," 533.

[8] Washington to Joseph Reed, January 14, 1776, cited in McCullough, *1776*, 79.

[9] Parry et al., *The Real George Washington*, 272.

[10] Marshall and Manuel, *The Light and Glory*, 406.

[11] Washington to John Banister, April 21, 1778, cited in Washington, *The Writings of George Washington*, 11:291.

[12] Cited in Marshall and Manuel, *The Light and Glory*, 365.

[13] Washington to Thomas McKean, November 15, 1781, cited in Ballard, *The American Covenant*, 1:265.

[14] Tallmadge, *Memoir*, 63–64; emphasis in original.

[15] Parry et al., *The Real George Washington*, 431, 522.

[16] Washington to Lund Washington, June 11, 1783, and Washington to Robert Lewis, August 18, 1799, cited in Washington, *The Writings of George Washington*, 27:3 and 37:339.

[17] Speech to Congress, December 23, 1783, cited in ibid., 27:284.

Section Five: Writing the Charter of Freedom

[1] The dollars in circulation in a national economy must be balanced with the goods and services available for purchase. When more dollars are added without adding more goods or services, the buying power of each dollar lessens, requiring more dollars to transact the purchase. For more on inflation, see Section 8.4.

[2] Washington to James Madison, November 5, 1786, cited in Washington, *The Writings of George Washington*, 29:51–52.

[3] Hamilton et al., *The Federalist*, no. 15.

[4] Madison to Edmund Pendleton, April 22, 1787, cited in Madison, *The Writings of James Madison*, 2:355.

[5] Speech in Constitutional Convention, June 30, 1787, cited in Bowen, *Miracle at Philadelphia*, 131.

[6] Adams to Joseph Hawley, November 25, 1775, cited in Bowen, *Miracle at Philadelphia*, 91.

[7] Bowen, *Miracle at Philadelphia*, 195.

[8] Pierce's notes on the Constitutional Convention, cited in Bowen, *Miracle at Philadelphia*, 98.

[9] Cited in Bowen, *Miracle at Philadelphia*, 260.

[10] Jefferson, *The Writings of Thomas Jefferson*, ed. Washington, 40–41.

[11] All quotations in this paragraph are cited in Bowen, *Miracle at Philadelphia*, 93.

[12] Bowen, *Miracle at Philadelphia*, 55.

[13] Speech before the Pennsylvania legislature, October 6, 1787, cited in Ketcham, *The Anti-Federalist Papers and The Constitutional Convention Debates*, 188.

[14] Speech to the Constitutional Convention, June 1787, cited in Ketcham, *The Anti-Federalist Papers and The Constitutional Convention Debates*, 43.

[15] Speech to the Constitutional Convention, June 2, 1787, cited in Bowen, *Miracle at Philadelphia*, 61.

[16] Speech to the New York Historical Society, September 4, 1816, cited in Bowen, *Miracle at Philadelphia*, 236.

[17] Franklin to Peter Collinson, May 28, 1754, cited in Franklin, *The Papers of Benjamin Franklin*, ed. Labaree et al., 5:332.

[18] Speech given in the Constitutional Convention, June 28, 1787, cited in Bowen, *Miracle at Philadelphia*, 258.

[19] Speech given in the Constitutional Convention, September 17, 1787, cited in Bowen, *Miracle at Philadelphia*, 255.

Section Six: The Fight for Ratification

[1] Beck and Charles, *The Original Argument*, xxiv.

[2] Jefferson to James Madison, November 18, 1788, cited in Beck and Charles, *The Original Argument*, xxv.

[3] Speech to the Massachusetts ratifying convention, January 1788, cited in Bowen, *Miracle at Philadelphia*, 287–88.

[4] Speech to the Virginia ratifying convention, June 5, 1788, cited in Bowen, *Miracle at Philadelphia*, 297.

[5] *The Pennsylvania Gazette*, August 29, 1787, cited in Bowen, *Miracle at Philadelphia*, 225.

[6] *The Pennsylvania Packet*, September 19, 1787, cited in Bowen, *Miracle at Philadelphia*, 267.

[7] Washington to John Armstrong, April 25, 1788, cited in Bowen, *Miracle at Philadelphia*, 305.

[8] Rush to Elias Boudinot, July 9, 1788, cited in Bowen, *Miracle at Philadelphia*, 310. Rush apparently used the same statement five days earlier in an Independence Day address in Philadelphia. Some sources attribute this quotation to James Wilson.

Section Seven: Basic Governing Principles

[1] Acton to Mandell Creighton, April 5, 1887, cited in Dalberg-Acton, *Historical Essays and Studies*, 504.

[2] Hamilton et al., *The Federalist*, no. 55.

[3] This quotation, widely attributed to Washington as early as 1910, cannot be found in any of his extant speeches or letters. However, it has been quoted and paraphrased in speeches in Congress as recently as 1998. It appears here as cited in Skousen, *The 5000 Year Leap*, 120.

[4] Allison, *The Real Thomas Jefferson*, 74.

[5] Jefferson to Charles Hammond, August 18, 1821, cited in Jefferson, *The Writings of Thomas Jefferson*, 15:332.

[6] Speech before the Virginia ratifying convention, 1787, cited in Elliot, *The Debates in the Several State Conventions on the Adoption of the Federal Constitution,* 3:563.

[7] Adams to John Taylor, April 15, 1814, cited in Adams, *The Works of John Adams,* 6:453–54.

[8] Cleveland, *Essays on Liberty,* 3:254–55.

[9] Address to the officers of the first brigade, third division, of the militia of Massachusetts, October 11, 1798, cited in Adams, *The Works of John Adams,* 9:229.

[10] Franklin to the Abbés Chalut and Arnaud, April 17, 1787, cited in Franklin, *The Writings of Benjamin Franklin,* ed. Smyth, 9:569.

[11] Cited in Newquist, *Prophets, Principles and National Survival,* 33.

[12] Coolidge, *The Price of Freedom: Speeches and Addresses,* 390.

[13] Coolidge, *Foundations of the Republic,* 149, 153.

[14] Franklin to Ezra Stiles, March 9, 1790, cited in Franklin, *The Life and Writings of Benjamin Franklin,* 1:623.

Section Eight: Economic Freedom

[1] Skousen, *The 5000 Year Leap,* 132.

[2] Skousen, *The 5000 Year Leap,* 133.

[3] "Regulation Nation: Drowning in Rules, Businesses Brace for Cost and Time for Compliance," www.foxnews.com report, published September 12, 2011, accessed August 8, 2012, reports that regulations on new businesses are increasing at the rate of ten per week. The *Federal Register,* which records government regulations, is 81,405 pages long and contains 180 million words—more than anyone could read in a lifetime. It costs small businesses $10,585 per employee per year to meet government regulations. Copy in my possession.

[4] Reply to a committee from the Workingmen's Democratic Republican Association of New York, March 21, 1864, cited in Lincoln, *The Papers and Writings of Abraham Lincoln,* 7:33.

Section Nine: The Constitution: Making the Laws

[1] Jefferson, *The Writings of Thomas Jefferson,* ed. Bergh, 3:227.

[2] Jefferson, *The Writings of Thomas Jefferson,* ed. Bergh, 17:445.

[3] Bowen, *Miracle at Philadelphia,* 203.

[4] Jackson, "Slavery and the Founding Fathers."

[5] Dwinell, *The Story of Our Money,* 84.

[6] Much of the information in this subsection came from Skousen, "The Development of the United States Monetary System," which was a major influence on Reaganomics. See also Griffin, *The Creature from Jekyll Island.*

[7] Bastiat, *The Law,* 21.

[8] Ellis, *The Life of Colonel David Crockett,* 138–39.

[9] Jefferson, *The Writings of Thomas Jefferson,* ed. Ford, 4:414.

[10] On its home page (accessed August 10, 2012), www.themoneymasters.com proposed a "Two-Step Plan to National Economic Reform and Recovery" as follows: "Step 1: Directs the Treasury Department to issue U.S. Notes (like Lincoln's

Greenbacks; can also be in electronic deposit format) to pay off the National debt. Step 2: Increases the reserve ratio private banks are required to maintain from 10% to 100%, thereby terminating their ability to create money, while simultaneously absorbing the funds created to retire the national debt. These two relatively simple steps, which Congress has the power to enact, would extinguish the national debt, without inflation or deflation, and end the unjust practice of private banks creating money as loans (i.e., fractional reserve banking). Paying off the national debt would wipe out the $400+ billion annual interest payments and thereby balance the budget. This Act would stabilize the economy and end the boom-bust economic cycles caused by fractional reserve banking." Printed copy in my possession. This is only one possibility; others have also been proposed.

[11] See Corwin, *The Constitution and What It Means Today*, 152.

[12] Schuettinger and Butler, *Forty Centuries of Wage and Price Controls*, front flyleaf.

[13] Skousen, *The Making of America*, 444–45.

[14] Skousen, *The Making of America*, 459.

[15] Skousen, *The Making of America*, 429.

Section Ten: The Constitution: Enforcing and Interpreting the Law

[1] Skousen, *The Making of America*, 508.

[2] Jefferson to M. M. Coray, October 21, 1823, cited in Jefferson, *The Writings of Thomas Jefferson*, ed. Bergh, 15:489.

[3] Hamilton et al., *The Federalist*, no. 74.

[4] Speech in Constitutional Convention, June 2, 1787, cited in Madison, *The Debates in the Federal Convention of 1787 Which Framed the Constitution of the United States of America*, 44.

[5] Speech in Constitutional Convention, July 19, 1787, cited in Elliot, *The Debates in the Several State Conventions on the Adoption of the Federal Constitution*, 5:337.

[6] Drafts of the Kentucky Resolutions, November 1798, cited in Jefferson, *The Writings of Thomas Jefferson*, ed. Ford, 8:475.

[7] Jefferson to Spencer Roane, March 9, 1821, cited in Jefferson, *The Writings of Thomas Jefferson*, ed. Ford, 10:189.

[8] Georgia v. Brailsford, 156 US 51 (1794), dissenting opinion, cited in Skousen, *The Making of America*, 627.

[9] Hamilton et al., *The Federalist*, no. 83.

[10] Hamilton et al., *The Federalist*, no. 28.

[11] George Washington to "the People of the United States," September 19, 1796, cited in Washington, *The Writings of George Washington*, 35:229.

[12] Skousen, *The Making of America*, 645.

[13] Speech in Constitutional Convention, September 17, 1787, cited in Bowen, *Miracle at Philadelphia*, 255.

Section Eleven: The Bill of Rights and the Amendments

[1] Randolph, *Early History of the University of Virginia, as Contained in the Letters of Thomas Jefferson and Joseph C. Cabell*, 441–42, 472–75.

[2] Address delivered at the J. Reuben Clark Law Society Conference, Provo, Utah, February 11, 2010; emphasis in original.

[3] William Blackstone, *Commentaries on the Laws of England* (1827 New York ed.), 2:109, cited in Norton, *Undermining the Constitution: A History of Lawless Government*, 199.

[4] Speeches to Virginia ratification convention, June 14, 1788, cited in Senate Subcommittee on the Constitution, *The Right to Keep and Bear Arms*, v, 4, 5, 54, 58.

[5] Cited in Senate Subcommittee on the Constitution, *The Right to Keep and Bear Arms*, v, 5.

[6] Senate subcommittee on the Constitution, *The Right to Keep and Bear Arms*, 12.

[7] Senate Subcommittee on the Constitution, *The Right to Keep and Bear Arms*, vii.

[8] Speech to the Virginia ratifying convention, June 14, 1788, cited in Senate Subcommittee on the Constitution, *The Right to Keep and Bear Arms*, 5. Slight variations in the quotation appear in other sources.

[9] For background on this issue, see Section 9.4.

Section Twelve: The Bill of Rights and the Amendments

[1] Wilson, *The Works of the Honourable James Wilson*, 1:104–6.

[2] Washington to the mayor and council of Philadelphia, April 20, 1789, cited in Washington, *The Writings of George Washington*, 30:289.

[3] de Tocqueville, *Democracy in America*, 1:55.

[4] Olasky, *The Tragedy of American Compassion*, 193–94.

[5] Samuel L. Blumenfeld, in his article "Humanism and Public Education," posted at Death from Ritalin: The Truth about ADHD, http://www.ritalindeath.com/Education/humanism-and-public-education.htm, accessed August 22, 2012, quotes the following from an article by John J. Dunphy in the January/February 1983 issue of *The Humanist:* "I am convinced that the battle for humankind's future must be waged and won in the public school classroom by teachers who . . . convey humanist values in whatever subject they teach . . . The classroom must and will become an arena of conflict between the old and the new—the rotting corpse of Christianity, together with its adjacent evils and misery, and the new faith of humanism, resplendent in its promise of a world in which the never-realized Christian ideal of 'love thy neighbor' will finally be achieved." Copy of the article in my possession.

[6] de Tocqueville, *Democracy in America*, 1:407.

[7] Rousas J. Rushdoony, *The Messianic Character of American Education* (Nutley, NJ: Craig Press, 1968), 32.

[8] John Dewey, "Soul Searching," *Teacher Magazine*, September 1933, 33.

[9] Griffin, *The Creature from Jekyll Island*. For more on the two central banks, see Sections 9.8 and 10.9. In 1913, the Rothschild organization established the Federal Reserve Bank; see Section 9.8.

[10] Raymond B. Bragg, "Humanist Manifesto I" (1933), fourteenth principle,

reads: "A socialized and cooperative economic order must be established to the end that the equitable distribution of the means of life be possible." Posted at American Humanist Association: Good without a God, accessed August 21, 2012, http://www. americanhumanist.org/Humanism/Humanist_Manifesto_I. Printed copy in my possession.

[11] See Section 12.3.

[12] See Section 12.15.

[13] Skousen, *The Majesty of God's Law*, 494–95. The quotation from de Tocqueville appears as Skousen cited it.

[14] Paul Kurtz and Edwin H. Wilson, "Humanist Manifesto II" (1973), fifteenth principle, reads: "Extreme disproportions in wealth, income, and economic growth should be reduced on a worldwide basis." Posted at American Humanist Association: Good without a God, accessed August 21, 2012, http://www.americanhumanist.org/ humanist/humanist_manifesto_ii. Printed copy in my possession.

[15] See Sections 9.6–7 and 11.7.

[16] See Section 7.7, note 10.

[17] "Abortion Facts," The Center for Bio-Ethical Reform, accessed August 21, 2012, http://www.abortionno.org/Resources/fastfacts.html. Printed copy in my possession.

[18] "Internet Pornography Statistics," accessed August 21, 2012, http://internet-filter-review.toptenreviews.com/internet-pornography-statistics.html. Printed copy in my possession.

[19] "Academic Cheating Fact Sheet," ETS Ad Council, accessed August 21, 2012, http://www.glass.castle.com/clients/www-nocheating-org/adcouncil/research/ cheatingfacts. Printed copy in my possession.

[20] Statistics in this and the next paragraph come from "Family Debt—Statistics," The Ethics and Religious Liberty Commission, last modified December 2, 2005, accessed August 21, 2012, http://erlc.com/article/family-debt-statistics. Printed copy in my possession.

[21] Barton, *The Influence of the Bible on America*.

[22] Farewell Address, September 19, 1796, cited in Washington, *The Writings of George Washington*, 35:229.

[23] "New Statistics on Church Attendance and Avoidance," Barna Group, last modified March 3, 2008, accessed August 21, 2012, http://www.barna.org/ congregations-articles/45-new-statistics-on-church-attendance. Printed copy in my possession.

[24] "For Women under 30, Most Births Occur outside Marriage," *New York Times*, last updated February 21, 2012, accessed August 21, 2012, http://www.nytimes. com/2012/02/18/us/for-women-under-30-most-births-occur-outside-marriage. html?pagewanted=all. Printed copy in my possession.

[25] Adams to James Warren, February 12, 1779, cited in Marshall and Manuel, *The Light and the Glory*, 11.

[26] Adams to Zabdiel Adams, June 21, 1776, cited in Marshall and Manuel, *The Light and the Glory*, 12.

[27] Cited in R. H. Markham, *Tito's Imperial Communism* (1947; reprint, [Whitefish, MT]: Kessinger Publishing, 2005), 65.

²⁸ Interview by Sean Hannity on *Fox News*, FOX, February 9, 2012. In this remark, Levin echoed a statement of Montesquieu, quoted three times in his book *Ameritopia*, on pages 128, 167, and 198: "In a popular state there must be . . . virtue . . . In a popular government when the laws have ceased to be executed, as this can come only from the corruption of the republic, the state is already lost."

²⁹ Paul Kurtz and Edmund H. Wilson, "Humanist Manifesto II" (1973), eleventh principle, reads: "Individuals should be encouraged to contribute to their own betterment. If unable, then society should provide means to satisfy their basic economic, health, and cultural needs, including . . . a minimum guaranteed annual income." Posted at American Humanist Association: Good without a God, accessed August 21, 2012, http://www.americanhumanist.org/humanist/humanist_manifesto_ii. Printed copy in my possession.

³⁰ Grover Cleveland was also our twenty-fourth president—the only president to serve two nonconsecutive terms.

³¹ Cleveland to Congress, bill veto, February 16, 1887, cited in Newquist, *Prophets, Principles and National Survival*, 345.

³² Olasky, *The Tragedy of American Compassion*, 8.

³³ "Arator" [pseudonym for Franklin] to "the Public," in Franklin, *The Writings of Benjamin Franklin*, ed. Smyth, 5:538.

³⁴ Jefferson, *The Writings of Thomas Jefferson*, ed. Bergh, 2:184.

³⁵ The Supreme Court has long determined that "obscene" materials are not protected by the First Amendment right to freedom of speech. However, in order for obscene materials to be removed from circulation, they must be proven obscene. The actions of the Supreme Court have made it difficult to prove obscenity, thus making it difficult to eliminate offensive materials.

In 1966, the Court substantially diminished the government's power to prosecute obscenity cases. In *Memoirs v. Massachusetts*, 383 US 413 (1966), the Court set a new test of obscenity: "It must be established that (a) the dominant theme of the material taken as a whole appeals to a prurient interest in sex; (b) the material is patently offensive because it affronts contemporary community standards relating to the description or representation of sexual matters; and (c) the material is utterly without redeeming social value." This requires the prosecution to prove a negative—that the material was "utterly without redeeming social value," which is virtually impossible under our criminal standards of proof.

Seven years later, in *Miller v. California*, 413 US 15 (1973), the court modified the *Memoirs* decision, but only slightly. In the *Miller* case, the Supreme Court set the modern standard of what may be found "obscene": "(a) whether 'the average person, applying contemporary community standards' would find that the work, taken as a whole, appeals to the prurient interest; (b) whether the work depicts or describes, in a patently offensive way, sexual conduct specifically defined by the applicable state law; and (c) whether the work, taken as a whole, lacks serious literary, artistic, political, or scientific value." This definition makes obscenity very hard for a prosecutor to prove beyond a reasonable doubt. All of the quotes above come from the text of the *Miller* case.

WORKS CITED

Adams, John. *The Quotable John Adams*. Edited by Randy Howe. Guilford, CN: Globe Pequot Press, 2008.

---. *The Works of John Adams*. Edited by Charles Francis Adams. 10 volumes. Boston: Little, Brown, 1856.

Alder, Gary, and Carolyn Alder. *The Evolution and Destruction of the Original Electoral College: Including an Examination of Federalist No. 68 (Alexander Hamilton Defends the Electoral College)*. Salt Lake City: GCA Ventures, 2010.

Allison, Andrew M. *The Real Thomas Jefferson*. 2nd edition. American Classic Series, 1. Washington, DC: National Center for Constitutional Studies, 1983.

Allison, Andrew M., et al. *The Real Benjamin Franklin*. American Classic Series, 2. Salt Lake City: Freemen Institute, 1982.

American Oratory: or Selections from the Speeches of Eminent Americans. Philadelphia: Desilver, Thomas, 1836.

Andersen, Hans Verlan. *The Legal Basis of a Free Society*. 2nd edition. 1974. Reprint. Heber, UT: Archive, 2009.

Anderson, Fred. *The War That Made America: A Short History of the French and Indian War*. New York: Viking Penguin, 2005.

Arbon, Val. *Which Presidential Selection Process?* Which Way, America? series. Recorded 2012. James Madison Institute. Digital video disc.

"Audit of the Federal Reserve Reveals $16 Trillion in Secret Bailouts." Unelected. Accessed November 21, 2011. http://www.unelected.org/audit-of-the-federal-reserve-reveals-16-trillion-in-secret-bailouts. Hard copy in my possession.

Ballard, Timothy. *The American Covenant: One Nation under God*. New York: Digital Legend, 2011.

Barbé-Marbois, François, Marquis de. *Our Revolutionary Forefathers: The Letters of François, Marquis de Barbé-Marbois during His Residence in the United States as Secretary of the French Legation, 1779–1785*. Edited by Eugene Parker Chase. New York: Duffield at the Cornwall Press, 1929.

Barton, David. *Faith, Character, and the Constitution*. Recorded 1998. WallBuilders. Compact disc.

---. *The Influence of the Bible on America*. Recorded 1998. WallBuilders. Compact disc.

---. *The Jefferson Lies: Exposing the Myths You've Always Believed about Thomas Jefferson*. Nashville, TN: Thomas Nelson, 2012. Recent criticism of this book for "factual inaccuracies" is unfounded. The disputed information comes from original documents in its author's possession about which the critics knew nothing.

Bastiat, Frédéric. *The Law: The Classic Blueprint for a Free Society*. 3rd edition. Irvington-on-Hudson, NY: Foundation for Economic Education, 2010.

Beach, Stewart. *Samuel Adams: The Fateful Years, 1764–1776.* New York: Dodd, Mead, 1965.

Beck, Glenn, and Joshua Charles. *The Original Argument: The Federalists' Case for the Constitution, Adapted for the 21st Century.* New York: Threshold Editions, Simon and Schuster, 2011.

Benjamin Rush: Signer of the Declaration of Independence. Edited by David Barton. Aledo, TX: WallBuilders, 1999.

Benson, Ezra Taft. *An Enemy Hath Done This.* Compiled by Jerreld L. Newquist. 1969. Reprint. Heber City, UT: Archive, 2010.

---. *The Constitution: A Heavenly Banner.* Compiled by Dan P. Hunter. 1986. Reprint. Heber City, UT: Archive, 2012.

---. *This Nation Shall Endure.* 1977. Reprint. Heber City, UT: Archive, 2011.

Bowen, Catherine Drinker. *Miracle at Philadelphia: The Story of the Constitutional Convention, May to September, 1787.* Boston: Little, Brown, 1966.

Bradford, William. *Of Plymouth Plantation, 1620–1647.* Edited by Samuel Eliot Morison. New York: Alfred A. Knopf, 1952.

Bremer, Francis J. *John Winthrop: America's Forgotten Founding Father.* New York: Oxford University Press, 2003.

Burnett, Edmund Cody, editor. *Letters of Members of the Continental Congress.* 8 volumes. Washington, DC: Carnegie Institute of Washington, 1921–36.

Carmack, Patrick S. J. "Towards Ideal Monetary Reform Legislation." The Money Masters. Accessed 15 June 2012. http://www.themoneymasters.com. Hard copy in my possession.

Carrington, Henry B. *Battles of the American Revolution, 1775–1781: Historical and Military Criticism, with Topographical Illustration.* 1888. Reprint. [Whitefish, MT]: Kessinger Legacy Reprints, [2010].

Chadwick, Michael Loyd, editor. "International Banking." Special issue, *The Freemen Digest,* 1981.

---. "Tax-Exempt Foundations: Their Impact on the World." Special issue, *The Freemen Digest,* June 1978.

Cleveland, Grover. *Essays on Liberty.* 12 volumes. Irvington-on-Hudson, NY: Foundation for Economic Education, 1952–65.

Cleveland, H. A., editor. *Golden Sheaves: Gathered from the Fields of Ancient and Modern Literature.* Philadelphia: Zeigler, McCurdy, 1869.

Cobb, Sanford H. *The Rise of Religious Liberty in America.* New York: Macmillan, 1902.

Coolidge, Calvin. *Foundations of the Republic: Speeches and Addresses.* 1926. Reprint. Stratford, NH: Ayer Publishing, 1968.

---. *The Price of Freedom: Speeches and Addresses.* 1924. Reprint. Amsterdam: Fredonia Books, 2001.

Corwin, Edwin S. *The Constitution and What It Means Today.* 13th edition, revised. Princeton, NJ: Princeton University Press, 1973.

Dalberg-Acton, John Emerich Edward. *Historical Essays and Studies.* Edited by John Neville Figgis and Reginald Vere Laurence. London: Macmillan, 1907.

de Tocqueville, Alexis. *Democracy in America.* Translated by Henry Reeve. Edited by Francis Bowen. 3rd edition. 2 volumes. Cambridge: Sever and Francis, 1863.

Dranias, Nick. "Debunking Myth of the 'Runaway' Convention." E-mail message to Goldwater Institute list. 4 November 2010. http://goldwaterinstitute.org/blog/debunking-myth-runaway-convention.Hard copy in my possession.

Dwinell, Olive Cushing. *The Story of Our Money.* 2nd edition. Boston: Forum Publishing, 1946.

Eidsmore, John. "The Framers of the Constitution: Christians or Deists?" *CWA Newsletter,* July 1987, 3–13.

Elliot, Jonathan, editor. *The Debates in the Several State Conventions on the Adoption of the Federal Constitution.* 2nd edition. 4 volumes. Washington, DC: Jonathan Elliot, 1836.

Ellis, Edward S. *The Life of Colonel David Crockett.* Philadelphia: Porter and Coates, 1884.

Farrand, Max, editor. *The Records of the Federal Convention of 1787.* 3 volumes. New Haven: Yale University Press, 1911.

Flurry, Gerald. "Our Educators Have a Dangerous Contempt for Authority." *The Philadelphia Trumpet,* March 2010, 1.

Force, Peter. *American Archives: A Documentary History of the English Colonies in North America.* Fourth Series of Six. 9 volumes. Washington, DC: M. St. Clair Clarke and Peter Force, 1837.

Franklin, Benjamin. *The Memoirs [Life and Writings] of Benjamin Franklin.* Edited by William Temple Franklin and William Duane. 2 volumes. Philadelphia: McCarty and Davis, 1834.

---. *The Papers of Benjamin Franklin.* Edited by Leonard W. Labaree et al. 46 volumes projected. New Haven, CN: Yale University Press, 1959–.

---. *The Writings of Benjamin Franklin.* Edited by Albert Henry Smyth. 10 volumes. New York: Macmillan, 1905–7.

Goodman, Stanley E. "Squanto." In *They Knew They Were Pilgrims: Essays in Plymouth History,* edited by L. D. Geller, 25–31. New York: Poseidon Books, 1971.

Goodrich, Charles A. *Lives of the Signers to the Declaration of Independence.* 5th edition. New York: Thomas Mather, 1836.

Griffin, G. Edward. *The Creature from Jekyll Island: A Second Look at the Federal Reserve.* 5th edition. Westlake Village, CA: American Media, 2010.

Hamilton, Alexander, James Madison, and John Jay. *The Federalist: A Commentary on the Constitution of the United States.* Edited by Robert Scigliano. New York: Modern Library, Random House, 2000.

Horowitz, Jerome. *The United States Has Two Constitutions: How to Identify and Promote the True Constitution, including Text of Constitution and Amendments with Explanatory Comments.* 1995. Reprint. Heber City, UT: Archive, 2010.

Jackson, Al. "Slavery and the Founding Fathers: History Based on Factual Information." Presentation given at Lehi, UT, January 27, 2012.

Jefferson, Thomas. *The Papers of Thomas Jefferson.* Edited by Julian P. Boyd et al. 60 volumes projected. Princeton, NJ: Princeton University Press, 1950–.

---. *The Writings of Thomas Jefferson.* Edited by Albert Ellery Bergh. 20 volumes. Washington, DC: Thomas Jefferson Memorial Association, 1905–7.

---. *The Writings of Thomas Jefferson.* Edited by Paul Leicester Ford. 10 volumes. New York: G. P. Putnam, 1892–99.

---. *The Writings of Thomas Jefferson.* Edited by H. A. Washington. Volume 1. Washington, DC: Taylor and Maury, 1853. This volume includes Jefferson's autobiography.

Ketcham, Ralph, editor. *The Anti-Federalist Papers and The Constitutional Convention Debates.* New York: Signet Classic, 1986.

Kunhardt, Philip B. Jr., Philip B. Kunhardt III, and Peter W. Kunhardt. *The American President.* Putnam, NY: Riverhead Books, Penguin, 1999.

Lane, Arthur Bliss. *I Saw Poland Betrayed: An American Ambassador Reports to the American People.* Indianapolis: Bobbs-Merrill, 1948.

Lemisch, L. Jesse, editor. *Benjamin Franklin: The Autobiography and Other Writings.* Signet Classics. New York: New American Library, 1961.

Levin, Mark R. *Ameritopia: The Unmaking of America.* New York: Threshold Editions, Simon and Schuster, 2012.

Lincoln, Abraham. *The Papers and Writings of Abraham Lincoln.* Edited by Arthur Brooks Lapsley. Constitutional Edition. 7 volumes. New York: G. P. Putnam's Sons, 1905.

Lipsky, Seth. "The Floating Dollar as a Threat to Property Rights." *Imprimis* 40.2 (2011): 1–5.

Locke, John. *Second Treatise of Government.* New York: Barnes and Noble, 2004.

Lossing, Benson John. *Lives of the Signers of the Declaration of Independence.* 1848. Reprint. Aledo, TX: WallBuilders, 1998.

Madison, James. *The Debates in the Federal Convention of 1787 Which Framed the Constitution of the United States of America.* Edited by Gaillard Hunt and James Brown Scott. New York: Oxford University Press, 1920.

---. *The Writings of James Madison.* Edited by Gaillard Hunt. 9 volumes. New York: G. P. Putnam, 1900–1910.

Marshall, Peter, and David Manuel. *The Light and the Glory: 1492–1793.* Revised and expanded edition. Grand Rapids, MI: Revell, 2009.

Mather, Cotton. *Magnalia Christi Americana: or, The Ecclesiastical History of New-England.* Edited by Thomas Robbins. 2 volumes. Hartford, CT: Silas Andrus, 1853.

McCullough, David G. *1776.* New York: Simon and Schuster, 2005.

---. *John Adams.* New York: Simon and Schuster, 2001.

McDonald, Larry. "The Liberty Amendment: Questions and Answers." Quoted from the Congressional Record—House, October 9, 1975. http://libertyamendment. org/mcdonald.html. Accessed July 21, 2012. Hard copy in my possession.

Meyer, Herbert E. "Revolution." *americanthinker.com*. Last updated May 20, 2009. http://www.americanthinker.com/2009/05/revolution.html. Accessed July 21, 2012. Hard copy in my possession.

Moreau de Saint-Méry, Médéric Louis Élie. *Voyage aux États-Unis de l'Amérique, 1793–1798*. Edited by Stewart L. Mims. New Haven, CN: Yale University Press, 1913.

Natelson, Robert G. "Amending the Constitution by Convention: A Complete View of the Founders' Plan." *Policy Report, Goldwater Institute*, 1st series, 241 (September 16, 2010): 1–43.

Newquist, Jerreld L. *Prophets, Principles and National Survival*. Salt Lake City: Publishers Press, 1964.

Niles, H. *Principles and Acts of the Revolution in America*. 1822. Reprint. Boston: Pinkham Press, 1929.

Noebel, David A. "The Socialization of America." *Schwarz Report* 49.5 (2009): 1–5.

Norton, Thomas James. *Undermining the Constitution: A History of Lawless Government*. New York: Devin-Adair, 1950.

Novak, Michael. *On Two Wings: Humble Faith and Common Sense at the American Founding*. San Francisco: Encounter Books, 2002.

Olasky, Marvin. *The Tragedy of American Compassion*. Washington, DC: Regnery Gateway, 1992.

Parry, Jay A., et al. *The Real George Washington*. American Classic Series, 3. Washington, DC: National Center for Constitutional Studies, 2008.

Pratt, Mara L. *American History Stories—You Never Read in School—but Should Have*. 2 volumes. 1889. Reprint. Centerville, UT: Randall, 1993–2004. In this edition, unlike other editions of this set, the first volume, rather than the second, contains stories of the Revolutionary War.

Randolph, John William, editor. *Early History of the University of Virginia, as Contained in the Letters of Thomas Jefferson and Joseph C. Cabell*. Richmond, VA: J. W. Randolph, 1856.

Rhodehamel, John H. *The Great Experiment: George Washington and the American Republic*. San Marino, CA/New Haven, CN: Henry E. Huntington Library and Art Gallery/Yale University Press, 1998.

Romney, Mitt. *No Apology: The Case for American Greatness*. New York: St. Martin's, 2010.

Rowlandson, Mary White. *The Sovereignty and Goodness of God: Together with the Faithfulness of His Promises Displayed: Being a Narrative of the Captivity and Restoration of Mrs. Mary Rowlandson*. Boston: Bedford Books, 1997.

Schlafly, Phyllis. "Barack Obama's Radical Rogue's Gallery." *Schwarz Report* 50.1 (2010): 1–2.

Schuettinger, Robert L., and Eamonn F. Butler. *Forty Centuries of Wage and Price Controls: How Not to Fight Inflation.* Washington, DC: Heritage Foundation, 1979.

Sherrill, Charles Hitchcock. *French Memories of Eighteenth-Century America.* New York: Charles Scribner's Sons, 1915.

Skousen, W. Cleon. "The Development of the United States Monetary System." National Center for Constitutional Studies. Accessed August 10, 2012. http://www.nccs.net/monetary_reform1.html. Hard copy in my possession.

---. *The 5000 Year Leap: 28 Great Ideas That Changed the World.* 1981. Reprint. Franklin, TN: American Documents, 2009.

---. *The Majesty of God's Law.* 1996. Reprint. Riverton, UT: Ensign, 2010.

---. *The Making of America: The Substance and Meaning of the Constitution.* 1985. Reprint. [Malta, ID]: National Center for Constitutional Studies, 1991.

Slover, Tim. *A More Perfect Union.* Digital video disc. Directed by Peter N. Johnson. Provo, UT: Brigham Young University, 1989. This motion picture was officially recognized by the Commission on the Bicentennial of the United States Constitution.

Smith, Adam. *The Wealth of Nations.* London: Penguin, 1986.

Spalding, Matthew. "Revolutionary Truths That Work." The Heritage Foundation. Last updated November 25, 2009. http://www.heritage.org/research/commentary/2009/11/revolutionary-truths-that-work?query=Revolutionary+Truths+That+Work. Accessed July 21, 2012. Hard copy in my possession.

---. "The Rediscovery of America: Here's the Best Ground from Which to Repulse the Whole Progressive Project." The Heritage Foundation. Last updated November 3, 2009. http://www.heritage.org/research/commentary/2009/11/the-rediscovery-of-america-heres-the-best-ground-from-which-to-repulse-the-whole-progressive-project?query=The+Rediscovery+of+America:+Here's+the+Best+Ground+from+Which+to+Repulse+the+Whole+Progressive+Project. Accessed July 21, 2012. Hard copy in my possession.

Stansbury, Arthur J. *A Catechism on the United States Constitution: 332 Questions with Basic Answers Every Citizen Should Know.* Edited by W. Cleon Skousen. Cedar City, UT: God, Family, Country, 2009.

Stevenson, Deborah G. "Bulletin #67: The Parental Rights Amendment." National Home Education Legal Defense, April 1, 2009. http://www.nheld.com/BTN67.htm. Accessed July 21, 2012. Hard copy in my possession.

Tallmadge, Benjamin. *Memoir of Col. Benjamin Tallmadge.* New York: Thomas Holman, 1858.

Thacher, James. *A Military Journal during the American Revolutionary War.* Boston: Richardson and Lord, 1823.

Thornton, John Wingate. *The Pulpit of the American Revolution: or, The Political Sermons of the Period of 1776*. Boston: D. Lothrop, 1876.

United States. Militia Act of 1903, 32 Stat. 775 (1903).

United States. Senate. Committee on the Judiciary. Subcommittee on the Constitution. *The Right to Keep and Bear Arms*. Senate Report, 97th Congress, 2nd Session. Washington, DC: United States Government Printing Office, 1982.

Walsh, Lorena S. "New Findings about the Virginia Slave Trade." *Colonial Williamsburg Interpreter* 20.2 (1999): n. pag. Hard copy in my possession.

Washington, George. *The Writings of George Washington from the Original Manuscript Sources, 1745–1799*. Edited by John C. Fitzpatrick. 39 volumes. Washington, DC: Government Printing Office, 1931–44.

West, Thomas G. *Vindicating the Founders: Race, Sex, Class, and Justice in the Origins of America*. Lanham, MD: Rowman and Littlefield, 1997.

Wilson, James. *The Works of the Honourable James Wilson*. Edited by Bird Wilson. 3 volumes. Philadelphia: Lorenzo Press for Bronson and Chauncey, 1804.

Winthrop, John. *The History of New England from 1630 to 1649*. Edited by James Savage. 3 volumes. Boston: Phelps and Farnham, 1825.

Witherspoon, John. "The Dominion of Providence over the Passions of Men." In *Political Sermons of the American Founding Era, 1730–1805*, edited by Ellis Sandoz, 1:531–60. Indianapolis, IN: Liberty Fund, 1998.

INDEX

☙